CWSG Library

Gift of:

Triumph at the James

My best regards,
Donald E. Waldemer

Triumph at the James:
the Checkmate of General R.E. Lee

Donald E. Waldemer
St. Louis, MO

"**Triumph At The James**"

Copyright © 1998 by Donald E. Waldemer

Published by: Donald E. Waldemer
32 Middlesex Drive
St. Louis, MO 63144

All rights reserved. No part of this book may be reproduced in any form by any electronic or mechanical means without permission in writing from the publisher, except by a reviewer who may quote brief passages in a review.

Cover and Art Work
by Kathy Waldemer and Lucy Ryan

Produced by Windsor Associates, San Diego, CA

Printed in the United States of America

Also by Donald E. Waldemer:

Fireflies of My Days
Wind Chimes
Paper Airplanes
Postcards

Mathew Brady

Ulysses S. Grant

The Army of the Potomac crossing the James River near Fort Powhattan on pontoons   (E. Forbes June 17/'64)

This book is dedicated to my children, Mark, Lucy, Dean and Daniel, whose great, great grandfathers,

Daniel Whittenberg Johnson, Illinois 44th

and

Joel Dandy Carter, 7th Alabama Cavalry (Malone's)

fought against each other in the Civil War at the Battle of Stone's River, Tennessee, on December 31, 1862, survived the war and now lie buried 100 yards apart in a graveyard in Ashley, Illinois.

Acknowledgements

No book is the product of a single hand.

The person whose encouragement and steadfast devotion has contributed the most to this volume is my wife, Jean. Without her it would never have been completed.

Second, is my brother-in-law, Frank Kirtz, whose insight, suggestions, and criticism were of significant help at a time when it was most needed.

Dear friends who have taken the time to read the manuscript and made suggestions were Merle Sumner, Lowell Reidenbough, James Schiele, Harry Hammer, Donald Schaeffer and Dr. William Costen.

For technical development of the text I am indebted to William Congdon and Jim Waldemer.

Donald E. Waldemer

Mark D. Waldemer, Editor

Author's note:

All communications and letters shown in this book are authentic and their sources are documented with footnotes.

Certain lines in the letters were underlined by the author to emphasize the significance of a passage as it relates to the text. Some letters were excerpted to spare the reader unrelated details. The complete letters can be found through the footnotes. Other letters were reprinted in their entirety as they were written.

D.E.W.

CONTENTS

Chapter 1	Cold Harbor Aftermath	1
Chapter 2	Final Preparations	49
Chapter 3	Crossing the James	85
Chapter 4	Assaults on Petersburg	139
Chapter 5	Afterward	155
Appendix A	Grant's Plan/Lincoln's Plan	199
Appendix B	Grant and Sherman/Grant and Meade	217
Appendix C	The BIG Secret: Confederate Casualties	235
Appendix D	Cold Harbor Letters	263
Bibliography		286

Key Maps:

Area of Operations	10, 11
Crossing the James	88, 89

INTRODUCTION

Few Civil War historians have grasped the key maneuver that won the Civil War for the Union. Once Grant placed the Army of the Potomac south and east of Petersburg, in an impregnable, entrenched position, Lee was finished. Lee had no choice. He had to rush south with his army and occupy the trenches defending Petersburg or lose his vital railroads. But, having occupied the trenches, Lee found that he had fallen into a trap that he could not get out of.

The trap was this: Lee had to hold Richmond, the capital of the Confederacy. In order to hold Richmond, Lee had to defend Petersburg, 20 miles south, the railroad center for Richmond. To hold on to all this territory, Lee had to stretch his depleted army over thirty-five miles of trenches. Offensive action was out of the question. Concentration of his army was impossible. Lee was reduced to fighting delaying actions to defend his railroads as his army wasted away to starvation and desertion. Grant had him completely "checkmated", while other Federal armies cut up the South.

General Grant was perfectly positioned to hold Lee in place and attack at the same time. His army was lavishly supplied by sea through City Point. Grant could easily shift forces along the extended front and attack Lee here, there, and everywhere. Steadily the roads and railroads fell into Union hands as the noose tightened. Grant had achieved his "line further South" which he had proposed to Lincoln in his letter of January 19, 1864. Once the Army of Northern Virginia was trapped in siege in Petersburg, it had no future. No one understood that better than Robert E. Lee.

The Virginia campaign was the most important of the Civil War. It lasted only 46 days (May 4-June 18, 1864.)

Lee was driven eighty-five miles south to Petersburg by Grant. He suffered 35,000 casualties, half of his army. Lee lost northern Virginia, central Virginia and a considerable part of southern Virginia. Lee had been trapped in his terminal siege, the position he most wanted to avoid. Once Grant established the Union army in an entrenched position southeast of Petersburg, Lee believed that his own situation was hopeless.

Headquarters Army No. VA
Near Petersburg, VA.
June 19th 1864

His excellency Jefferson Davis
President Confed States

Mr. President:

".... My greatest apprehension at present is the maintenance of our communications south. It will be difficult, and I fear impracticable to preserve it uninterrupted. The enemy's left now rests on the Jerusalem road, and I fear it would be impossible to arrest a sudden attack aimed at a distant point. In addition the enemy's cavalry, in spite of all our efforts, can burn the bridges over the Nottoway and its branches, the Meherrin & even the South side road is very much exposed, and our only dependence seems to be on the Danville."

Most respectfully and truly yours,
R. E. Lee, Gen.[1]

...And further on June 21, 1864 General Lee writes:

Petersburg *June 21, 1864*

Mr. President:
"...I hope your Exc' will put no reliance in what I can do individually, for I feel that will be very little. The enemy has a strong position & is able to deal us more injury than from any other point he has ever taken..."

"...I fear he will not attack us but advance by regular approaches. He is so situated that I cannot attack him...."

Praying that you may enjoy all health & happiness,

I remain most respy, & truly,
R.E. Lee, Genl.[2]

---

1 Freeman, Douglas Southall, editor, "Lee's Dispatches" page 250.
2 Freeman, Douglas Southall, editor, "Lee's Dispatches" page 253.

The Virginia campaign has received the least competent analysis of any Civil War campaign. Contemporary historians have failed completely to grasp the strategy that brought General Robert E. Lee's active military career to a close and set the stage for the end of the war.

James M. McPherson, author of "Battle Cry of Freedom," renders this judgment:

> "Thus ended a seven week campaign of movement and battle whose brutal intensity was unmatched in the war. Little wonder that the Army of the Potomac did not fight at Petersburg with "the vigor and force" it had shown in the Wilderness—it was no longer the same army. Many of its best and bravest had been killed or wounded....."[3]

By simply stating this and giving no other facts, Mr. McPherson is implying that the Union army accomplished nothing in 46 days, and that the Confederacy had a future.

Noah Andre Trudeau, author of "Bloody Roads South," renders much the same judgment:

> "Forty-seven days before, Lincoln had wished Grant well and asked "that any great disaster or the capture of our men in great numbers shall be avoided." What Grant had provided for Lincoln was a succession of nightmares: the Wilderness, Spotsylvania, Cold Harbor. His strategy had resulted in massive casualty lists...."[4]

Mr. Trudeau does what Mr. McPherson does: tells only a small part of the story, and leaves out the important facts. But it was all over by June 18th. The Confederacy had lost the war. Lee's army, reduced by fifty percent, was hopelessly trapped in a terminal siege at Petersburg, a siege from which it could never escape. Gradually, steadily, Lee's army starved.

(Telegram from Headquarters A. N. VA.)
HEADQUARTERS ARMY OF NORTHERN VIRGINIA,
January 11, 1865.

HON. J. A. SEDDON:
There is nothing within reach of this army to be impressed. The country is swept clear; our only reliance is upon the railroads. We have but two days supplies.

R. E. LEE.[5]

---

3 McPherson, James M, "Battle Cry of Freedom", p. 742
4 Trudeau, Noah Andre, "Bloody Roads South", p. 321
5 Jones, J. W., "Life & Letters of Gen. Robert E. Lee," p. 348.

Through the letters, orders and reports written by Grant and Lee as the fighting was taking place, the story of the Virginia campaign is told. The strategy of the first truly modern campaign, planned from the start to finish in great detail, is fully explained. Lee and Grant come to life as they reveal themselves in their own written words. This book directly challenges the conventional understanding of this key campaign. It tells what happened and why.

Lee told General Early in May, 1864:
"We must destroy this army of Grant's before he gets to the James River. If he gets there it will become a siege, and then, it will be a mere question of time."[6]

D.E.W.
January 1998

---

6   Jones, J. Williams, "Personal Reminiscences of General Robert E. Lee" p. 40.

FROM OUR SPECIAL WAR CORRESPONDENT.

"CITY POINT, VA., *April* —, 8.30 A.M.
"All seems well with us."—A. LINCOLN.

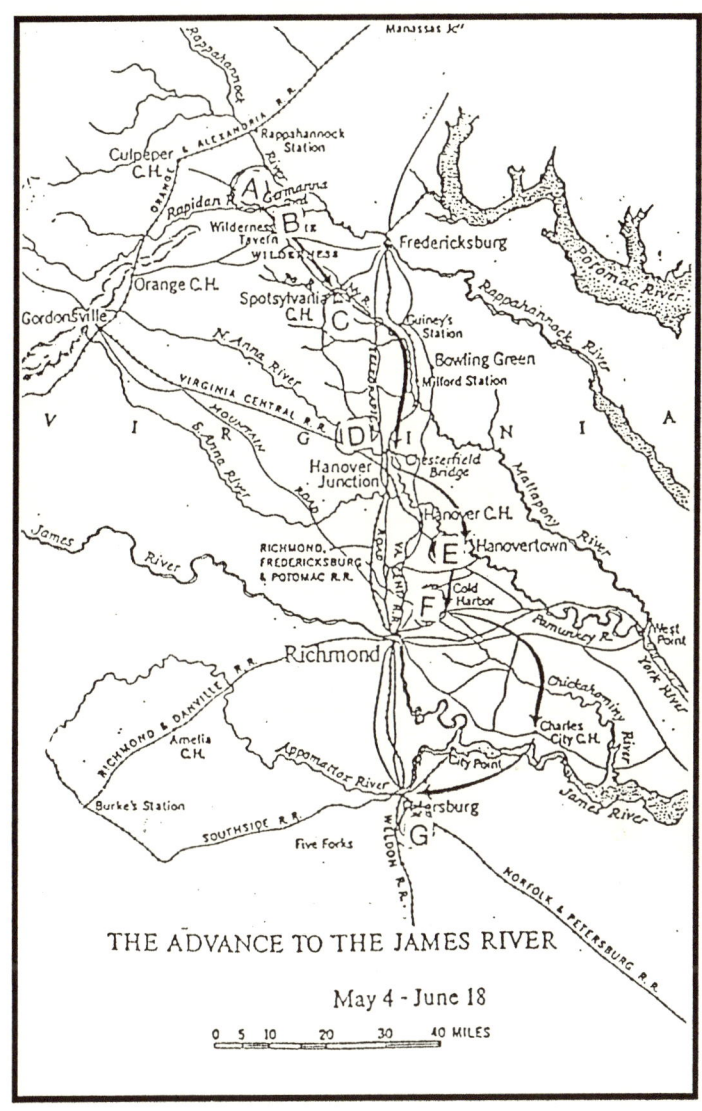

THE ADVANCE TO THE JAMES RIVER
May 4 - June 18

A. Crossing the Rapidan — May 4, 1864
B. Wilderness — May 5,6,7, 1864
C. Spotsylvania — May 8-20, 1864
D. North Anna — May 23-25, 1864
E. Totopotomy Creek — May 26,27,28, 1864
F. Cold Harbor — June 1-12, 1864
G. Crossing the James-Attacks on Petersburg — June 14-18, 1864

I
COLD HARBOR AFTERMATH
JUNE 4, 1864 TO JUNE 7, 1864

Napoleon said that war is a struggle between two men. He believed it was a mental contest between opposing generals, each attempting to read the mind of the other, each attempting to impose his will on the other. The general who understood his opponent best gained the victory.

The supreme test of this theory can be seen in the confrontation between Grant and Lee in Virginia in 1864. Grant relentlessly pushed south. Lee fought desperately to stop him

In January of 1864, Grant had outlined for Lincoln his preference for a seaborne invasion of North Carolina to lessen the casualties. Such a move would have forced Lee to abandon Virginia and come south to attack him. Grant would have had the advantage of fighting defensively:

CONFIDENTIAL.] HDQRS MIL. DIV. OR THE Mississippi,
Nashville, Tenn., *January 19, 1864.*

Maj. Gen. H. W. HALLECK,
General-in-Chief of the Army, Washington, D. C.:

GENERAL: I would respectfully suggest whether an abandonment of all previously attempted lines to Richmond is not advisable, and in lieu of these one be taken farther south, I would suggest Raleigh. N.C. as the objective point and Suffolk as the starting point. Raleigh once secured, I would make New Berne the base of supplies until Wilmington is secured.

A moving force of 60,000 men would probably be required to start on such an expedition. This force would not have to be

Cold Harbor Aftermath

increased unless Lee should withdraw from his present position. In that case the necessity for so large a force on the Potomac would not exist. <u>A force moving from Suffolk would destroy first all the roads about Weldon or even as far north as Hicksford. From Weldon to Raleigh they would scarcely meet with serious opposition.</u> Once there, the most interior line of railway still left to the enemy, in fact the only one they would then have, would be so threatened as to force him to use a large portion of his army in guarding it. <u>This would virtually force an evacuation of Virginia and indirectly of East Tennessee. It would throw our armies into new fields, where they could partially live upon the country and would reduce the stores of the enemy.</u> It would cause thousands of the North Carolina troops to desert and return to their homes. It would give us possession of many negroes who are now indirectly aiding the rebellion. It would draw the enemy from campaigns of their own choosing, and for which they are prepared, to new lines of operations never expected to become necessary. <u>It would effectually blockade Wilmington, the port now of more value to the enemy than all the balance of their seacoast. It would enable operations to commence at once by removing the war to a more southern climate, instead of months of inactivity in winter quarters.</u> Other advantages might be cited which would be likely to grow out of this plan, but these are enough. From your better opportunities of studying the country and the armies that would be involved in this plan, you will be better able to judge of the practicability of it than I possibly can. I have written this in accordance with what I understand to be an invitation from you to express my views about military operations, and not to insist that any plan of mine should be carried out. Whatever course is agreed upon, I shall always believe is at least intended for the best, and until fully tested will hope to have it prove so.

                      I am, general, very respectfully,
                      your obedient servant,
                      U.S. GRANT,
                      Major-General.[1]

---

1 Official Records, Vol. XXXIII Series I, Ser. No. 60, p. 394.

Cold Harbor Aftermath

But President Lincoln had wanted a direct attack on General Robert E. Lee. President Lincoln did not want the Army of the Potomac divided and a repetition of McClellan's Peninsula campaign.

Lincoln wanted the Army of the Potomac, his army, used as a mighty axe wielded by a resolute general to deal Lee a mortal blow. Lincoln believed the elimination of Lee essential to winning the war. General Halleck, Lincoln's military secretary, wrote Grant in the midpoint of the campaign to reemphasize that point:

HEADQUARTERS OF THE ARMY,
Washington, May 23, 1864

Lieutenant-General Grant,
Army of the Potomac:

GENERAL; Your dispatch from Bethel Church, dated 6.30(8) p.m. yesterday, is received. In accordance with your previous directions Generals Meigs and Barnard were sent to the James River, with orders to report by telegraph how many troops could be spared and on the means of water transportation. The moment I receive it I will give the orders for the proposed movement....If the enemy retreats behind the South Anna, West Point would be the proper place to occupy, but until he does so I think it would be unwise and exceedingly hazardous to attempt to hold both City Point and West Point, as the enemy might concentrate on either and crush it out. I shall, therefore, order any troops that Meigs and Barnard think can be spared from Butler's command to Rappahannock or Port Royal; to the latter if you are still in the vicinity of Bowling Green or the North Anna. Whatever I can raise here will be sent to same place till further orders. <u>Permit me to repeat what I have so often urged, that in my opinion every man we can collect should be hurled against Lee, wherever he may be as his army, not Richmond, is the true objective point of this campaign. When that army is broken Richmond will be of very little value to the enemy.</u> Demonstrations on that place exhaust us more than they injure the rebels, for it will require 2 men outside to keep 1 in Richmond. I once thought that this could be more than compensated for by destroying their lines of supply, but experience has proved that they can repair them just about as fast as we can destroy them; such at least was the case

Cold Harbor Aftermath

under Dix and Foster, and I think Butler's operations will have no better result. I have no doubt we shall soon have loud calls for re-enforcements in West Virginia, but I shall not send any unless you so order, for I have very little faith in these collateral operations. The little good they accomplish seldom equals their cost in men and money. <u>If you succeed in crushing Lee all will be well; if you fail, we immediately lose whatever we may have gained in West Virginia or around Richmond.</u> I therefore propose to send to you everything I can get without regard to the calls of others, until you direct otherwise.

Very respectfully, your obedient servant,
H. W. HALLECK.
Major-General and Chief of Staff [2]

General Grant had done exactly what President Lincoln had wanted in the month of May. Lee's army had been struck many times.

General Lee never understood Grant's strategy. Lee never knew where Grant was going. He never knew what Grant intended to do. At the conclusion of the battle of Spotsylvania on May 22nd, General Lee wrote President Davis:

> ....The enemy night before last commenced to withdraw from his position & to move towards Bowling Green —The movement was not discovered until after daylight, & in a wooded country like that in which we have been operating, where nothing is known beyond what can be ascertained by feeling, a day's march can always be gained—The enemy left in his trenches the usual amount of force generally visible, & the reports of his movement were so vague & conflicting that it required some time to sift the truth. It appeared however that he was endeavoring to place the Matapony river between him and our army, which secured his flank, & by rapid movements to join his cavalry under Sheridan to attack Richmond-I therefore thought it safest to move to the Annas to intercept his march, and to be within easy reach of Richmond. As soon therefore as his forces in my front C4 be disposed of, I withdrew the army from its position, & with two

---

[2] Official Records, Vol. XXXVI Pt. III, Ser. No. 69, p. 114.

Cold Harbor Aftermath

corps arrived here this morning - The 3rd corps (Hills) is moving on my right & I hope by noon to have the whole army behind the Annas. I should have preferred contesting the enemy's approach inch by inch; but my solicitude for Richmond caused me to abandon that plan...[3]

This was General Lee's explanation of his loss of Northern Virginia and the 25 mile retreat south through central Virginia after the battle of Spotsylvania to the North Anna River. In this retreat Lee abandoned all of central Virginia without a fight.

On May 22, 1864, after the two great battles in Northern Virginia had ended, Wilderness (May 5-7) and Spotsylvania (May 8-22), General Lee had suffered an estimated 25,000 casualties, of which 7,500[4] were actual prisoners in hand which were shipped North. After the two great battles the Confederate army could only fight defensively from trenches. General Lee apparently believed that General Grant had the same military objectives as the Union generals who had preceded him: to avoid giving battle to the Confederate army and to advance on Richmond and attack it. With this belief, General Lee's strategy was first to attack the Union army in the Wilderness and, after his own army had been crippled, to intervene between the Union army and Richmond as Grant moved South.

General Lee states his belief that Grant's primary objective is to attack Richmond. This was not true. Nowhere in Grant's correspondence is there any hint that Grant intended to attack Richmond. Instead Richmond was to serve as a fulcrum on which to turn Lee. Grant's stated intention from first to last was to take his army south of Lee and destroy Lee's railroads. Fourteen days before, in the midst of the heavy fighting at Spotsylvania in northern Virginia, Grant sent this report to Washington:

HEADQUARTERS,
Piney Branch Church,
May 8, 1864-11:30 a.m.
(Received 3:15 p.m.)

Maj. Gen. H. W. HALLECK;
The army commenced moving south at 9 p.m. yesterday, and when closed up to the position assigned for first day's march

---

[3] Freeman, Douglas Southhall, editor, "Lee's Dispatches to Jefferson Davis, 1862-65," G. P. Putnam & Sons, N.Y., 1957, p. 190.
[4] Frassanito, William A., "Grant and Lee," Charles Scribners, 1983, p. 57.

Cold Harbor Aftermath

will stand thus: General Warren's corps at Spotsylvania Court-House Hancock's at Todd's Tavern; Sedgwick's on road from Piney Branch Church to Spotsylvania, and General Burnside at Alrich's. It is not yet demonstrated what the enemy will do, but the best of feeling prevails in this army, and I feel at present no apprehension for the result. <u>My efforts will be to form a junction with General Butler as early as possible and be prepared to meet any enemy interposing.</u> The results of the three days' fight at Old Wilderness was decidedly in our favor. The enemy having a strong entrenched position to fall back on when hard pressed, and the extensive train we had to cover, rendered it impossible to inflict the heavy blow on Lee's army I had hoped. <u>My exact route to the James River I have not yet definitely marked out.</u>

U.S. GRANT,
Lieutenant-General.[5]

The fact that the James River was Grant's objective in the campaign could not have been stated more clearly. Far from a mere after thought, it was the heart of his strategy. Previous historians have been wrong. The widely held concept that Richmond was the military objective is without foundation.

General Lee did not understand Grant's strategy. On May 9th, the day after Grant's report, Lee wrote President Davis:

> We have succeeded so far in keeping on the front flank of the army, and impeding its progress, <u>without a general engagement</u>, which I will not bring on unless a favorable opportunity offers, or as a last resort. Heavy attack made upon us has been repelled and considerable damage done to the enemy. With the blessing of God, I trust we shall be able to prevent Gen. Grant from reaching Richmond, and I think this army could render no more effectual service.[6]

---

5 Official Records, Vol. XXXVI pt. III, Ser. No. 68, p. 526.
6 Freeman, Douglas Southall, editor, "Lee's Dispatches to Jefferson Davis, 1862-65, " G.P. Putnam & Sons, N.Y., 1957, p. 174.

Cold Harbor Aftermath

The contrast between these two reports is amazing. General Grant's report is quite frank and honest. Grant refers to the "three days fight in Old Wilderness" and states his belief that it "was decidedly in our favor." General Lee's report is misleading. Lee tells President Davis:

We have succeeded so far in keeping on the front flank of that army and impeding its progress without a general engagement.

General Lee had just fought a major battle in the Wilderness on May 5, 6, and 7. In the battle of the Wilderness the Confederate army suffered 11,000 casualties, 16% of Lee's entire force of 67,000. Lee is stating to Davis that there has not been a general engagement, in other words, there was no major battle. Lee's purpose in this mis-statement is unclear. It is possible that he did not want to reveal the extent of the major damage to his army to President Davis. By May 9th, General Lee was two days into the battle of Spotsylvania where he would suffer an additional 12,000 casualties.

General Lee never did grasp Grant's threefold strategy in the 46-day Virginia campaign: (1) attack and cripple the Confederate army in Northern Virginia (Wilderness, Spotsylvania, 25,000 casualties). Then (2) maneuver the Confederate army south, away from Washington and destroy the North/South railroads (North Anna, Totopotomy Creek) and (3) pass around Lee and establish the Union army in a position south of Lee where it would attack and destroy the Southern railroads (Cold Harbor and the Crossing of the James):

HEADQUARTERS ARMIES OF THE UNITED STATES,

Cold Harbor, VA., June 5, 1864

Major-General Halleck,
Chief of Staff of the Army, Washington, D.C.:

GENERAL: A full survey of all the ground satisfies me that it would not be practicable to hold a line northeast of Richmond that would protect the Fredericksburg railroad, to enable us to use it for supplying the army. To do so would give us a long vulnerable line of road to protect, exhausting much of our strength in guarding it, and would leave open to the enemy all of his lines of communication on the south side of the James. <u>My idea from the start has been to beat Lee's army, if possible, north of Richmond, then, after destroying his lines of communication</u>

Cold Harbor Aftermath

<u>north of the James River, to transfer the army to the south side and besiege Lee in Richmond, or follow him south if he should retreat.</u> I now find, after more that thirty days of trial, that the enemy deems it of the first importance to run no risks with the armies they now have. They act purely on the defensive, behind breastworks, or feebly on the offensive immediately in front of them. Without a greater sacrifice of human life than I am willing to make, all cannot be accomplished that I had designed outside of the city. I have, therefore, resolved upon the following plan: I will continue to hold substantially the ground now occupied by the Army of the Potomac, taking advantage of any favorable circumstance that may present itself, until the cavalry can be sent west to destroy the Virginia Central Railroad from about Beaver Dam for some 25 or 30 miles west. When this is affected, <u>I will move the army to the south side of James River, either by crossing the Chickcahominy and marching near to City Point, or by going to the mouth of the Chickahominy on the north side and crossing there.</u> To provide for this last and most probable contingency six or more ferryboats of the largest class ought to be immediately provided. <u>Once on the south side of the James River I can cut off all sources of supply to the enemy, except what is furnished by the canal.</u> If Hunter succeeds in reaching Lynchburg that will be lost to him also. Should Hunter not succeed I will still make the effort to the canal by sending cavalry up the south side of the river with a pontoon train to cross wherever they can. The feeling of the two armies now seems to be that the rebels can protect themselves only by strong entrenchments, while our army is not only confident of protecting itself without entrenchments, but that it can beat and drive the enemy wherever and whenever he can be found without this protection.

Very respectfully,
U. S. GRANT,
Lieutenant-General [7]

---

7 Official Records, Vol. XXXVI, Pt. 111, Ser. No. 69, p. 598. Note General Grant's message was delivered by Col. Babcock of his staff. There were suspected security problems with telegraph.

Cold Harbor Aftermath

General Grant's letter of June 5, 1864 is a brilliant analysis of the Virginia campaign, far better than the analysis of most historians. Grant's strategic concept had remained constant throughout the campaign: General Lee's destruction was best accomplished by putting the Union army South of Lee and destroying his source of supply—the railroads.

The only question that remained — was Grant a sufficiently skilled general to move 100,000 men south of Lee and across the James River without Lee knowing it?

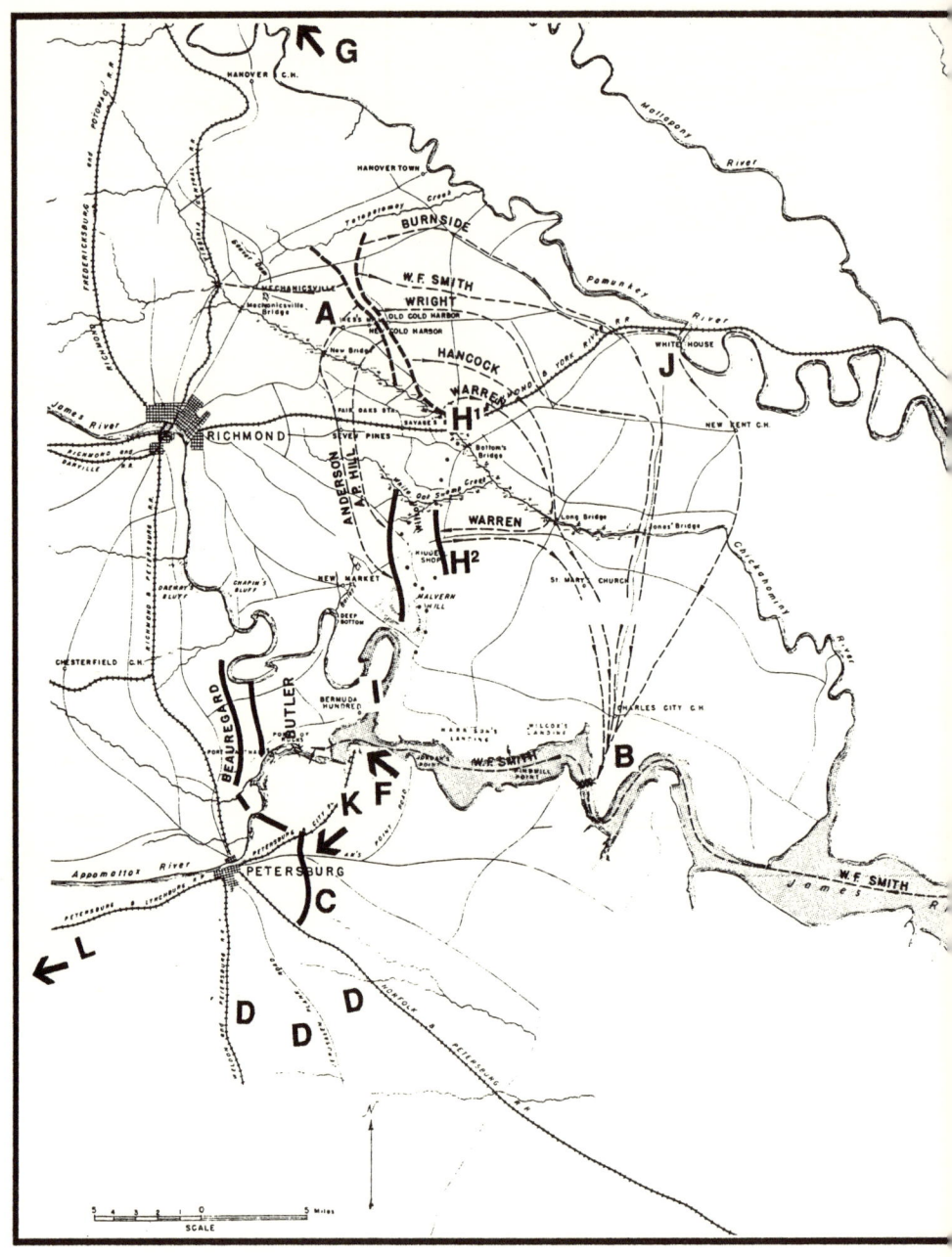

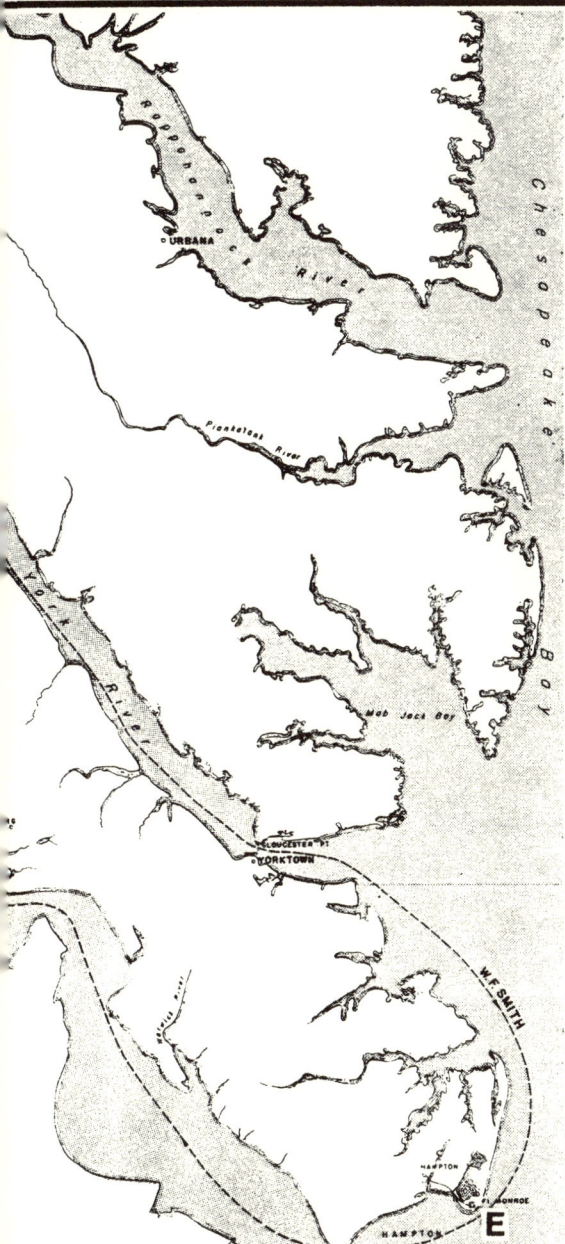

Virginia Theater of Operations— June, 1864

A. Cold Harbor Battlefield Scene of Battle on June 3, 1864

B. The Great Bridge—One half mile military bridge over the James River

C. Confederate defense line for the railroad center of Petersburg

D. Confederate railroads south of Petersburg—General Grant's ultimate objective

E. Fortress Monroe—A Union enclave at the end of the Peninsula

F. Landing point of Union General Smith's eighteenth corps (15,000 men) to spearhead the attack on Petersburg

G. General Sheridan's cavalry raid on Charlottesville which drew the bulk of Confederate Cavalry away from the area of operations

H^1. General Warren's fifth corps in rest area prior to the crossing of the James

H^2. General Warren's fifth corps in position at Riddell Shop blocking Lee's army from the area of the crossing

I. Union Headquarters of General Butler's Army of the James at Bermuda Hundred prior to Grant's crossing of the James

J. Embarkation point of Smith's eighteenth corps for the 140 mile ride by ship to Bermuda Hundred so that fresh troops could attack Petersburg on June 15th

K. Diversionary attack by Union General Gillmore with 2,000 troops on June 9th to convince Confederates that Petersburg was not the Union objective

L. Union attack on Lynchberg by General Hunter's Valley army which compelled Lee to send 8,000 badly needed Confederate troops

Saturday June 4, 1864
Cold Harbor
D day minus 8

The task facing General Grant was enormous. He must overcome the inertia of a 100,000 man army closely engaged with the enemy. He must steal away undetected in the night. There was always the disastrous possibility that the enemy could attack his army in motion. Grant had to avoid ambush as he moved South with five infantry divisions, 49 artillery batteries, 1,200 caissons and ammunition wagons, herds of cattle, a division of cavalry and an immense column of supply wagons for a distance of fifty miles. He must use primitive country roads. He faced potential unknown enemy forces. The army must build bridges across the Chickahominy River, cross and then press on to the greatest obstacle of all the mighty James River.

The James was a tidal estuary one-half mile wide, and 100 feet deep. It possessed a strong current and a tidal rise and fall of four feet. The James had never been bridged. No military bridge of the proportions needed had ever been built. Grant's engineers would have to build the longest, strongest yet most flexible bridge in history. All of the materials for the bridge had to be brought to the spot from distant areas, some for a distance of one hundred miles.

The bridge must be constructed in the shortest possible time. The army had to cross before the enemy was alerted as to what was happening. The Confederates had powerful rams upstream on the James that could descend the river and destroy the bridge. Time was of vital importance.

Once across the James the army must press on and attack the railroad hub of Petersburg, the final military objective. Movements of the units of the 100,000 man army must be coordinated with the action of navy ships and their commanders, engineers and General Butler's Army of the James at Bermuda Hundred. All must work with precision. A few mistakes would spell disaster.

On June 4, 1864 General Grant's staff and General Meade's staff went into high gear on all bridging equipment. The entire movement would fail if the Army of the Potomac could not cross the James River in three days. General Grant wanted to know the exact location and status of bridging equipment.

D Day Minus 8

Brigadier General Benham was Chief Engineer of the Army of the Potomac.

General S. Williams was Assistant Adjudant General for General Meade. Any commmunication by Williams was an order from Meade or Grant.

HEADQUARTERS ARMY OF THE POTOMAC,
June 4, 1864-7.12 a.m.

Brigadier-General BENHAM,
Commanding Engineer Brigade,
Fort Monroe, Va.:

The commanding general desires you to send in a report showing what bridging material and entrenching tools have been brought by you to Fort Monroe, what you expect to receive in addition, and the disposition made of the property in your charge.
S. WILLIAMS[8]
Assistant Adjutant-General

The Chief Engineer of the Army of the Potomac replied quickly:

HEADQUARTERS ENGINEER BRIGADE,
Fort Monroe, *June 4, 1864.*
(Received 4:55 p.m.)

General S. WILLIAMS,
Asst. Adjutant-General, Hdqrs, Army of the Potomac:

In reply to your dispatch of this date, just received, I would state that brought here about 1,460 feet of wooden bridging, all for which I had the chess. This was sent up to General Butler on the day of its arrival: June 1, by order of General Halleck. I am expecting here tomorrow, if the weather permits it to come out of York River, the bridge that was at Fredericksburg, last placed under General Abercrombie. This was over 400 feet. I have also here for an emergency fifteen canvas boats but no other bridging, as I had not the chess. In addition I have here in the barges the sandbags, tools, lumber, and other material ordered by General Humphreys, according to Major Duane's schedule, on the 16th

---

8 Official Records, Vol. XXXVI Pt. 111, Ser. Nl. 69, p. 592.

D Day Minus 8

of April. I would further state that the bridging that arrived at Washington from New York since I left, I believe about 1,200 feet, has been sent, as Colonel Pettes telegraphs today, to Bermuda Hundred by order of the War Department, and I presume it to be in a raft that I saw passing Rip at 9 a.m today. There is no more bridging of any consequence now at the deport, and I expect no more at present.

H. W. BENHAM, [9]
Brigadier-General

Grant was specific in his orders. General Benham was in charge and completely responsible for the bridge. There must be a concentration of all bridging equipment at Fortress Monroe. No specific reason was given. The telegraph was often tampered with. Fortress Monroe, a Union enclave on the Peninsula, is 60 miles east of the anticipated point of crossing. The Navy would quickly bring the equipment up the James when it was needed.

Grant directed:

HEADQUARTERS ARMY OF THE POTOMAC,
June 4 1864-12 a.m.
(Received 6:20 p.m.)

Brig. Gen H. Q. Benham,
Commanding Engineer Brigade:

Your dispatch of 7 p.m. June 3 received. The commanding general directs that you collect at Fortress Monroe all the bridging material at your command, including that just sent to Washington from New York, and that you hold the same by readiness to be moved at very short notice, unless you receive instructions of a contrary tenor from authority superior to the commanding general, and in that event you will promptly communicate to these headquarters any orders that may be sent you by such superior authority.

S. WILLIAMS,
Assistant Adjutant-General[10]

---

9 Official Records, Vol. XXXVI Pt. 111, Ser. No. 69, p. 593.

10 Official Records, Vol. XXXVI Pt. III Ser. No. 69, p. 593.

D Day Minus 8

At Cold Harbor General Grant's headquarters and General Lee's headquarters were separated by five miles of trenches, troops, cannon, corpses and wounded men still lying on the battlefield. The Union army had attacked the Confederate trenches at dawn on June 3rd and suffered 7,500 casualties within an hour. The entrenched Confederates suffered only 1500 casualties. It was Pickett's charge in reverse.

Most of the Confederate casualties were in their own trenches; they were easily recoverable. Many of the Union wounded still lay on the battlefield because Confederate soldiers fired on litter bearers with white flags who tried to remove them. There was a heartlessness here not perceived on other battlefields:

HEADQUARTERS SECOND DIVISION,

June 4, 1864-3 p.m.

MAJOR-GENERAL HANCOCK;
GENERAL: The sharpshooters I sent out this morning have discovered the body of Colonel McKeen lying in front of the enemy's works in a position from which they will not be able to remove it until after dark. They succeeded, however, in removing the papers (by which the body was recognized), watch, Etc. which are to be brought to me this evening.

John Gibbon,
Brig. Gen. Of Volunteers,[11]
Commanding Division

June 5, 1864

General WILLIAMS,
Assistant Adjutant-General, Army of the Potomac:
General Gibbon reports that Colonel Symth's brigade left some of its wounded very near the enemy's works, and that others were wounded in the attempt to get them off. It is probable that a considerable number of dead remain behind the line.

D. B. BIRNEY,
Major-General.[12]

---

11 Official Records, Vol. XXXVI Pt. 111, Ser. No. 69, p. 574.
12 Official Records, Vol. XXXVI Pt. 111, Ser. No. 69, p. 608.

D Day Minus 8

At the close of the day on June 4, 1864 the Confederate army was secure in elaborate trenches at Cold Harbor. All attempts of the Union army to recover casualties from the bloody June 3 assault had been themselves repelled viciously. Richmond, the capital of the Confederacy, the supposed target of the June 3 attack at dawn, appeared to be safe. Lee made this report:

HEADQUARTERS ARMY OF NORTHERN VIRGINIA,
June 4, 1864-8:30 p.m.

Hon. SECRETARY OF WAR,
Richmond Va.

SIR: Last night, after the date of my dispatch, Generals Breckinridge and Finegan were attacked by the enemy as they were preparing to re-establish their skirmish line. The enemy was soon repulsed. Immediately afterward, an attack was made upon General Hoke's front, with a like result. Up to the time of writing nothing has occurred along the lines today except skirmishing at various points. The position of the army is substantially unchanged.

Very respectfully,
your obedient servant,
R. E. LEE.,
General[13]

---

13 Official Records, Vol. XXXVI pt. 111, Ser. No. 69, p. 874.

Sunday June 5, 1864
Cold Harbor
D day minus 7

Grant's move south across the James would violate Lincoln's guideline of keeping the Union Army between Washington, D.C., and Lee.

In reality, Grant had already provided for Washington's protection. He had destroyed the North/South railroads in central Virginia. General Lee could never go North again. In addition, General Grant had struck the Confederate army so hard at the Wilderness and Spotsylvania that Lee was now incapable of taking the offensive.

The answer by President Lincoln to Grant's letter of June 5th (page 7) can be found in General Halleck's reply of June 7th.

HEADQUARTERS OF THE ARMY,
Washington, *June 7, 1864.*

Lieutenant-General Grant,
In the Field:
GENERAL: Your letter of the 5th, by Lieutenant-Colonel Babcock, was received last evening. General Meigs has been advised of your wishes in regard to ferryboats. He will keep all he has or can procure in the vicinity of Fort Monroe subject to your orders. Many of the side-wheel boats in the quartermaster's department will also answer all the purposes of ferryboats. The barges will also be excellent for teams and stores, and can be towed by the tugs. <u>Everything will be sent forward as soon as you direct.</u> They are now mostly engaged as transports to White House. Nothing has recently been heard of Generals Hunter and Crook. Sherman is still doing well, but some apprehension has been felt about Forrest's movements to cut off his communications. General Canby has sent forces to Memphis to assist in driving Forrest out of the country. Nothing recently from Steele. I enclose a list of the troops forwarded from this department to the Army of the Potomac since the campaign opened-48,265 men. I shall send you a few regiments more, when all resources will be exhausted till another draft is made.
Very respectfully, your obedient servant,
H. W. HALLECK,
Major-General and Chief of Staff[14]

---

14 Official Records, Vol. XXXVI Pt. 111, Ser. No. 69, p. 665.

D Day Minus 7

In the statement in line 7, "Everything will be sent forward as soon as you direct," lay President Lincoln's approval. By providing General Grant all of the resources he needed to move South, President Lincoln was demonstrating his confidence in Grant's strategy.

On June 5, 1864 General Grant issued the first of a series of orders that would create four diversions to distract General Lee's attention away from the crossing of the James and force him to order troops to move away from the Union army's area of operations. Every effort would be made to deceive General Lee as to Grant's true objective. The diversions would come from four directions.

The importance of these planned diversions to the success of the crossing of the James has largely been ignored by historians. These actions have been treated just as separate battles that happened to occur at the same time. Nothing could be further from the truth. General Grant orchestrated his big planned movements with a series of planned minor actions that confused the enemy as to his intent. Grant wanted Lee to look in four directions and see a Union force advancing on him.

The first diversion would come from the North. General Sheridan would lead his cavalry in a raid on Charlottesville and the Virginia Central railroad on June 8th. This movement by the Union cavalry would pull most of the Confederate cavalry—the "eyes" of Lee's army-away from the Cold Harbor area. With his available cavalry diminished, General Lee's chances of discovering the crossing of the James by the Army of the Potomac were greatly reduced.

The second diversion would be a movement by General Warren's 5th Corps to the Riddell's Shop area on June 12th to create the impression that Richmond was threatened from the Southeast. This would draw the Confederate army to that area to establish a defensive position.

The third diversion would be a demonstration by a small force from the Army of the James against Petersburg on June 9th in which Union forces would first advance and then withdraw quickly after testing the defenses of Petersburg. This demonstration was to discredit the idea that Petersburg was the ultimate military target, which in fact it was.

The fourth and last diversion would be an attack on Lynchburg, Southeast of Petersburg, by General Hunter and his Valley army. This threat was to draw Confederate infantry from Lee's army to defend Lynchburg. Lee sent 8,000 men.

The first diversion, General Sheridan's cavalry raid on Charlottesville, was set in motion by General Grant:

D Day Minus 7

HEADQUARTERS ARMIES OF THE UNITED STATES,
Cold Harbor, Va., *June 5, 1864.*

Major-General MEADE,
Commanding Army of the Potomac:

GENERAL: The subject of the cavalry expedition to Charlottesville and Gordonsville is to effectually break up the railroad connection between Richmond and the Shenandoah Valley and Lynchburg. To secure this end they should go as far as Charlottesville, and work upon the Lynchburg branch and main line to Staunton for several miles beyond the junction. This done they could work back this way to where the road is already destroyed, <u>or until driven off by a superior force</u>. It is desirable that every rail on the road destroyed should be so bent or twisted as to make it impossible to repair the road without supplying new rails. After the work is accomplished, herein directed, the cavalry will rejoin the main army, keeping north of the Pamunkey until the position or the army is known to them. It may be found to be necessary to keep on the north side as far down as West Point. Instructions will be sent to General Hunter by the cavalry expedition. He will be required to join his force to General Sheridan's and return with him to the Army of the Potomac. If it is found practicable, whilst the cavalry is at the most westerly point reached by it, to detach a brigade or more to go over to the James River and destroy the canal, it will be a service well repaying for three or four days' detention.

U. S. GRANT.
Lieutenant-General.[15]

The second diversion, the movement of General Warren's 5th Corps to the Riddell's Shop area on June 12th, concurrent with the crossing of the James, was begun by withdrawing the 5th Corps from the battleline and putting it in reserve so that the men would be well rested:

[ORDERS.] HEADQUARTERS ARMY OF THE POTOMAC,
June 5, 1864-4 p.m.

The following movements and changes are ordered for tonight, and will commence as soon after dark as practicable:

---
15 Official Records, Vol. XXXVI Pt. 111, Ser. No. 69, p. 599.

D Day Minus 7

<u>1. Major-General Warren will withdraw and move by way of Old Church to the vicinity of Leary's, about 2 miles in rear of Cold Harbor, where he will remain in reserve, prepared to move wherever required.</u>

2. Major-General Burnside will change his position, keeping his left united with General Smith's right, in the best manner the ground admits of, and extend along Roundabout Creek and the Matadequin, past Allen's Mill, toward the fork of Old Church road, near the crossing of the Matadequin.

3. Major General Smith will modify his right in the manner required by this change of position of General Burnside.

4. Brigadier-General Ferrero will hold his command ready to move on the morning of the 6th.

5. Major-General Hancock will extend his picket or skirmish line, with strong supports, to the nearest point of the Chickahominy, relieving the cavalry pickets in that space.

6. Major-General Sheridan will hold two divisions of his cavalry ready to carry out, at the time to be indicated, the special instructions which will be given him. A brigade of the remaining division will be posted at Old Church, and picket from the right of General Burnside to the Pamunkey. The other brigade will picket the Chickahominy from the left of General Hancock. The changes in the position of the cavalry will be made at such time and by such routes as not to interfere with the movements of the infantry.

By command of Major-General Meade:
S. WILLIAMS,
Assistant Adjutant-General.[16]

As the 5th Corps was placed in reserve, General Burnside's 9th Corps was moved South to fill the vacuum.

On June 5th messages continued from the Union army headquarters regarding bridging equipment, where it was located and who was responsible for it. The communications were guarded. None of the communications revealed a precise use for the bridging, a date or a location. Grant operated only on a need to know basis.

General Butler at Bermuda Hundred discretely inquired of the quartermaster regarding sawmills in the area. (See Map 1, page 10, Pt. 1.) Sawmills were essential for making planking, balks and chesses for bridges.

---
16 Official Records, Vol. XXXVI Pt. I 1 1, Ser. 69, p. 603.

D Day Minus 7

HEADQUARTERS DEPARTMENT, Sec.
In the Field. June 5, 1864

Lieutenant-Colonel Biggs,
Chief Quartermaster:

COLONEL General Butler directs me to inquire whether the sawmills at Sewell's Point, Tanner's Creek, Warwick, Portsmouth, Newport News and others, if any are running. Also, whether you can supply lumber for the use of this army. If you cannot supply lumber, he desires to be informed of the reason. I am, colonel, very respectfully, your obedient servant,

C. J. PAINE,
Colonel and Acting Chief of Staff[17]

The navy appeared to be aware that something was in the wind:

FARRAR'S ISLAND, VA.,
June 5, 1864-10 p.m.
(Received 4.15 p.m. 6th.)

Hon. GIDEON WELLES,
Secretary of the Navy:

If General Grant swings around to James River, a dredging machine to deepen the channel heretofore cut through Trent's Reach bar will be wanted immediately to enable the monitors to pass up. Nothing new.

S. P. LEE.
Acting Rear-Admiral.[18]

Involved as he was in planning the movement of the Army of the Potomac that would end the campaign, General Grant had all the duties of General in Chief.

---

17 Official Records, Vol. XXXVI Pt. 111, Ser. 69, p. 635.
18 Official Records, Vol. XXXVI Pt. 111, Ser. No. 69, p. 634.

D Day Minus 7

> COLD HARBOR, VA.,
> *June 5, 1864-7 p.m.*
> (Received 6th)

MAJOR-GENERAL HALLECK.
Chief of Staff
    The object of sending troops to Mobile now would not be so much to assist General Sherman against Johnson as to secure for him a base of supplies after his work is done. Mobile also is important to us and would be a great loss to the enemy. Let the 100-days' men, such of them as you have to spare, move on.
> U. S. GRANT,
> *Lieutenant-General*[19]

During these preparations, the task of recovering Union wounded from the battlefield continued. The Confederate soldiers continued to fire on unarmed litter parties. In frustration, General Hancock turned to General Meade for help. At this point the commanding general became involved in a matter heretofore resolved at a Corps or division level by frontline troops:

> SECOND CORPS,
> *June 5, 1864-1 p.m.*

General WILLIAMS:
    Can any arrangement be made by which the wounded in front of Barlow can be removed? I understand men wounded on the 3d are still lying there.
> WINF'D S. HANCOCK,
> *Major-General, Commanding*[20]

(First endorsement)

Respectfully referred to Lieutenant-General Grant.
    Is it possible to ask under flag of truce for permission to remove the wounded now lying between our lines, and which the enemy's sharpshooters prevent me bringing off?

---

[19] Official Records, Vol. XXXVI Pt. 111, Ser. No. 69, p. 599.
[20] Official Records, Vol. XEVI Pt. 111, Ser. No. 69, p. 603.

D Day Minus 7

The wounded are lying in front of the Second, Sixth, and Eighteenth Corps.

> Respectfully,
> GEO. G. MEADE,
> *Major-General.*

(*Second endorsement*)

A flag might be sent proposing to suspend firing where the wounded are, until each party got their own. I have no objection to such a course.

> U. S. Grant,
> *Lieutenant-General.*[21]

General Meade replied to General Grant.

> HEADQUARTERS ARMY OF THE POTOMAC,
> *June 5 1864-1.30 p.m.*

Lieutenant-General Grant:

GENERAL: Any communication by flag of truce will have to come from you, as the enemy do not recognize me as in command whilst you are present.

> GEO. G. MEADE,
> *Major-General.*[22]

This was the first time that Grant was informed that Union wounded were still on the field. Without the slightest hesitation Grant sent the following message to Lee:

---

21 Official Records, Vol. XEVI Pt. 111, Ser. No. 69, p. 604.
22 Official Records, Vol. XXXVI Pt. 111, Ser. No. 69, p. 599.

D Day Minus 7

COLD HARBOR, VA.,
June 5, 1884.

General R. E. Lee,
Commanding Confederate Army

 It is reported to me that there are wounded men, probably of both armies, now lying exposed and suffering between the lines occupied respectively by the two armies. Humanity would dictate that some provision should be made to provide against such hardships. I would propose, therefore, that hereafter when no battle is raging either party be authorized to send to any point between the pickets or skirmish lines, unarmed men bearing litters to pick up their dead or wounded without being fired upon by the other party. <u>Any other method equally fair to both parties you may propose for meeting the end desired will be accepted by me.</u>

U. S. GRANT,
Lieutenant-General.[23]

 The difficulty of getting messages across the no man's land of the Cold Harbor battlefield cannot be overstated. It took a minimum of three hours to cross an active battlefield, pass all the sentries posted and communicate from Grant's headquarters to Lee's headquarters. At three o'clock on June 5, 1864 General Meade summoned Col. Lyman to his tent and gave him the following orders:

> Lyman, I want you to take this letter from General Grant and take <u>it by a flag of truce</u>, to the enemy's lines. General Hancock will tell you where you can carry it out.[24]

 Col. Lyman experienced long delays in getting through the Confederate lines and obtaining a response from the Confederate command. At 7:10 p.m. Col. Lyman had still not been received by Lee:

---

[23] Official Records, Vol. XXXVI Pt. 111, Ser. No. 69, p 600
[24] Agassiz, George R. editor, "Meade's Headquarters"
(Letters of Theodore Lyman), Atlantic Monthly 1922, p. 149

D Day Minus 7

>HEADQUARTERS SECOND ARMY CORPS,
>*June 5, 1864-7.10 p.m.*

General Williams:

Colonel Lyman sends word that he has communicated with the enemy, and is waiting to know how soon he will be received.

>WINF'D S. HANCOCK,
>*Major-General.*[25]

At 10 p.m. that night General Meade was trying to locate Col. Lyman.

>HEADQUARTERS ARMY OF THE POTOMAC,
>*June 5, 1864-10 p.m.*

GENERAL HANCOCK:

What has become of Lyman? He need not wait for an answer. We can receive and forward it when delivered.

>GEO. G. MEADE,
>*Major-General, Commanding.*

>HEADQUARTERS. SECOND ARMY CORPS,
>*June 5, 1864.*

GENERAL MEADE:

Nothing has been heard of Colonel Lyman since he went beyond my picket-line with one of my staff. I do not know that I will be able to communicate with him.

>WINF'D S. HANCOCK,
>*Major-General*[26]

When General Lee's first response to General Grant's appeal was received it appeared reasonable and cooperative. Lee had modified Grant's proposal:

---

25 Official Records, Vol. XXXVI, Part 111, Ser. No. 69, p. 607.
26 Official Records, Vol. XXXVI, Part 111, Ser. No. 69, p. 608.

D Day Minus 7

HEADQUARTERS ARMY OF NORTHERN VIRGINIA,
June 5, 1864.

Lieut. Gen. U. S. GRANT,
Commanding U.S. Armies:

GENERAL: I have the honor to acknowledge the receipt of your letter of this date proposing that hereafter, except in time of action, either party be at liberty to remove the dead and wounded from between the lines. I fear that such an arrangement will lead to misunderstanding and difficulty. I propose, therefore, instead, that when either party desires to remove their dead or wounded, a flag of truce be sent, as is customary. It will always afford me pleasure to comply with such a request as far as circumstances will permit.

Very respectfully,
your obedient servant,
R. E. LEE,
General[27]

General Grant's response went back to General Lee very quickly, early on the morning of June 6th by messenger under flag of truce:

COLD HARBOR, VA.,
June 6, 1864.

General R. E. LEE,
Commanding Army of Northern Virginia:

Your communication of yesterday's date is received. I will send immediately, as you propose, to collect the dead and wounded between the lines of the two armies, and will also instruct that you be allowed to do the same. I propose that the time for doing this be between the hours of 12 m. and 3 p.m. today. I will direct all parties going out to bear a white flag, and not to attempt to go beyond where we have dead or wounded, and not beyond or on ground occupied by your troops.

U. S. GRANT,
Lieutenant-General[28]

---

[27] Official Records, Vol. XXXVI Pt. 111, Ser. No. 69, p. 600.
[28] Official Records, Vol. XXXVI Pt. 111 Ser . No. 69 p. 638.

D Day Minus 7

The entire Army of the Potomac was notified that a truce was being negotiated and that preparations must be made for recovering the wounded on June 6th:

CIRCULAR.] HEADQUARTERS FOURTH BRIGADE.
June 5, 1864

<u>Regimental commanders are informed that a flag has been sent out from army headquarters proposing a cessation of hostilities* for a short time to enable our troops to bring off the wounded in our front.</u> The command will be held in readiness to cease firing at a moment's notice. During the truce, not a man or officer will be permitted outside the works, nor will they show themselves to the enemy in any manner. Regimental commanders will be held rigidly responsible that these orders are fully carried out. Notice will be given in due time if the truce is agreed upon. This information is published for the present for the information of regimental commanders only.

By order of Colonel Beaver, commanding brigade:

CHAS. P. HATCH,
Lieutenant and Acting
Assistant Adjutant-General.[29]

*Note: The term "cessation of hostilities" is used in the Union army communication. There was no effort made to have it appear to be anything other than what it was. General Grant had proposed a truce with General Lee for the recovery of the dead and wounded.

It appeared to General Grant that the nightmare was over. The men wounded on June 3rd would be recovered. General Lee had suggested the use of a flag of truce in a request "to remove their dead or wounded." Surely Confederate soldiers would not fire on unarmed litter bearers on June 6th:

---

29 Official Records Vol. XXXVI Pt. 111, Ser. No. 69, p. 608.

D Day Minus 7

General Lee reported to Richmond at the end of the day:

> Headquarters Army of Northern Virginia
> *June 5, 1864-8:30 p.m.*
>
> Hon. Secretary of War
> *Richmond, Va.*
>   SIR: Nothing has occurred on the lines today except slight skirmishing. There is no apparent change in the position of the enemy. No movement on his part has been discovered.
>
>   Very respectfully,
>   your obedient servant,
>   R. E. LEE,
>   General[30]

---

30 Official Records Vol. XXXVI Pt. 111, Ser. No. 69 p. 875

Monday June 6, 1864
Cold Harbor
D day minus 6

On June 6, 1864 preparations for the big movement across the James continued. One of the key players would be General Butler, commander of the Army of the James, headquarters at Bermuda Hundred. General Butler must coordinate the movements of specific units and provide information on the area of the James River. To insure that there would be no misunderstanding General Grant sent two key members of his staff, Col. Comstock and Col. Porter, to General Butler along with this letter:

COLD HARBOR, VA.,
June 6, 1864.

Major-General BUTLER,
Commanding Dept. of Virginia and North Carolina:
An expedition under General Hunter is now on its way up the Shenandoah Valley, and a large cavalry force will leave here tomorrow under General Sheridan to join him, for the purpose of utterly destroying the enemy's lines of communication on the north side of James River. When this is done it is my intention to transfer all the force now with me to the south side. To do this I may be compelled to go to the mouth of the Chickahominy. I now send Colonel Comstock, of my staff, to you to see what preparations are necessary to secure the rapid crossing of the river, and to learn if your position will be secure during the time the enemy would necessarily be able to spare a large force to operate with against you before re-enforcements could reach you. Colonel Comstock will explain to you fully the situation here.
U. S. GRANT.
Lieutenant-General.[31]

General Butler had commanded a previous diversionary attack on Richmond on May 4, 1864, by leading an army up the James River at the same time that the Army of the Potomac attacked Lee along the Rapidan. The movement by General Butler had been stopped in the area of Bermuda Hundred on the James River by Confederate General Beauregard. Butler had occupied the Bermuda Hundred position all

---

31 Official Records, Vol. XXXVI Pt. 111, Ser. No. 69, p. 662.

D Day Minus 6

through the month of May. Now, in the final move of the campaign, General Butler would play a key role.

Colonel Porter recalls the mission to General Butler:

> In the afternoon of June 6 the general* called Colonel Comstock and me into his tent, asked us to be seated, and said with more impressiveness of manner than he usually manifested: "I want you to undertake an important mission preliminary to moving the army from its present position. I have made up my mind to send Smith's corps by a forced night march to Cole's Landing on the Chickahominy, there to take boats and be transferred to Butler's position at Bermuda Hundred. These troops are to move without their wagons or artillery. Their batteries will accompany the Army of the Potomac. That army will be held in readiness to pull out on short notice, and by rapid marches reach the James River and prepare to cross. I want you to go to Bermuda Hundred, and explain the contemplated movement fully to General Butler, and see that the necessary preparations are made by him to render his position secure against any attack from Lee's forces while the Army of the Potomac is making its movement. You will then select the best point on the river for the crossing, taking into consideration the necessity of choosing a place which will give the Army of the Potomac as short a line of march as practicable, and which will at the same time be far enough downstream to allow for a sufficient distance between it and the present position of Lee's army to prevent the chances of our being attacked successfully while in the act of crossing. You should be guided also by considerations of the width of the river at the point of crossing, and of the character of the country by which it will have to be approached."[32]

*Note: General Grant

    Col. Comstock and Col. Porter left Cold Harbor early on the morning of June 7th.
    General Grant made himself the focal point for suggestions from staff officers. They felt free to offer advice because they were well received. General Hunt offered his vast knowledge of artillery.

---

32 Porter, Gen. Horace, "Campaigning with Grant," p. 187.

D Day Minus 6

Quartermasters General Meigs and General Ingals were particular favorites of General Grant. Their recommendations got a good hearing. Now, in this crucial stage of the campaign, General Barnard, Chief Engineer, gave his suggestions:

HEADQUARTERS ARMIES OF THE UNITED STATES.
Cold Harbor, June 6, 1864.

Lieut. Gen. U. S. Grant,
General-in-Chief:

GENERAL: It is quite probable that the present campaign may result in heavy siege work, and your own experience at Vicksburg must have shown you the need of a sufficient number of engineer officers. Every corps should have an engineer officer at headquarters, and so far as practicable every division. I would recommend that all the engineer officers not now in the field, fit for field duty, and whom it may be possible to spare from the duties on which they are engaged, be ordered to the Army of the Potomac. Brigadier - General Woodbury (lieutenant colonel of engineers) now commanding at Key West, would from his ability and knowledge of this country, be a great acquisition. The only objection in his case, and that of some others, would be the want of rank in the present meritorious and capable chief engineer of the Army of the Potomac, Major Duane. I noticed the great value of Coehorn mortars in the trenches of this position. Whether needed here or not, similar circumstances may arise elsewhere, and I mention them under the impression that if needed the Ordnance Department may not be able to furnish them at short notice. In view of possible siege operations it would be well to collect a siege train at Fort Monroe.

I am, very respectfully, your most obedient servant,
J. G. BARNARD.
Chief Engineer Armies in the Field.[33]

The prospect of the campaign ending in siege was prevalent in the minds of Union commanders. They were well aware of the massive slave-built fortifications surrounding Richmond and Petersburg. There was nothing in the personality or character of General Robert E. Lee that

---
33 Official Records, Vol. XXXV1 Pt. 111, Ser. No. 69, p. 637.

D Day Minus 6

indicated he would surrender his army while it was still capable of resistance.

On June 6th the recovery of the men wounded on June 3rd and still lying on the battlefield was uppermost in the minds of the Army of the Potomac. The time specified for the truce in Grant's letter was 12 noon to 3 PM. Preparations were made for parties of litter bearers to move out on the battlefield. Ambulances and medical facilities were made ready. Nothing happened. There was no reply from General Lee confirming the truce. The hours dragged by. The noon deadline came and went. Late in the afternoon General Burnside inquired of General Meade regarding the delay in the truce:

> HEADQUARTERS NINTH ARMY CORPS.
> *June 6, 1864.*
>
> Major-General HUMPHREYS;
>   Has the proposition for flag of truce been accepted? If so, for what time?
> A. E. BURNSIDE,
> *Major-General.*[34]

> HEADQUARTERS ARMY OF THE POTOMAC,
> *June 6, 1864-3:10 p.m.*
> (Received 3.50 p.m.)
>
> Major-General BURNSIDE,
> *Commanding Ninth Corps:*
>   The commanding general directs me to say that you will be notified as soon as the flag of truce is accepted.
> A.A. HUMPHREYS,
> Major-General and Chief of Staff.[35]

As late as 3:10 PM Lee had not bothered to reply to Grant's proposal for a truce which had been delivered to Lee's headquarters around 7 AM that morning. Finally a letter came across the battlefield from General Lee. It was one of the strangest letters of the Civil War. It reveals a side of Lee's character that has remained hidden and is at sharp variance with the popular concept of Robert E. Lee:

---

34 Official Records, Vol. XXXVI Pt. 111, Ser. No. 69 p. 655.
35 Official Records Vol. XXXVI Pt. 111, Ser. No. 69, p. 655.

D Day Minus 6

HEADQUARTERS ARMY OF NORTHERN VIRGINIA,
June 6, 1864.

Lieut. Gen. U. S. GRANT:
Commanding U. S. Army:

GENERAL: I have the honor to acknowledge the receipt of your letter of this date and regret to find that I did not make myself understood in my communication of yesterday. <u>I intended to say that I could not consent to the burial of the dead and the removal of the wounded between the armies in the way you propose,</u> but that when either party desire such permission it shall be asked for by flag of truce in the usual way.

Until I receive a proposition from you on the subject to which I can accede with propriety, <u>I have directed any parties you may send under white flags as mentioned in your letter to be turned back.</u>
Very respectfully, your obedient servant,

R.E. LEE,
General.[36]

Lee is frankly admitting that his troops will fire on unarmed litter parties. No wounded Union troops were to be recovered from the battlefield. Lee called off the recovery of the wounded because he did not like the wording in which the request was made.

Grant had no other choice but to make another attempt to reach the dying men. Grant wrote promptly:

COLD HARBOR, VA.,
June 6, 1864.

General R. E. Lee,
Commanding Army of Northern Virginia;

The knowledge that wounded men are now suffering from want of attention, between the two armies compels me to ask a suspension of hostilities for sufficient time to collect them in, say two hours. Permit me to say that the hours you may fix upon for this will be agreeable to me, and the same privilege will be extended to such parties as you may wish to send out on the same duty, without further application.

U. S. GRANT,
Lieutenant-General[37]

---

36 Official Records Vol. XXXVI Pt. III, Ser. No. 69, p. 638.
37 Official Records Vol. XXXVI Pt. III, Ser. No. 69, p. 638

D Day Minus 6

If there is any doubt as to Lee's lack of sincerity in getting the wounded men off the battlefield, Lee's letter of June 6, 1864 should dispel it. Lee's letter written at 7:00 p.m. could be expected to take three hours to make its way back across the battlefield to Grant's headquarters:

HEADQUARTERS ARMY OF THE NORTHERN VIRGINIA,
June 6, 1864-7 p.m.

Lieut. Gen. U. S. GRANT, *Commanding U. S. Armies:*

GENERAL: I regret that your letter of this date asking a suspension of hostilities to enable you to remove your wounded from between the two armies was received at so late an hour as to make it impossible to give the necessary directions so as to enable you to effect your purpose by daylight.

In order that the suffering of the wounded may not be further protracted, I have ordered that any parties you may send out for the purpose between the hours of 8 and 10 p.m. today shall not be molested, and will avail myself of the privilege extended to those from this army to collect any of its wounded that may remain upon the field.

I will direct our skirmishers to be drawn close to our lines between the hours indicated, with the understanding that at the expiration of the time they be allowed to resume their positions without molestation, and that during the interval all military movements be suspended.

Very respectfully, your obedient servant,

R E. LEE,
General.[38]

After four days of barring the Union army from its wounded at gunpoint, Lee had sent Grant a worthless piece of paper:

Note in Letter Book, Headquarters Armies of the United States
This last letter of General Lee was not delivered at the outposts of General Hancock until after 10 o'clock, the hour fixed by General Lee for the expiration of the armistice. Notwithstanding, the rebel pickets were drawn in as proposed, and a burial party sent out shortly after 8 o'clock, but as our pickets had received

---

38 Official Records, Vol. XXXVI Pt. 111, Ser. No. 69, p 639.

D Day Minus 6

no instructions on the subject, the party was captured. On the report of these facts, General Grant has just sent the subjoined letter to the rebel commander.[39]

Grant's letter of reply to Lee dated June 7, 1864 - 10:30 AM., reflects Grant's realization of Lee's duplicity:

Cold Harbor, VA.,
June 7, 1864-10:30 a.m.

General R. E. LEE,
Comdg. Army of Northern Virginia.

I regret that your note of 7 p.m. yesterday should have been received at the nearest corps headquarters to where it was delivered after the hour that had been given for the removal of the dead and wounded had expired. 10:45 p.m. was the hour at which it was received at corps headquarters, and between 11 and 12 it reached my headquarters. As a consequence, it was not understood by the troops of this army that there was a cessation of hostilities for the purpose of collecting the dead and wounded, and none were collected. Two officers and six men of the Eighth and Twenty-fifth North Carolina Regiments, who were out in search of the bodies of officers of their respective regiments, were captured and brought into our lines owing to this want of understanding. I regret this, but will state that as soon as I learned the fact I directed that they should not be held as prisoners, but must be returned to their commands. These officers and men having been carelessly brought through our lines to the rear, I have not determined whether they will be sent back the way they came or whether they will be sent by some other route.

<u>Regretting that all my efforts for alleviating the sufferings of wounded men left upon the battlefield have been rendered nugatory,</u>

I remain, Etc.,

U. S. GRANT,
Lieutenant-General.[40]

---

39 Official Records, Vol. XXXVI Pt. 111, Ser. No. 69, p. 666.
40 Official Records, Vol., XXXVI Pt. 111, Ser. No., 69, p. 666.

D Day Minus 6

It was Grant's conclusion that the correspondence had come to an end. Surprisingly, Lee responded:

> HEADQUARTERS ARMY OF NORTHERN VIRGINIA,
> *June 7, 1864-2 p.m.*
>
> Lieut. Gen. U. S. GRANT,
> *Commanding U. 5. Armies:*
>   GENERAL; Your note of 10:30 a.m. today has just been received. I regret that my letter to you of 7 p.m. yesterday should have been too late in reaching you to effect the removal of the wounded.
>   I am willing, if you desire it, to devote the hours between 6 and 8 this afternoon to accomplish that object upon the same terms and conditions as set forth in my letter of 7 p.m. yesterday. If this will answer your purpose, and you will send parties from your lines at the hour designated with white flags, I will direct that they be recognized and be permitted to collect the dead and wounded.
>   I will also notify the officers on my lines that they will be permitted to collect any of our men that may be on the field. I request you will notify me as soon as practicable if this arrangement is agreeable to you. Lieutenant McAllister, Corporal Martin, and two privates of the Eighth North Carolina Regiment, and Lieutenant Hartman, Corpl. T. Kinlow, and Privates Bass and Grey were sent last night, between the hours of 8 and 10 p.m., for the purpose of recovering the body of Colonel Murchison, and as they have not returned, I presume they are the men mentioned in your letter. I request that they be returned to our lines.
> Very respectfully, your obedient servant,
>   R. E. LEE,
>   *General.*[41]

Again, Lee's latest letter deserves close scrutiny. Grant's letter to Lee was marked June 7 1864, 10:30 a.m. Lee's letter of response was marked June 7, 1864, 2:00 p.m. Surely, Lee could see that if it took four hours for him to receive and respond to Grant's letter brought by messenger over a battlefield it would also take his own letter at least three hours to reach Grant. The truce he is offering Grant expires at almost the moment it is delivered. Notice the irony of Lee's conditional

---
41 Official Records, Vol. XXXVI Pt. 111, Ser. No. 69, p. 667.

D Day Minus 6

statement: "....if you desire it...." Grant has written four times to General Lee about his desire to recover Union wounded and Lee has the gall to say "if you desire it".

In his reply to Lee, Grant points out the obvious impossibility of complying with Lee's timing:

Cold Harbor, VA.,
June 7, 1864-5:30 p.m.

General R. E. LEE,
Commanding Army of Northern Virginia:

Your note of this date just received. It will be impossible for me to communicate the fact of the truce by the hour named by you (6 p.m.) but I will avail myself of your offer at the earliest possible moment, which I hope will not be much after that hour. The officers and men taken last evening are the same mentioned in your note and will be returned.

U. S. GRANT,
Lieutenant-General.[42]

The last truce that General Lee proposed on June 7, 1864, 2:00 p.m. was in the exact terms that Grant had originally proposed to Lee on June 6th and which Lee had refused. Lee has twice sent Grant meaningless truce proposals designed to expire before they can be carried out. Lee has done nothing to help. Lee was aware that wounded men were dying.

Nonetheless the Union army made use of whatever means were available to retrieve its wounded:

[*Endorsement*]

June 7, 1864.

Referred to General G. G. Meade commanding Army of the Potomac.

I will notify General Lee that hostilities will cease from 6 to 8 for the purposes mentioned. You may send the officers and men referred to as you deem best. Please return this.

U. S. GRANT,
Lieutenant-General.[43]

---
42 Official Records, Vol. XXXVI Pt. 111, Ser. No. 69, p. 667.
43 Official Records, Vol. XXXVI Pt. 111, Ser. No. 69, p. 667.

D Day Minus 6

CIRCULAR.] HEADQUARTERS ARMY OF THE POTOMAC,
June 7, 1864.

Corps commanders are notified that a flag of truce exists from 6 to 8 p.m. today and they will immediately send out under a white flag, medical officers with stretcher-bearers to bring in the dead and wounded. No other officers or men will be permitted to leave the lines, and no intercourse of any kind will be held with the enemy, and the medical officers and attendants will be enjoined not to converse upon any subject connected with the military operations or likely to give information to the enemy. By command of Major-General Meade:
S. WILLIAMS,
Assistant Adjutant-General[44]

HEADQUARTERS NINTH ARMY CORPS,
June 7 1864-8:30 p.m.

General HUMPHREYS;
The enemy in my front did not respect the flag of truce. My medical director was fired upon as he advanced with a white flag, and a continual fire kept up by the enemy during the whole period covered by the flag.
Respectfully,
A. E. BURNSIDE,
Major-General.[45]

Despite Lee's effort to frustrate the proceedings, some of the Union wounded were recovered as several of the Confederate units felt compassion for the wounded, and granted an unofficial truce in the section of the battlefield held by General Wright's 6th Corps. This informal truce occurred at approximately 1:00 p.m. June 6th 1864.

---

44 Official Records, Vol.XXXVI Pt. 111, Ser. No. 69, p. 669.
45 Official Records, Vol. XXXVI Pt. 111, Ser. No. 69, p. 684.

D Day Minus 6

HEADQUARTERS ARMY OF THE POTOMAC,
June 7, 1864-11 a.m.

Major-General WRIGHT,
Sixth Corps.

I am informed unofficially, based on the report of Colonel Tompkins, that there was yesterday some time on your lines a suspension of hostilities, or some kind of informal agreement between your forces and the enemy, during which your dead and wounded were removed. You will please report whether you have any knowledge of the existence of such a state of affairs, of any communications being held with the enemy, and, if so by whose authority the same was done.

Respectfully, yours,
GEO G. MEADE,
Mayor-General

(Same to Major-General Smith., Eighteenth Corps.)

HEADQUARTERS SIXTH ARMY CORPS,
June 7, 1864-11:05 a.m.

Major-General Meade:

I had already inquired into the report referred to in your dispatch of 11 a.m. and am assured that no agreement whatever was entered into with the enemy for a cessation of hostilities, but that some time before the cannonading of yesterday afternoon men from both sides brought in their dead lying between the lines; both parties refraining from firing as if by tacit consent and that this condition of things existed for an hour or more, when the fire of the enemy above alluded to commenced, and was followed by firing along the line. I shall call on Colonel Tompkins for a further report in the matter.

H. G. WRIGHT,
Major-General, Commanding[46]

A second informal truce occurred along the section of the battlefield held by General Smith's 18th Corps. This informal truce was in the afternoon of June 6th.

---

46 Official Records, Vol. XXXVI Pt. 111, Ser. No. 69, p 679.

D Day Minus 6

HEADQUARTERS EIGHTEENTH CORPS,
June 7, 1864

Major-General MEADE,
Commanding Army of the Potomac:

GENERAL; I have the honor to acknowledge receipt of your dispatch of 11 a.m., and in answer to furnish the following information: General Brooks, commanding First Division, states that an officer went out from his front during yesterday p.m. and at his own risk brought in a wounded man. General Martindale, commanding Second Division, states that the enemy ceased firing and stood upon their works and our men did likewise, supposing a cessation of hostilities was going on according to the request of the commanding general of the army. A rebel officer advanced and informed one of the officers of Second Brigade that unless work was suspended on a battery we were building hostilities would be resumed. Our men and the enemy then resumed their old positions. General Ames, commanding Third Division, states there was no communication along his front.

During the afternoon of yesterday, between 2 and 3 o'clock, I visited my lines, and was informed by the troops of the first line that an informal agreement had been made with the enemy in their front to stop picket-firing. As this was very much in accordance with my own ideas, I expressed a wish that this state of affairs would extend all along my lines, as my men in the rear lines were suffering adversely from such firing. While I was down there an officer of my corps went out under fire to exchange papers. During the night, while our dead were being buried, our men were so near as to hear a rebel officer give orders not to fire on burying parties. This is all with regard to cessation of hostilities or communication with the enemy on my front that I am informed of officially or otherwise.

I am, general, very respectfully, your obedient servant,
WM. F. SMITH,
Major-General, Commanding.[47]

---

47 Official Records, Vol. XXXVI Pt. 111, Ser. No. 69, p 687.

D Day Minus 6

There is no record that General Lee was aware that these unofficial truces had occurred. During all of the negotiations with General Lee over the recovery of wounded from the battlefield, Grant continued the complex preparations for the crossing of the James, turning his attention to the fourth diversion, an attack coming from the west against Lynchburg. General Hunter commanded a Union force that had moved up the Shenandoah Valley and occupied Lexington. Grant now wanted Hunter to aid in the crossing of the James by attacking Lynchburg and forcing Lee to divert troops there:

Headqrs Armies of the U.S.
Cold Harbor Va. June 6th 1864.

Maj. Gen D. HUNTER
COMD'G DEPT WEST VA.
GENERAL

General Sheridan leaves here tomorrow morning with instructions to proceed to Charlottesville Va, and to commence there the destruction of the Va. Cen. Rail road, destroying this way as much as possible. The complete destruction of this road and of the Canal on James River is of great importance to us. <u>According to the instructions I sent to Gen Halleck for your guidance you were to proceed to Lynchburg: and commence there. It would be of great value to us to get possession of Lynchburg for a single day.</u> But that point is of so much importance to the enemy that in attempting to get it, such resistance may be met as to defeat your getting on to the road or canal at all. I see in looking over my letter to Gen Halleck on the subject of your instructions that it rather indicates that your route should be from Staunton via Charlottesville. If you have so understood it, you will be doing just what I want. The direction I would now give is that if this letter reaches you in the valley between Staunton and Lynchburg, you immediately turn east by the most practicable road until you strike the Lynchburg branch of the Va Central road. From there move Eastward along the line of the road, destroying it completely and thoroughly until you join Gen Sheridan. After the work laid out for Gen Sheridan and yourself is thoroughly done proceed to join the Army of the Potomac by the route laid out in Gen Sheridans instructions.

D Day Minus 6

If any portion of your force, especially of your Cavalry, is needed back in your Dept. you are authorized to send it back.

If on receipt of this you should be near to Lynchburg and deem it practicable to reach that point, you will exercise your judgment about going there.

If you should be on the rail road between Charlottesville and Lynchburg, it may be practicable to detach a cavalry force to destroy the Canal. Lose no opportunity to destroy the Canal.

Very Respectfully Your Obt Svt
U.S. GRANT Lt Gen[48]

At the close of the day on June 6th General Lee reported:

HEADQUARTERS ARMY OF NORTHERN VIRGINIA
June 6, 1864-8:30 p.m.

Hon. Secretary of War
Richmond, Va.

SIR: There has been very little skirmishing on the lines today. It was discovered early this morning that the enemy had withdrawn from the front of General Early, on our left, and from most of the front of General Anderson, in the center,

Very respectfully, your obedient servant,
R. E. LEE
General.[49]

---

48 Symon, John Y. "The Papers of Ulysses S. Grant, Vol. 11, p. 24.
49 Official Records, Vol. XXXVI Pt. 111, Ser. No. 69, p. 887.

Tuesday, June 7, 1864
Cold Harbor
D day minus 5

On June 7th, 1864 General Sheridan left Cold Harbor with 8,000 Yankee cavalrymen and headed northwest for Charlottesville. His mission was threefold: to destroy the Virginia Central railroad, to possibly form a link with General Hunter in the Shenandoah Valley, and to draw the bulk of Confederate cavalry from the Cold Harbor area where it could interfere with the crossing of the James by the Army of the Potomac. In his first objective, destroying the railroad, Sheridan was only partially successful. In his second objective of linking up with General Hunter, Sheridan failed. He never reached Hunter. But in his third objective of drawing off the Confederate cavalry from Cold Harbor, General Sheridan more than earned his pay. On June 9th General Wade Hampton and 5,000 Confederate troopers left Cold Harbor in pursuit of Sheridan. That was 5/7th of Lee's cavalry. General Lee's ability to discover Union moves to the South was greatly diminished.

The preparation of the army for the crossing of the James continued. Each movement would be long and arduous. The army would march constantly for fifty miles. Everything possible must be done to rest the troops and get them in shape. Offensive operations were suspended.

[CIRCULAR] HEADQUARTERS ARMY OF THE POTOMAC.
June 7, 1864.

The major-general commanding directs that corps commanders suspend pushing their works up to the enemy, limiting their operations to completing those necessary for their security that have been commenced.

A. A. HUMPHREYS
Major-General and Chief of Staff[50]

Grant was always focused on achieving the ultimate military objective that would bring the Civil War to an end. Routine matters, paperwork, details, were handled by a competent staff. General Grant invented the modern military staff:

---

50 Official Records, Vol. XXXVI Pt. 111, Ser. No. 69, p. 669.

D Day Minus 5

GENERAL ORDERS, WAR DEPT., ADJT. GENERAL'S OFFICE,
No. 155. *Washington April 8, 1864.*

The General-in-Chief announces the following-named officers as composing his staff in the field:
Brig. Gen. John A. Rawlins, chief of staff.
Lieut. Col. T. S. Bowers, assistant adjutant-general
Lieut. Col. C. B. Comstock, senior aide-de-camp.
Lieut. Col. O. E. Babcock, aide-de-camp
Lieut Col. F. T. Dent, aide-de-camp.
Lieut. Col. Horace Porter, aide-de-camp.
Lieut. Col. W. L. Duff, assistant inspector-general.
Lieut. Col. W. R. Rowley, secretary.
Lieut. Col. Adarn Badeau, secretary.
Capt. E. S. Parker, assistant adjutant-general.
Capt. George K. Leet, assistant adjutant general, in charge of office at Washington.
Capt. P. T. Hudson. aide-de-camp.
Capt. H. W. Janes, assistant quartermaster, on special duty at headquarters.
First Lieut. W. M. Dunn, jr., Eighty-third Indiana Volunteers, acting aide-de-camp.
By command of Lieutenant-General Grant.

E. D. TOWNSEND,
Assistant Adjutant-General.[51]

While Lee labored long into the night on mountains of paperwork assisted by only three colonels, Col. Walter H. Taylor, C.S.A., Col. Charles Marshall, C.S.A., and Col. Charles S. Venable, C.S.A., Grant was able to concentrate on prosecuting the war.

Grant placed great importance on railroads as sources of supply both for his armies and the enemy armies. Where he needed railroads, he built them. Where railroads supported the Confederate Army, he destroyed them With his stategic plan to move the Union army South of the James River, General Grant did not want to leave behind anything that might be of use to the Confederates, especially railroads.

---

[51] Official Records, Vol. XXXIII, Ser. No. 60, p 820.

D Day Minus 5

COLD HARBOR, VA.
June 7, 1864

BRIG GEN. J.J. ABERCROMBE
COMDG U.S. FORCES WHITE HOUSE VA.
GENERAL.

    Capt. Parker, Asst. Adj Gen. goes to White House this morning for the purpose of ascertaining certainly the time when cars can commence moving and the probable time it would take thereafter to remove all the iron from the York river R. R. from the Chickahominy back to White House and place it on board of steamers. <u>I shall not want to use the railroad at all for supplying the army but will destroy it so that the enemy cannot use the iron for the purpose of relaying other roads.</u>

Very Respectfully
U.S. GRANT, Lt Gen[52]

During this whole period the watch on railroad traffic between Richmond and Petersburg by Union scouts was continued. It was important to know if any Confederate troops were being shifted South to Petersburg:

SPRING HILL SIGNAL STATION,
June 7, 1864-11.40 a.m.

Captain NORTON;

    Three very long trains passed toward Petersburg this a.m. They were composed almost entirely of freight cars, and from the sound and appearance I judge they were empty.

GARRETT.
Sergeant, Signal Corps, U.S. Army.[53]

---

52 Simon, John Y. "The Papers of Ulysses S. Grant," Vol. II, p. 28.
53 Official Records, Vol. XXXVI Pt. 111, Ser. No. 69, p. 692.

D Day Minus 5

SPRING HILL SIGNAL STATION,
June 7, 1864-1:15 p.m.

Captain NORTON;

Two trains have just passed toward Richmond. One was partially loaded with troops and the other entirely with freight. One empty train just passed toward Petersburg.

GARRETT,
Sergeant. Signal Corps, U.S. Army.[54]

SPRING HILL SIGNAL STATION,
June 7, 1864-4:10 p.m.

Captain NORTON:

A train of eight cars has just passed toward Richmond, with two of the cars loaded with troops and the rest with freight.

GARRETT,
Sergeant, Signal Corps.[55]

SPRING HILL SIGNAL STATION.
June 7, 1864-4:50 p.m.

Captain NORTON;

A small train has just passed toward Petersburg. It appears to be empty.

GARRETT,
Sergeant, Signal Corps.[56]

---

54 Official Records, Vol. XXXVI Pt. 111, Ser. No. 69, p. 692.
55 Official Records, Vol. XXXVI Pt. 111, Ser. No. 69, p. 693.
56 Official Records, Vol. XXXVI Pt. 111, Ser. No. 69, p. 693.

D Day Minus 5

At the close of the day on June 7, 1864 General Lee reported:

> HEADQUARTERS ARMY OF NORTHERN VIRGINIA,
> *June 7, 1864 7 p.m.*
>
> Hon. SECRETARY OF WAR,
> Richmond, Va.
>   SIR: the operations of today have been unimportant. Slight skirmishing has taken place along the lines.
>   Very respectfully, your obedient servant,
>   R. E. LEE,
>   *General.*[57]

---

[57] Official Records, Vol. XXXVI Pt. 111, Ser. No. 69, p. 877.

II

COLD HARBOR-FINAL PREPARATIONS D DAY MINUS 4

Wednesday, June 8, 1864

Moving an army engaged with the enemy on a six mile front without being detected would be extremely difficult.

The Army of the Potomac would begin its fifty mile march at night. Grant had been very successful in stealing a day's march on General Lee by night maneuvers during the campaign; two Confederate generals on the Bermuda Hundred front understood this:

JUNE 11, 1864.

General BEAUREGARD,
Commanding:

GENERAL: I am so much disturbed about our condition, but especially about our relations to Petersburg, that you must excuse me for a suggestion. It seems to me that there is but one way to save the country, and bring the authorities to their senses, and that is to say "I cannot guard Bermuda Hundred and Petersburg both, with my present forces. I have decided that Petersburg is the important point and will withdraw my whole command to that place tonight." <u>It is arrant nonsense for Lee to say that Grant can't make a night march without his knowing it. Has not Grant slipped around him four times already?</u> Did not Burnside retire from Fredericksburg, and Hooker from the Wilderness, without his knowing it? Grant can get 10,000 or 20,000 men to Westover and Lee know nothing of it. What then is to become of Petersburg? Its loss surely involves that of Richmond-perhaps of the Confederacy.

D Day Minus 4

An earnest appeal is called for now, else a terrible disaster may, and I think will, befall us.

> Very respectully,
> D. H. HILL,
> *Major-General and Aide-de-Camp.*

(Indorsement)

General HILL:

I fully concur in the above views, which have been already communicated to the Government in substance if not in words. I consider it useless again to do so, as it would produce no good results and my records are already "all right." I shall continue to hold "the lines" as long as there is the slightest hope of being able to do so with success and without endangering Petersburg.

> G. T. BEAUREGARD.[1]

In order to steal another night march on Lee in the final big movement of the campaign, Grant had to take every precaution. During the withdrawal of the Army of the Potomac from the fighting front after sundown on June 12th, there was always the danger that the Confederates would detect the movement and attack the Union army while it was in motion in marching columns. To forestall this possibility, a reserve line of fortifications had to be prepared behind the front line where a screening force could take position to protect the army's withdrawal:

> HEADQUARTERS ARMIES OF THE UNITED STATES,
> *June 8, 1864 7:40 p.m.*

Maj. Gen. G. G. MEADE,
Commanding Army of the Potomac:

GENERAL; To prepare for the withdrawal of the army from its present position, which will take place in a few days, a direct line from the present right to left should be marked out and partially fortified. Such a line can be occupied by the two divisions of the Fifth Corps, now loose, and a sufficient number from other corps, when the movement takes place, to perfectly cover such a withdrawal. General Barnard has been looking today

---

1 Official Records, Vol. XXXVI Pt. 111, Ser. No. 69, p. 896.

D Day Minus 4

with the view of locating such a line, and will direct your chief engineer in the work to be done.

Very respectfully,
U. S. GRANT,
Lieutenant-General.[2]

Very early in taking command, Grant established the logistical support for the Virginia campaign. In April 1864, he created a floating supply base to support his army as it moved south:

CONFIDENTIAL.
Brigadier-General MEIGS,

HEADQUARTERS OF THE ARMY
April 30, 1864.

Quartermaster - General : Lieutenant - General Grant wishes put afloat 1,000,000 of provision rations and 200,000 forage rations, ready to be sent in to the James, York or Rappahannock Rivers.

H. W. HALLECK,
Major-General and Chief of Staff[3]

As the Army of the Potomac progressed south, Grant constantly shifted his base of supplies. The first base had been Belle Plaines for the battle of the Wilderness and Spotsylvania. Then Grant shifted base to Port Royal, Virginia. In crossing the Pamunky River, it shifted to White House, Virginia. Now, as the army prepared to cross the James River, the question of retaining White House was considered:

June 8, 1864.

Col. E. SCHRIVER:

The commanding general directs that you at once proceed to make an inspection of the depot at White House, Va., and report upon the condition of the several branches of the service at the depot. A statement showing precisely what troops are at the White House, whether as permanent garrison or en route for this army, (and) also whether the troops composing the garrison are advantageously posted for the defense of the position. You will also report upon the

---

2 Official Records, Vol. XXXVI Pt. 111, Ser. No. 69, p. 695.
3 Official Records, Vol. XXXIII, Ser. No. 60, p. 1023.

D Day Minus 4

character of the field-works now being constructed at the White House, and how far they are advanced toward completion. The commanding general further directs that in your examination of the hospitals you ascertain whether any stragglers found their way down with the sick and wounded, and should such persons be found at the hospitals they will at once be turned over to the commander at the White House, to be by him returned to the army.

      Very respectfully, &tc.,
      S. WILLIAMS,
      Assistant Adjutant-General.[4]

Grant decided the main supply base for the Army of the Potomac would become City Point on the south bank of the James River. City Point would become one of the largest ports on the East coast for the balance of the war, overflowing with ships, warehouses and military supplies.

      HEADQUARTERS U. S. ARMIES,
    Cold Harbor, Va., *June 9, 1864-7:30 a.m.*
      (Received 3 a.m. 10th.)

Major Gen. H. W. HALLECK,
Chief of Staff:
 All re-enforcements sent hereafter please send to City Point.
      U. S. GRANT,
      Lieutenant-General.[5]

  HEADQUARTERS ARMIES OF THE UNITED STATES,
    Near Cold Harbor, Va., June 9, 1864.

Brig. Gen. J. J. ABERCROMBIE,
Commanding U. S. Forces, White House, Va.:
 GENERAL: Direct all organized troops arriving at the White House from and after to-day to proceed, without debarking from transports they may be in, to City Point or Bermuda Hundred, and there report to Major-General Butler, commanding.
 By command of Lieutenant-General Grant:
      JNO. A RAWLINS,
      Brigadier-General-and-Chief-of-Staff.[6]

---

4 Official Records, Vol. XXXVI Part 111. Ser. No.69, p. 695.
5 Official Records, Vol. XXXVI Pt. 111, Ser. No. 69, p. 709.
6 Official Records, Vol. XXXVI Pt. 111, Ser. No. 69, p. 716.

D Day Minus 4

Since Grant supplied his army by sea, he did not waste troops defending long overland supply lines. Supplies were unloaded from the ships into wagon trains. The wagon trains moved the supplies to the fighting front with military escorts. Confederate cavalry was never able to disrupt the logistical system of the Union army.

On June 8th the concentration of bridging equipment at Fortress Monroe and Bermuda Hundred continued:

>NAVY-YARD, WASHINGTON,
>*June 8, 1864-9:10 a.m.*

Brig. Gen. H. W. BENHAM,
Commanding Engineers:

The New York bridge sent to Bermuda Hundred, consisting of 33 pontoons, 1,000 chesses, 6 trestles, 400 common balks, 170 claw balks, and other material for bridges of 1,300 feet. The remainder, 27 boats and 300 chesses, were ordered stopped in transit, and have probably gone up the James River.

>WM. H. PETTES,
>*Colonel Fiftieth New York Vols.,*
>*Comdg. Engineers Depot.*[7]

The observation by Union scouts of the railroad traffic between Petersburg and Richmond continued; Grant wanted to know if any enemy troops were being shifted south of the James to Petersburg:

>SPRING HILL SIGNAL STATION,
>*June 8, 1864 1:20 p.m.*

Captain NORTON;

Two large freight trains have just passed toward Richmond, and one empty train toward Petersburg.

>GARRETT,
>*Sergeant, Signal Corps.*

---

[7] Official Records, Vol. XXXVI, Part 111, Ser. No. 69, p. 704.

D Day Minus 4

SPRING HILL SIGNAL STATION,
June 8, 1864-3:50 p.m.

Captain NORTON;
 The working party of rebels is not directly between my station and the railroad station, but off a little to the left. The number is about 25, and they are dressed in a variety of colors,

GARRETT,
Sergeant, Signal Corps.

SPRING HILL SIGNAL STATION,
June 8, 1864 4:10. p.m.

Captain NORTON;
 A train of six cars has just passed toward Richmond, partly loaded with troops.

GARRETT,
Sergeant, Signal Corps.[8]

On June 8, 1864, General Lee wrote his wife to comfort her over loss of personal property caused by Confederate reverses in the Shenandoah Valley:

Gaines' Mill
June 8, 1864

To HIS WIFE
Richmond, Virginia

I received today your note without date. It is useless for us to grieve for the calamity at Staunton or elsewhere. We must bear everything with patience that is inflicted on us. It will be impossible to remove the silver, etc., from Lexington. It will incur more danger in removal than in remaining. It must bide its fate. I hope you are all well. Give love to the girls & may God bless & preserve you all.

Truly & sincerely,
R. E. LEE.[9]

---

8 Official Records, Vol. XXXVI Pt. 111, Ser. No. 69, p. 705.
9 Dowdy, "The Wartime Papers of R E. Lee," p. 769.

54

D Day Minus 4

The third diversion, a demonstration against Petersburg by General Gillmore and a small force of troops (2,000 men) from General Butler's command based at Bermuda Hundred, began on the night of June 8th.

HEADQUARTERS TENTH ARMY CORPS,
In the Field, *June 8, 1864-10 p.m.*

Brigadier-General Terry,
Commanding First Division:

You will direct Colonel Hawley with his brigade to move at once across the Appomattox, by way of the pontoon bridge near General Butler's headquarters, calling there for a guide. Upon reaching the high ground on the other side of the Appomatox, Colonel Hawley will assume command of the Sixty-second Ohio Volunteers and the artillery under Lieutenant Sanger, First Artillery, and there await orders. The command should move without noise.

By order of Major-General Gillmore:

ED. W. SMITH,
Assistant Adjutant-General.[10]

June 8, 1864. (Received 11 p.m.)

General HINKS;

General Butler directs me to say that General Gillmore, with his column, will be at the pontoon bridge between 11 and 12 o'clock tonight. He directs that you have a staff officer at the bridge to guide the troops to the Jordan's Point road, to a good place to rest within the pickets. Also that you meet General Gillmore for consultation at the bridge at midnight. Please acknowledge receipt.

C. J. PAINE,
Colonel and Acting Chief of Staff.[11]

Colonel Paine is General Butler's Chief of Staff. This is an order from Butler.

---

10 Official Records, Vol. XXXVI Pt. 111, Ser. No. 69, p. 706.
11 Official Records, Vol. XXXVI Pt. 111, Ser. No. 69, p. 707.

D Day Minus 4

At the close of the day on June 8th General Lee reported:

> HEADQUARTERS ARMY OF NORTHERN VIRGINIA,
> June 8, 1864-8 p.m.
>
> Hon. SECRETARY OF WAR,
> Richmond, Va.:
>
> SIR: The enemy has been unusually quiet today along the whole extent of his lines, and nothing of importance has occurred. Two divisions of his cavalry, under General Sheridan. are reported to have crossed the Pamunkey yesterday at New Castle Ferry, and to have encamped last night at Dunkirk and Aylett's on the Mattapony. They were accompanied by artillery, ambulances, wagons, and beef-cattle.
>
> Very respectfully, your obedient servant,
>
> R. E. LEE,
> *General.*[12]

---

12 Official Records, Vol. XXXVI Pt. 111, Ser. No. 69, p. 879.

Thursday June 9, 1864
Cold Harbor
D day minus 3

On June 9, 1864, just three days away from the crossing of the James, Grant found time to write his friend, Representative Elihu Washburne of Illinois. Washburne had been an early patron of Grant and championed his cause in Washington as Grant rose in rank in the field. The letter, written not for publication, represents General Grant's appraisal of the military situation.

To Elihu B. Washburne

Cold Harbor Va. *June 9th/64*

HON. E. B. WASHBURNE
DEAR SIR;

Your two letters enclosing orders published by Maj. Gen Washburne have been received. I highly approve the course he is taking and am glad to see that Gen Slocum is pursuing a similar course about Vicksburg-....

....Every thing is progressing favorably but slowly. All the fight, except defensive and behind breast works, is taken out of Lee's army. <u>Unless my next move brings on a battle the balance of the campaign will settle down to a siege.</u>

All here are well and desire to be remembered to you. <u>When Congress adjourns, come down and see us.</u>

Yours Truly
U.S. GRANT
Lt. Gen.[13]

It is obvious from his letter that General Grant did not expect the war to end in the immediate future. He expected the campaign to end in a siege.

---

13 Simon, John Y. "The Papers of Ulysses S. Grant", Vol. XI, page 32.

D Day Minus 3

As he wrote to his wife:

June 6th

"This is likely to prove a very tedious job I have on hand but I feel very confident of ultimate success. The enemy keeps himself behind strong entrenchments all the time and seems determined to hold on to the last— [14]

In crossing the James River and either taking Petersburg or entrenching his army opposite Petersburg, Grant would force Lee into a new position: Lee would have to come south and fight for Petersburg and his railroads. Once in the trenches of Petersburg the Confederate army would be trapped. It could never leave.

The third diversion had begun:

GENERAL BUTLER'S HEADQUARTERS,
June 9, 1864-7:30 p.m. (Received 10th)

Lieutenant-General GRANT:

Will start back early in the morning. General Gillmore with 2,000 men started today to demonstrate on Petersburg, while Kautz with 1,500 cavalry was to go around, enter Petersburg, if practicable and destroy railroad bridges, and to go south on the railroad. Gillmore reconnoitered the enemy's works and has returned, finding them strong. Kautz has not yet been heard from.
C. B. COMSTOCK,
Lieutenant-Colonel and Aide-de-Camp.[15]

A more complete description of this minor action can be found in General Gillmore's own reports:

HEADQUARTERS TENTH ARMY CORPS,
Copsa's Va., June 9, 1864-5:30 a.m.

Major General BUTLER;

Colonel Hawley will approach Petersburg by the City Point Road, General Hinks on the Jordan's Point Road. General Kautz is well in advance with directions to approach on the Jerusalem

---

14 Simon, John Y., "The Papers of Ulysses S. Grant," Vol. XI, page 25. Letter to Julia Dent Grant dated June 6, 1864 from Cold Harbor.
15 Official Records, Vol. XXXVI Pt. 111, Ser. No. 69, p. 709.

D Day Minus 3

Road. I recommend that the pickets of the Spring Hill garrison be increased and thrown forward beyond Rushmore's as a demonstration.

Respectfully, &tc.,
Q. A. GILLMORE,
Major-General.

HEADQUARTERS,
Elick Jordan's, June 9, 1864-12:30 p.m.

Major-General BUTLER;

I found the enemy prepared for me, to all appearances. A prisoner says our movement was known at 1 this morning, and that re-enforcements arrived by railroad. General Hinks, on the Jordan's Point road, says he cannot carry the work in his front, and that since he arrived there at 7 a.m. two more regiments have been added to the entrenchments, coming from the city. In Hawley's front the works are as strong, I should think as our own on Terry's front. In my opinion, they cannot be carried by the force I have. Distant firing on my extreme left has been heard for the last hour and a half. I, therefore, judge that Kautz finds himself opposed. I am about to withdraw from under fire in the hopes of hearing from him.

Very respectfully, &tc.,
Q. A. GILLMORE,
Major-General.

JUNE 9, 1864-2:30 p.m.

General Gillmore:

Your dispatch of 12:30 received. I grieve for the delay in getting off the expedition this morning. I hope Kautz has been more successful in getting in. You do not speak of any loss. I send you a note from Surgeon McCormick which please preserve. Not on the ground, I cannot advise. No troops have passed over railroad or turnpike since 6 o'clock this morning.

Yours,
BENJ. F. BUTLER,
Major-General, Commanding.

D Day Minus 3

HEADQUARTERS,
Near Baylor's Saw-Mill, June 9, 1864.

Major-General BUTLER;

General Hinks, who was on the left, says the last firing from General Kautz was heard at 12 o'clock, apparently just where it commenced. After waiting under the entrenchments until about 1 o'clock to hear further from him I gradually withdrew to Baylor's, and then waited until 3:30 o'clock. Both General Hinks and myself think Kautz has gone to cut the railroad; that was understood to be his intention. As I was directed to return tonight, l do not feel justified in delaying here any longer.

Very respectfully, your obedient servant,

Q. A. GILLMORE,
Major-General.[16]

Whatever the merits of Gillmore's "demonstration" before Petersburg, his hasty withdrawal seemed to have convinced Lee that Beauregard's messages of alarm were ill founded. Beauregard, in command at Petersburg, repeatedly sounded the alarm and called for reinforcements. Lee believed Gillmore's advance was a diversion to cover the real objective. Lee still believed that Richmond was Grant's ultimate objective and that it was essential that the Confederate army remain between Grant and the capital:

To GENERAL BRAXTON BRAGG
Commanding Armies of the Confederate States

Headquarters, Army of Northern Virginia
June 9, 1864
2 1/2 p.m.

Telegrams of Gen. Beauregard received. I am aware of no troops having left Gen. Grant's army. The regiment of cavalry and infantry seen by Gen. Ware [for Henry A. Wise] is a small force. Gen. Hoke's troops are now in the trenches, and cannot be withdrawn until night under any circumstances. Gen. Ransom's brigade is on the right bank of Chickahominy protecting the batteries there posted. I know no necessity for the removal of these troops, but if directed will send them. No troops have left

---
16 Official Records, Vol. XXXVI Pt. 111, Ser. No. 69, p. 719.

D Day Minus 3

Gen. Grant's army to my knowledge, and none could have crossed James River without being discovered. I think it very improbable that he would weaken himself under existing circumstances. Stanton's dispatches state that all available troops had been drawn from Butler except enough to hold his lines. It is further stated in a letter apparently from some one connected with Gen. Butler, that certain troops collected at Point Lookout to reinforce Butler, were diverted to Grant.

Couriers seem to reach me from Richmond more promptly than telegrams.

R.E. LEE[17]

At the close on the day on June 9th General Lee reported:

HEADQUARTERS ARMY OF NORTHERN VIRGINIA,
June 9, 1864-9:30 p.m.
Hon. SECRETARY OF WAR,
Richmond, Va:

SIR: The enemy has been quiet to-day-apparently engaged in strengthening his entrenchments. Skirmishing on the lines has been very light.

Very respectfully, your obedient servant,

R.E. LEE,
General[18]

---

17 Dowdey, Wartime Papers of R.E. Lee, Message 769, p. 774.
18 Official Records, Vol. XXXVI Pt. 111, Ser. No 69, p. 883.

Friday June 10, 1864
Cold Harbor
D day minus 2

General Warren would command the 5th Corps which would block the Confederate Army at Riddell's Shop from attacking the Union army as it marched south:

> HEADQUARTERS ARMY OF THE POTOMAC,
> *June 10, 1864-7:30 p.m.*
>
> Major-General WARREN,
> *Commanding Fifth Corps:*
>   The major-general commanding directs that tomorrow, the 11th instant, you move the two divisions of your corps, now held in reserve near Leary's, to Moody's (on the New Kent Court-House and Bottom's bridge road), by way of Parsley's Mill, Prospect Church &tc., so as to avoid the observation of the enemy. In addition to the eight wooden pontoons you will take with you eight canvas pontoons. <u>You will be prepared to move your whole corps on Sunday evening, the 12th instant as soon as it is dark, to Long Bridge, by way of Emmaus Church, cross the Chickahominy, march to the vicinity of White Oak Swamp crossing, and hold that crossing and the Long Bridge road, looking toward the Charles City, Central and New Market roads.</u> It is important that the point designated should be reached at the earliest practicable moment after the movement begins. The engineers will establish as many bridges at Jones' Bridge as the locality admits of. The order for the movement of the army will be sent to you in due time. So much of this communication as relates to the movement on Sunday will be considered confidential.
>
>   A.A. HUMPHREYS,
>   Major-General and Chief of Staff.[19]

The 5th corps had been held in reserve and was rested.
General Hancock, commanding the 2nd corps, began to prepare the roads behind his position for the big move:

---

19 Official Records, Vol. XXXVI Pt. 111, Ser. No 69, p.730.

D Day Minus 2

HEADQUARTERS SECOND ARMY CORPS,

June 10, 1864-12:15 p.m.

Major-General BIRNEY,
Commanding Third Division:

GENERAL; The major-general commanding directs that you open the road from Livesay's house by Mrs. McGee's to Wicker's, as indicated in enclosed sketch, so that it will be practicable for a column. An examination of the road this morning shows that it is practicable for artillery and infantry if widened a little and cleared of undergrowth. A party of 125 or 160 axmen will be able to open it in three or four hours. If the sketch is not sufficiently plain, Mr. Livesay can give the officer in charge of the party the necessary information.

Very respectfully, your obedient servant,
C.H. Morgan,
Lieutenant-Colonel and Chief of Staff.[20]

The lumber for the great bridge across the James River also must be secured:

HEADQUARTERS ARMIES OF THE UNITED STATES,
Cold Harbor, Va., June 10, 1864-4 p.m.
(Received 1:45 a.m. 11th.)

Maj. Gen. H.W. Halleck,
Chief of Staff:

Please order Captain McAlester here if he can be spared from West Point; also order the sawmill at Fort Monroe to saw all the 2-inch lumber they can, and place it on board barges, subject to my order. The Coehorn mortar on transports leave where they are. We will not want them now.

U.S. GRANT,
Lieutenant-General.[21]

---

20 Official Records, Vol. XXXVI Pt. 111, Ser. No. 69, p.730.
21 Official Records, Vol. XXXVI Pt. 111, Ser. No. 69, p.722.

D Day Minus 2

The organizing of bridging equipment was now critical. Responsibility was fixed on General H.W. Benham, Chief Engineer of the Army of the Potamac located at Fort Monroe.

> HDQRS. DEPT. OF VIRGINIA AND NORTH CAROLINA,
> In the Field, *June 10, 1864.*
>
> *Officer in charge of pontoons,*
> *belonging to Army of the Potamac, at Bermuda Landing:*
> SIR; You will proceed at once with your command and pontoon trains to Fort Monroe and there report to General Benham.
> By order of General Butler:
> C.J. PAINE,
> *Colonel and Acting Chief of Staff.*

> HDQRS. DEPT. OF VIRGINIA AND N.CAROLINA,
> ENGINEER'S OFFICE,
> *June 10, 1864.*
>
> Brig. Gen. H.W. Benham,
> *Chief Engineer, Army of the Potomac:*
> SIR: I have, according to your request, this day turned over to Captain Robbins part of pontoon bridge trains Nos. 7 and 11 which were invoiced to me from Washington, subject to the order of Lieutenant-General Grant.
> I have the honor to be, general, very respectfully, your obedient servant,
> G. WEITZEL,
> *Brigadier-General-and-Chief, Engineer*[22]

General Weitzel was Butler's Chief Engineer.

General Weitzel's services would prove invaluable in the construction of the approaches to the great bridge on June 14, 1864.

In addition to bridging equipment a number of ships would be required for the crossing of the James. These were so ordered.

---

22 Official Records, Vol. XXXVI Pt. 111, Ser. No 69, p.740.

D Day Minus 2

WHITE HOUSE, VA.,
June 10, 1864-11p.m.
(Received 9 a.m. 11th)

General D.H. RUCKER, *Chief Quartermaster:*

To enable me to comply with orders just received from General Ingalls, chief quartermaster, Army of the Potomac, I shall require at least five steamers and five tugs in addition to those now here. The vessels arriving here today and those to arrive tomorrow, having on board infantry recruits for the army, are not unloaded but are sent to Bermuda Hundred to debark their troops. I telegraphed to you today asking that 3,000,000 (pounds) of grain be loaded in barges and sent to me. Please have the captains of the vessels towing them ordered to proceed to Fort Monroe with their tows, and await orders from me. Please reply.

P.P. PITKIN,
Captain and Quartermaster.

WHITE HOUSE, VA.,
June 10, 1864.
(Received 2:40 a.m. 11th.)

Capt. E.S. ALLEN,
Assistant Quartermaster, Washington D.C.:

Steamers Ocean Wave and Diamond State were ordered from this place to Bermuda Hundred, carrying the troops which they brought from Washington. No more troops will be debarked at this place. Transportation is required from this place to Bermuda Hundred for 3,000 troops now here. We also have 2,500 wounded yet to be removed. Please send the necessary transportation, if possible. Steamer S.R.

Spaulding will leave this place this p.m. with 1,000 prisoners of war for Point Lookout.

P.P. PITKIN,
Captain, Quartermaster[23]

---

23 Official Records, Vol. XXXVI Pt.111, Ser. No. 69, p.737.

D Day Minus 2

The crossings of the Chickahominy River had to be scouted by Union cavalry. The Confederates had destroyed all bridges. Maps were bad. Locations for pontoon bridges must be found. Everything must be marked clearly for night movement:

> HDQRS, SECOND BRIG. THIRD DIV., CAVALRY CORPS,
> In the Field, *June 10, 1864.*
>
> Capt. L. SIEBERT,
> *Asst. Adjt. Gen. Third Cavalry Division:*
>
> CAPTAIN; In answer to inquiries made by General Humphreys I have the honor to state that Turner's Crossing is about half a mile below Fisher's Ford, which is the last point known, I think, to the engineers at army headquarters, and is from 1 1/4 miles to 1 1/2 miles below Bottom's Bridge. There was formerly a bridge at Turner's but whether the river is fordable at that point or not I am not advised. The approach to the river at Turner's passes near an old abandoned house (the first on the river below Fisher's) and is good. The only crossing on the river between Bottom's Bridge and Long Bridge known to me are Fisher's and Turner's. I have not ascertained that there are any crossings between Long Bridge and Jones' Bridge except the ford a short distance above the last-named point, which is laid down on the map furnished from headquarters.
>
> I am, very respectfully, your obedient servant,
> GEO. H. CHAPMAN,
> *Colonel, Commanding Brigade.*
>
> I might mention that at Fisher's Ford a very light belt of timber skirts the river.[24]

Preparations for transporting of the 18th Corps commanded by General W.F. Smith by steamer to Bermuda Hundred were passed forward. The 18th Corps was to go by boat rather than a long march. The 18th Corps would spearhead the attack on Petersburg and must arrive in the very best condition:

---

24 Official Records, Vol. XXXVI Pt.111, Ser. No. 69, p.737.

D Day Minus 2

HEADQUARTERS ARMY OF THE POTOMAC,
OFFICE OF CHIEF QUARTERMASTER,
Camp near Cold Harbor, Va., June 10, 1864

Brig. Gen. S. Williams,
Assistant Adjutant-General, Army of the Potomac:

GENERAL: I have the honor to report for the information of the general commanding that probably most of the transports employed in transporting the Eighteenth Army Corps to White House have been unloaded and used to send away wounded and unserviceable property. Some are still at White House with stores which belong to the corps. Captain Pitkin had positive orders to detain no transports at that depot, but to keep all actively employed. In order, therefore, to insure the prompt movement of General Smith's command from the Chickahominy to Bermuda Hundred, on his arrival at Cole's Ferry, I would respectfully recommend that Lieut. Col. H. Briggs, chief quartermaster at Fort Monroe, or other competent officer, be ordered to assemble suitable transports, and to be at the time and place designated in person, to superintend the transportation. Colonel Biggs, for instance, will have it in his power to call in all the boats that may be available in the Potomac, Pamunkey, and James Rivers. If the means of embarkation are not good in the Chickahominy, time will be gained by sending the corps direct from the White House.

I am, very respectfully, your most obedient servant,
RUFUS INGALLS,
Brig. Gen. and Chief Quartermaster,
Army of the Potomac[25]

The 18th Corps had been on the Bermuda Hundred front and had not suffered the rigors of the Virginia campaign from Wilderness to Richmond. Except for the battle of Cold Harbor the 18th Corps had not experience heavy fighting.

General Grant always gave close attention to the logistics involved in military maneuvers and the crossing of the James was no exception:

---

25 Official Records, Vol. XXXVI, Pt. III, Ser. No. 69, p. 724.

D Day Minus 2

SPECIAL ORDERS
No. 158
HDQRS ARMY OF THE POTOMAC,
July 10, 1864

2. Until further orders four days' rations will be kept on the persons of the men and six days subsistence in the supply trains. Wagons appropriated to subsistence, not required to keep up these supplies will be used in bringing forward from the depot for issue to the troops the small rations, not included in the marching rations, and anti-scorbutics. Any other wagons that the quartermaster's department can provide for the purpose will also be used in bringing up these additional stores.

4. In anticipation of his appointment as colonel of the regiment, First Lieut. R.S. Mackenzie, Engineers, will at once assume command of the Second Regiment Connecticut Heavy Artillery.

By command of Major-General Meade:

S. WILLIAMS,
Assistant Adjutant-General.[26]

On the Confederate side of the battlefield General Lee was reporting to Richmond on enemy actions. It is apparent that Sheridan is now occupying the mind of the Confederate commander:

HEADQUARTERS,
Gaines' Mill, June 10, 1864.

HON. SECRETARY OF WAR.
Richmond, Va.:

SIR: I have the honor to acknowledge the receipt of your letter of yesterday. With my present information as to the movements of the enemy's cavalry I am unable to determine their destination. The last dispatch from General Hampton dated at Frederick's Hall today, states that they had encamped last night at New Market, which is on the road from Chilesburg to Waller's Church, General Hampton's own command being nearly west of them at Frederick's Hall. My first impression was that the object of the expedition was to cooperate with the forces under General Hunter in the valley, and there is nothing as yet in their movements

---

26 Offical Records, Vol. XXXVI, Pt. 111, Ser. No, 69, p.729.

D Day Minus 2

inconsistent with this idea. They may intend to strike for the James River above Richmond, and cross to the south side to destroy the Danville road. I think it very important that we should be on our guard against such an attempt, and that parties should be held in readiness to burn the bridges over the river upon their approach. These parties should be under the direction of intelligent and cool men, for fear the bridges might be prematurely fired; and good scouts sent out on the roads to give timely notice of the approach of the enemy. I suppose you will be able to obtain men of the character indicated among the reserve forces of that section.

I will keep you advised as far as I can of the enemy's movements and should he turn toward the river our cavalry under General Hampton will endeavor to protect the bridges, and unable to do so, will aid the parties charged with burning them. Under existing circumstances I think it would be best to make every preparation to repair the railroad and the bridges to be in readiness for a more favorable opportunity to restore travel, but it would not be prudent to begin the work now. I am glad to learn that you are exerting yourself to accumulate stores for the army. No effort should be spared to provide against such interruption of our transportation as the enemy's superiority in cavalry may enable him to effect. If practicable, I hope that provision will be made to continue the supply of vegetables. It greatly promotes the health and comfort of the men.

Very respectfully, your obedient servant,

R.E. LEE,
General.[27]

---

27 Official Records, Vol. XXXVI Pt. 111, Ser. No. 69, p. 888.

D Day Minus 2

At the close of the day on June 10th, General Lee reported:

> HEADQUARTERS ARMY OF NORTHERN VIRGINIA
> *June* 10, 1864-8:30 p.m.
>
> HON. SECRETARY OF WAR,
> *Richmond*:
>
> SIR: The enemy has made no movement today. The skirmishing alone the line has been somewhat more active and systematic than during the past two days.
>
> Very respectfully, your obedient servant,
>
> R.E. LEE,
> *General*.[28]

---

28 Official Records, Vol. XXXVI Pt. 111, Ser. No. 69, p. 887.

Saturday June 11, 1864
Cold Harbor
D day minus 1

Grant had kept General Meade in command of the Army of the Potomac after Grant became General in Chief. Grant wanted a man who was familiar with the army and could carry out the tactics Grant devised to support the strategy of the Virginia campaign. During the battles of the Wilderness and Spotslyvania, and in the movement to southern Virginia, Meade had performed well. Grant praised him. Grant promoted him. Grant still believed Meade was the best man for the job.

Now, in the key movement of the Virginia campaign, Grant entrusted Meade to perform a near flawless execution of the grand plan: the crossing of the James.

On June 11, 1864 Grant gave Meade his final orders for the move:

HEADQUARTERS ARMIES OF THE UNITED STATES,
Cold Harbor, Va., June 11, 1864

Major-General MEADE,
Commanding General of Army of the Potomac:
GENERAL: Colonel Comstock, who visited the James River for the purpose of ascertaining the best point below Bermuda Hundred, to which to march the army, has not yet returned. It is now getting so late, however, that all preparations may be made for the move tomorrow night without waiting longer. The movement will be made as heretofore agreed upon-that is, the Eighteenth Corps make a rapid march with the infantry alone, their wagons and artillery accompanying the balance of the army to Cole's Landing or Ferry, and there embark for City point, losing no time for rest until they reach the latter point. The Fifth Corps will seize Long bridge and move out the Long Bridge road to its junction with Quaker road, or until stopped by the enemy. The other three corps will follow in such order as you may direct, one of them crossing at Long bridge, and two at Jones' Bridge. After the crossing is effected the most practicable roads will be taken to reach about Fort Powhatan.* Of course this is supposing the enemy makes no opposition to our advance. The Fifth Corps, after securing the passage of the balance of the army, will join or follow in rear of the corps which crossed the

*Note: crossing point on the James River

D Day Minus 1

same bridge with themselves. The wagon trains should be kept well east of the troops, and, if a crossing can be found or made lower down than Jones' they should take it.

Very respectfully,
U.S. Grant
Lieutenant-General

P.S.-In view of the long march to reach Cole's landing, and the uncertainty of being able to embark so large a number of men there,...the direction of the Eighteenth Corps may be changed to White House. They should be directed to load up transports and start them as fast as loaded without waiting for the whole corps, or even whole divisions, to go together.

U.S.G.[29]

The orders to each unit of the army for the crossing of the James were carefully drawn up by General Meade. Preparations were meticulous:

    (see map on page 88, 89 for details of movements)

(Cavalry)

[Orders]
HEADQUARTERS ARMY OF THE POTOMAC
June 11, 1864

The following movements were ordered:

1. At dark on the evening of the 12th instant Brigadier-General Wilson will move the brigade of cavalry picketing the Chickahominy across that swamp at Long Bridge, or that vicinity, and out on the Long Bridge road toward the crossing of White Oak Swamp and toward the Charles City, Central and New Market roads. The brigade will move promptly and clear the road for the Fifth Corps. The pickets at the crossings of the Chickahominy will remain until relieved by infantry pickets.

(5th Corps)

2. During Saturday, the 11th instant, Major-General Warren will move the two divisions of his corps, now held in reserve, to

---
29 Official Records, Vol. XXXVI Pt. 111, Ser. No. 69, p. 745.

D Day Minus 1

Moody's by way of Parsley's Mill, Prospect Church, &tc., so as to avoid the observation of the enemy. At dark on the evening of the 12th instant he will move his whole corps to Long bridge by the shortest route, cross the Chickahominy, and move on the road to White Oak Swamp bridge (called Long Bridge road) and hold that road, looking toward the crossings of White Oak Swamp and the Charles City, Central, and New Market roads, during the passage of the army toward James River. He will follow the Second Corps toward Charles City Court-House. General Warren will picket the crossings of the Chickahominy on his flank while moving to Long Bridge, relieving the cavalry pickets.

(18th Corps)

3. Maj. Gen. W.F. Smith, Eighteenth Corps, will withdraw as soon after dark as practicable on the evening of the 12th instant, and move by way of Parsley's Mill, Prospect Church, Hopewell Church, Tunstall's Station, to White house, where he will embark and proceed to Bermuda Hundred. Upon reaching Tunstall Station his artillery and trains will join the main trains of the army.

(9th Corps)

4. Major-General Burnside, Ninth Corps, will withdraw as soon after dark as practicable on the evening of the 12th instant, and move by way of Allen's Mill (or by roads avoiding Smith's route); then north of the south fork of the Matadequin to Burton's, thence past Hughes' Watts', Clopton's, Turner's Store, &tc., to Tunstall's Station, or by adjoining route avoiding Smith's that may be found to Tunstall's Station. At Tunstall's station the corps of General Smith has precedence. When it has cleared the way, General Burnside will move to Jones' Bridge, taking care not to interfere with routes of other corps, past Baltimore Cross-Roads, and Emmaus Church. Where the routes of the Sixth and Ninth Corps unite, about 3 miles from Jones' Bridge, the corps that reaches the point first will have precedence. After crossing at Jones' Bridge Major-General Burnside will take the route passing east of Charles City Court-House, by Vandom's [Vaiden's], Clopton's and Tyler's Mill.

D Day Minus 1

(6th Corps)

    5. Major-General Wright, Sixth Corps, will withdraw as soon after dark as practicable on the evening of the 12th instant to the intrenched line in his rear, from Allen's Pond to Elder Swamp, and, in conjuntion with the Second Corps, hold that line until the roads for the Sixth and Second Corps are well cleared by the Fifth Corps, when the two corps will withdraw. General Wright will move by way of Cold Harbor, Taylor's J. P. Parsley's, Widow Via's, Goode's, and Hopkin's Mill to Moody's; and thence by way of Emmaus Church to Jones' Bridge, preceding or following the Ninth Corps, as already indicated, where the routes unite. After crossing the Chickahominy, General Wright will take the route to Charles City Court-House by Vandom's [Vaiden's].

(2nd Corps)

    6. Major General Hancock, Second Corps, will withdraw as soon after dark as practicable on the evening of the 12th instant to the entrenched line in his rear from Allen's Pond to Elder Swamp, and hold that line in conjunction with the Sixth Corps, until the roads for the Second and Sixth Corps are well cleared, when he will move by routes in his rear to the Dispatch Station road, avoiding the roads of the Sixth Corps, and by Dispatch Station and the shortest route to Long Bridge. He will look out for the crossings of the Chickahominy on his flank while passing. After crossing the Chickahominy, General Hancock will move toward Charles City Court-House, by way of Saint Mary's Church, Walker's &tc.

(Trains - Supply Wagons)

    7. Brigadier-General Ferrero will move his division at dark on the evening of the 12th instant to the trains of the army near White House or Cumberland, and cover them during the movement.

    8. The trains will move to the Windsor Shades, and cross the Chickahominy in that vicinity. They will take such routes as not to interfere with the movements of the troops.

    9. The brigade of cavalry on the right will withdraw at the same time as the Sixth and Second Corps, and close in on the rear of the army and cover it and the trains during the movement.

D Day Minus 1

(Details)

10. Corps commanders will see that every precaution is taken to insure the rapid execution of this movement, and that the troops move promptly and quickly on the march.

11. Headquarters during the movement will be at Pollard's or Cedar Grove, near Long Bridge, and until established there will be on the route of the Sixth Corps as far as Emmaus Church.

12. Eight canvas and eight wooden pontoons will accompany the Fifth Corps to Long Bridge. The engineers will establish bridges at Jones' Bridge with the remaining eight canvas pontoons and the wooden pontoons of the Sixth Corps. The wooden pontoons of the Second Corps will accompany the main trains of the army.

13. The pickets of the several corps will be withdrawn at the same hour from the line of entrenchments before daylight of the 13th instant, and will follow the routes of their respective corps.

14. The corps will take with them on the march merely those light headquarters wagons, ammunition wagons, ambulances, &tc., specified for the march across the Rapidan. All others will be sent at once to the main trains of the army.

(Base of Supply)

15. The depot at White House will be continued for the present with its permanent garrison, but all supplies, &tc, for this army will be moved to the James River, leaving 50,000 rations of subsistence and 30,000 rations of forage, in addition to supplies for the garrison. On the arrival of Major-General Sheridan and Hunter, the post White House will be broken up and transferred to Yorktown, from which place the commanding officer will report his arrival to these headquarters.

By command of Major-General Meade:
S. WILLIAMS,
Assistant Adjutant-General.[30]

In his original orders to Meade and Butler, Grant said he would combine the Army of the Potomac under Meade with the Army of the James under Butler in a position of enormous strength south of Richmond. The movement across the James would bring these two powerful armies together as a combined force in the rear of Lee's army.

---
30 Official Records, Vol. XXXVI, Part 111, Ser. No 69, p. 745.

D Day Minus 1

Grant went to great pains to make clear to Butler the role that he was about to play in the combined operation:

HEADQUARTERS ARMIES OF THE UNITED STATES,
Cold Harbor, Va., *June 11, 1864.*
Maj. Gen. B.F. BUTLER,
Comdg, Dept of Virginia and North Carolina:
GENERAL: The movement to transfer this army to the south side of James River will commence after dark tomorrow night. Colonel Comstock, of my staff was sent especially to ascertain what was necessary to make your position secure in the interval, during which the enemy might use most of his force against you, and also to ascertain what point on the river we should reach to effect a crossing, if it should not be practicable to reach this side of the river at Bermuda Hundred. Colonel Comstock has not yet returned, so that I cannot make instructions as definite as I would wish, but the time between this and Sunday night being so short in which to get word to you, I must do the best I can.

Colonel Dent goes to make arrangements for gunboats and transportation to send up the Chickahominy to take to you the Eighteenth Corps. This corps will leave its position in the trenches as early in the evening tomorrow as possible, and make a forced march to Cole's Landing of Ferry, where is should reach by 10- a.m. the following morning. The corps numbers now 15,300 men. They take with them neither wagons nor artillery, these latter marching with the balance if the army to the James River. The remainder of the army will cross the Chickahominy at Long Bridge and at Jones' and strike the river at the most practicable crossing below City Point. I directed several days ago that all re-enforcements for the army should be sent to you. I am not advised of the number that many have gone, but suppose you have received from 6,000 to 10,000. General Smith will also reach you as soon as the enemy could going by way of the Richmond. The balances of the force will not be more than one day behind, unless detained by the whole of Lee's army, in which case you will be strong enough.

I wish you to direct the proper staff officers, your chief engineer and chief quartermaster to commence at once the collection of all the means in their reach for crossing the army on its arrival. If there is a point below City Point where a pontoon bridge can be thrown, have it laid. <u>Expecting the arrival of the Eighteenth Corps</u>

D Day Minus 1

<u>by Monday night, if you deem it practicable from the force you now have to seize and hold Petersburg, you may prepare to start on arrival of troops to hold your present lines.</u> I do not want Petersburg visited, however, unless it is held, nor a attempt to take it unless you feel a reasonable degree of confidence of success. If you should go there, I think troops should take nothing with them except what they carry, depending upon supplies being sent after the place is secured. If Colonel Dent should not succeed in securing the requisite amount of transportation for the Eighteenth Corps before reaching you, please have the balance supplied.

I am, general, very respectfully, your obedient servant,

U.S. GRANT,
Lieutenant-General.

P.S. - On reflection, I will send the Eighteenth Corps by way of White House. The distance which they will have to march will be enough shorter to enable them to reach you about the same time, and the uncertainty of navigation on the Chickahominy will be avoided.

U.S.G.[31]

It was clear in Grant's orders to Butler that the reason for transporting General Smith and the 18th Corps rapidly by boat to Bermuda Hundred was that they move aggressively to capture Petersburg before it could be reinforced. Butler's subsequent orders to General Smith made it clear that Butler understood the need for rapid movement and aggressive attack.

In preparation on June 12th for the withdrawal of the Army of the Potomac from the battlefield at Cold Harbor, the individual Corps commanders sent pioneer troops to prepare the roads South and East of their positions which they would have to use in darkness on the night of June 12th.

(5th Corps)

HEADQUARTERS FIFTH ARMY CORPS,
Moody's House, *June 11, 1864-6:30 p.m.*

Major-General HUMPHREYS:

My command is all in camp as ordered. I have had roads repaired so far and will work again tomorrow beyond here. I

---
31 Official Records, Vol. XXXVI Pt. 111, Ser. No. 69, p. 754.

D Day Minus 1

think the country is such that we can move the two divisions that are here so as to be at the river at dark, if necessary, without observation. I picket all around my camp to prevent my men from straying out or spies from getting through our lines as far as I am able. I have sent you some deserters today. Can get no information of enemy being south of White Oak Swamp, except near James River, where the bluffs are fortified. Hill's corps is supposed to be between Savage Station and the Chickahominy or thereabouts. Deserters are from Heth's division.

G.K. WARREN.[32]

(6th Corps)

[ORDERS]

HEADQUARTERS SIXTH CORPS
June 11, 1864-6:30 a.m.

Brigadier-General Russell, commanding First Division, will detail 650 men, Brigadier-General Neill, commanding Second Division, will detail 700 men, Brigadier Ricketts, commanding Third Division, will detail 500 men, and Major Beers, commanding Engineer Battalion, will detail 150 men, with the proper number of commissioned and non-commissioned officers, to report this morning punctually at 9 o'clock to Captain Michler, U.S. Engineer, at Cold Harbor. A field officer will be placed in command of the detail from each division. Each detail will be sent, under charge of a staff officer, to Cold Harbor, where they will be received by a staff officer from these headquarters, and the senior officer place in command of the whole. Major Beers, commanding Engineer Battalion, will send 1,400 spades, 500 picks, 100 axes to the same place at the same hour.

By command of Major-General Wright:

C.H. WHITTELSEY,
Assistant Adjutant-General.[33]

On June 11, 1864 General Robert E. Lee was looking at a very confusing chess board. Many pieces had been lost. The next move of his opponent was not at all clear. General Lee was facing threats from many different directions. He was faced with the perplexing problem of how to

---

32 Official Records, Vol. XXXVI Pt. 111, Ser. No. 69, p. 750.
33 Official Records, Vol. XXXVI Pt. 111, Ser. No. 69, p. 750.

D Day Minus 1

allocate his diminishing manpower to meet each threat and also to distinguish which of the threats was the key to General Grant's next move.

Directly in front of General Lee lay the Army of the Potomac, 100,000 strong, undiminished in strength by thirty days of combat. General Grant had received 48,265 troops[34] as reinforcements from Washington during the course of the campaign and, whereas the Confederate Corps of the Army of Virginia were reduced to one half strength from heavy fighting. The Confederate 2nd Corps which had entered the Wilderness on May 4, 1864, with 17,000 men, left Cold Harbor for Charlottesville on June 13, 1864 with 8,000 men after being reinforced. Lee could ill afford to split the Confederate Army in face of Grant.

What was equally bad was that Lee was running out of room to maneuver. His options were growing fewer. Lee had been pushed 60 miles south by the Union Army from his defense line of the Rapidan River to the gates of Richmond. Behind Lee's army at Cold Harbor lay the massive fixed fortifications of Richmond.

If Lee retreated into the fortifications of Richmond, his army would be immobilized. The very last thing General Lee wanted was to be forced to retire into fixed fortifications and endure siege. Lee believed that if he were forced into siege and lost all ability to maneuver, the Union army would in time cut his supply line and the Confederate army would fall apart.

On June 11th, 1864 General Hunter's army entered Lexington, Virginia in the Shenandoah Valley. This presented a very visible threat to Lee's rear. If General Hunter were not stopped he would reach Lynchburg and the vital railroads to the southwest.

At the close of the day in June 11th General Lee reported:

HEADQUARTERS ARMY OF NORTHERN VIRGINIA,
June 11, 1864-6:30 P.M.

HON. SECRETARY OF WAR,
Richmond:

SIR: The enemy has been quiet today, with the usual skirmishing along the lines.

Very respectfully, your obedient servant,

R.E. LEE,
General.[35]

---

34 Official Records, Vol. XXXVI Pt. 111, Ser. No. 69, p. 665.
35 Official Records, Vol. XXXVI Pt. 111, Ser. No. 69, p. 894.

Sunday June 12, 1864
Cold Harbor
D Day!

The success of General Hunter's diversion cannot be overstated. On June 12th, 1864, Lee ordered Early with 8,000 desperately needed soldiers to march before dawn on June 13th to Lynchberg and defend the Valley. Early's departure would take nearly 20% of Lee's manpower.[36] Lee would face Grant with two divisions.[37]

Colonel Comstock and Colonel Porter arrived at Cold Harbor from their exploration of the James River at 1:30 am on June 12th. They went immediately to General Grant's tent and gave him their report.* Col. Porter describes the scene:

> General Grant had been anxiously awaiting our return, and had in the meantime made every preparation for withdrawing the army from its present position. On our arrival we went at once to his tent, and were closeted with him for nearly an hour discussing the contemplated operation. While listening to our verbal report and preparing the orders for the movement which was to take place, the general showed the only anxiety and nervousness of manner he had ever manifested on any occasion. After smoking his cigar vigorously for some minutes, he removed it from his mouth, put it on the table, and allowed it to go out, then relighted it, gave a few puffs, and laid it aside again. In giving him the information he desired, we could hardly get the words out of our mouths fast enough to suit him. He kept repeating, "Yes, yes," in a manner which was the equivalent to saying, "Go on, go on", and the numerous questions he asked were uttered with much greater rapidity than usual. This would not have been noticed by persons unfamiliar with his habit; but to us it was evident that he was wrought up to an intensity of thought and action which he seldom displayed. At the close of the interview he informed us that he would begin the movement that night.[38]

*Note: It is apparent from the Official Records that Grant & Meade kept no regular hours.

---

36 Trudeau, Noah Andre, "Bloody Roads South," p. 314.
37 Dowdy, Clifford, "The Wartime Papers of R.E. Lee," p. 741
38 Porter, Horace, "Campaigning with Grant," p. 189.

D Day!

Although the Army of the Potomac's orders were not to move before darkness the evening of June 12, 1864, General W.F. Smith wanted to get an early start. It was his Corps that would spearhead the attack on Petersburg.

HEADQUARTERS EIGHTEENTH ARMY CORPS
June 12, 1864

Brigadier-General WILLIAMS:
Is there any objection to my relieving such troops as may be moved without attracting the attention of the enemy, and sending them to the White House today?

WM. F. Smith
Major-General

HEADQUARTERS ARMY OF THE POTOMAC
June 12, 1864-8:15 a.m.

Maj. Gen. W.F. Smith,
Commanding Eighteenth Corps:
Your dispatch received. The commanding general desires that you relieve such of your troops as can be removed without attracting the attention of the enemy and send them to the White House today, as suggested by you.

S. WILLIAMS,
Assistant Adjutant-General.[39]

The success of the operation hung on the James River bridge:

COLD HARBOR, VA., *June 12, 1864*

Colonel BIGGS,
Chief Quartermaster, Eighteenth Corps:
Lieutenant-Colonel Dent, of my staff, has gone to Fort Monroe and Bermuda Hundred to make, or rather communicate, the necessary orders for securing the crossing of the army over James River at Port Powhatan. Special instructions were not given, however, to send ferryboats, pontoons, &tc., that may be at Fort Monroe. This will be understood, no doubt, by General Butler

---

39 Official Records, Vol XXXVI Pt. 111, Ser. No. 69, p. 766.

D Day!

from the instructions that have gone to him; but to expedite, I now direct that you forward up the James River all things within your charge , and request the engineer officer at Fort Monroe, for me, to send all the pontoon bridge material he may have on hand. Send also all the lumber you can, particularly the 2-inch plank. This will not be construed to interfere with sending the amount of transportation to the White House heretofore called for.

U.S. GRANT.
Lieutenant-General.[40]

On June 12 artillery had to be withdrawn to the rear so that it was ready to move with the army at nightfall:

HEADQUARTERS EIGHTEENTH CORPS
[*June* 12, 1864.]

Captain ELDER,
Chief of Artillery:

The general commanding directs that you withdraw your batteries, as the second line of our troops moves to take up the line of entrenchments resting on the redoubt in rear of this camp, moving them to Tunstall's Station, there to join the Eighteenth Corps wagon train, with which you will continue to march (with Captain Cameron's squadron as escort} to the James River. You will send all but your three batteries back to their commands on withdrawing. On arriving at James River you will await further orders from these headquarters, unless you receive them from higher authority. You will not wait for the infantry to move to Tunstall's Station after withdrawing, but proceed on your road at once with your escort.

Respectfully, &tc.,
N. BOWEN,
Assistant Adjutant-General[41]

There are 56 artillery horses for you at Tunstall's.

---

40 Official Records, Vol. XXXVI Pt. 111, Ser. No. 69, p. 769.
41 Official Records, Vol. XXXVI Pt. 111. Ser. No. 69, p. 766.

D Day!

The ships needed to transport General Smith's 18th Corps for 140 miles from White House to Bermuda Hundred had to be ready. The 18th Corps, must be fresh for the assault on Petersburg.

WHITE HOUSE,
June 12, 1864.
(Received 2:15 p.m.)

Brig. Gen. M.C. MEIGS,
Quartermaster-General:

Transportation by water for 16,000 troops will be required from this place tomorrow. The movement is very important, and it is necessary that all vessels suitable for transporting troops, which have been sent from this place to Washington and Alexandria, be returned at once, together with such other vessels as can be spared. General Ingalls authorized me to telegraph you.

P.P. PITKIN,
Captain, Assistant Quartermaster.[42]

General Smith's 18th Corps would be landing at Bermuda Hundred on the night of June 14th and the roads leading away from the river towards Petersburg must be put in shape for the leading Corps to move quickly. General Butler was directed to get the required work done. "Corduroy" consisted of logs laid transversely over swampy areas to create a hard roadbed:

HEADQUARTERS ARMIES OF THE UNITED STATES,
Cold Harbor, *June 12, 1864.*

Major-General BUTLER:

Go on with the corduroy suggested by Comstock. A staff officer is on way with letter of instructions to you, but did not leave here until last night. Your chief engineer will understand what the corduroy meant.

GRANT,
Lieutenant-General.[43]

The giant Army of the Potomac was coiled like a spring ready to explode south. 100,000 men prepared to move out into the darkness.

---

42 Official Records, Vol. XXXVI Pt. 111, Ser. No.69, p. 769.
43 Official Records, Vol. XXXVI Pt. 111, Ser. No.69, p. 769.

III
CROSSING THE JAMES
NIGHTFALL - JUNE 12, 1864

Grant had always taken them to battle and not away from it. With General Grant there would be no retreat, no turning back. In darkness, the entire Union army stirred. Bands played all along the six mile front to cover the noise of an army in motion. Each Corps moved according to plan. The roads had been well scouted in advance and improved and widened by pioneer troops.

The vanguard of the army's move South was General Wilson's cavalry division. Moving ahead of General Warren's 5th Corps, it was General Wilson's mission to clear away Confederate pickets and patrols and to secure the roads and river crossings for the infantry that followed. The first obstacle was 15 miles south, the Chickahominy river. The cavalry must secure the crossing at Long Bridge so that the engineers could construct a pontoon bridge across the river:

(see map p. 88, 89 for details of movements)

HEADQUARTERS THIRD DIVISION, CAVALRY CORPS,
Near Long Bridge,
June 12, 1864-11:15 p.m.

Maj. Gen. A.A. HUMPHREYS
Chief of Staff:

GENERAL: After a sharp resistance, in which we lost several men, the advance of Chapman's brigade, two regiments, succeeded in passing both branches of the Chickahominy on logs and drifts, and driving the enemy from his rifle-pits, and are

Crossing the James

now well out on the other side, covering the construction of the bridges. As there is an island across which the road runs, with bad approaches, the bridges will probably not be done before midnight. Our advance crossed about 9 p.m. We will clear the way for the infantry as soon as possible.

Very respectfully, your obedient servant,

J.H. Wilson,
Brigadier-General, Commanding-Division.[1]

Although it was a moonlit night, the troops could barely see because the roads were clogged with dust. The 100 degree Virginia heat was unbearable. The guides leading each unit had to locate bridges by feeling for them.

At dawn on June 13, 1864 the Army of the Potomac was gone. It had disappeared from Cold Harbor.

Confederate pickets moved forward and probed the Union trenches. They were empty. General Lee was beside himself. As Noah Andre Trudeau describes it:

At daybreak, Robert E. Lee learned that Grant's army had slipped away during the night. According to Eppa Hunton, one of General Pickett's brigadiers, 'It was said that General Lee was in a furious passion - one of the few times during the war. When he did get mad he was mad all over.'[2]

Confederate scouts pushed several miles East but found nothing. They returned and reported. General Grant's army was well away from the Cold Harbor area but exactly where he had gone no one seemed to know.

By the end of the day General Lee had regained his composure. He reported as follows:

To: JAMES A. SEDDON
Secretary of War

Headquarters, Army of Northern Virginia
June 13, 1864 10 p.m.

Sir: A dispatch just received from Maj. Genl. Hampton states that he defeated the enemy's cavalry near Trevillian* with heavy loss, capturing 500 prisoners, besides the wounded. The enemy

---
1 Official Records, Vol. XXXVI Pt. 111, Ser. No. 69, p. 767.
2 Trudeau, Noah Andre, "Bloody Roads South," Little Brown & Co., 1989, p. 316.

Crossing the James

retreated in confusion, apparently by the route he came, leaving his dead and wounded on the field.

At daybreak this morning it was discovered that the army of Genl. Grant had left our front. Our skirmishes were advanced between one and two miles, but failing to discover the enemy were withdrawn, and the army was moved to conform to the route taken by him. He advanced a body of cavalry and some infantry from Long Bridge to Riddell's Shop, which were driven back this evening nearly two miles, after some sharp skirmishing.

Very resply, your obt servt
R.E. LEE
Gen.[3]

*Note: This refers to a Battle fought between Confederate General Wade Hampton's cavalry and General Sheridan's cavalry Northwest of Richmond, on the Virginia Central Railroad on June 11, 1864. Sheridan's cavalry movement towards Trevillian Station drew off most of Lee's cavalry leaving him bereft of reconnaisance support at this crucial moment.

---

3   Dowdey, Clifford, Editor, "The Wartime Papers of R.E. Lee," Little Brown, 1961, p. 776.

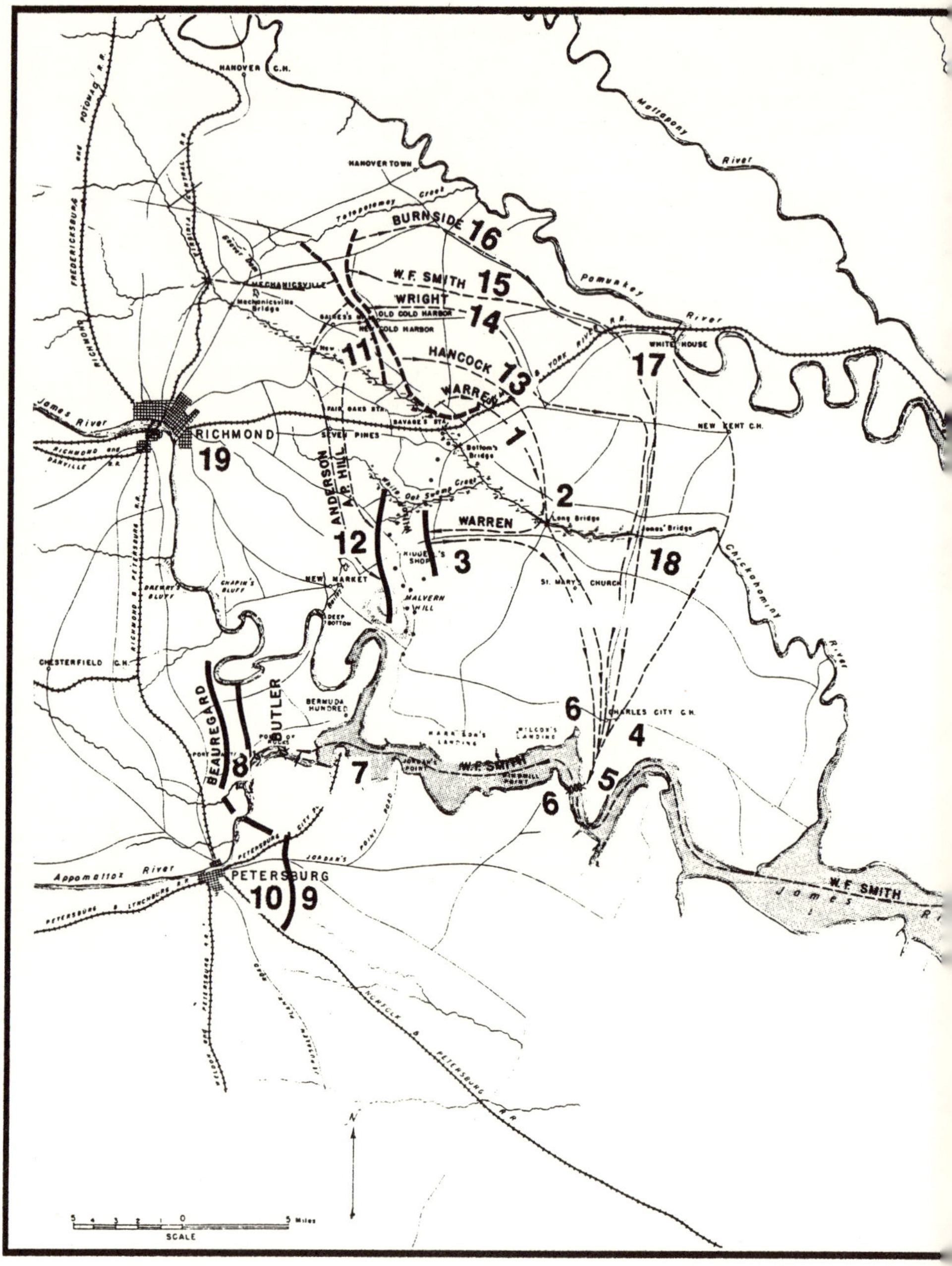

HANOVER C.H.
HANOVER TOWN
Mattapony River
Pamunkey River
Totopotomoy Creek
BURNSIDE 16
W.F. SMITH 15
WRIGHT
14
MECHANICSVILLE
Mechanicsville Bridge
OLD COLD HARBOR
NEW COLD HARBOR
11
HANCOCK 13
WARREN
1
WHITE HOUSE
17
YORK RIVER R.R.
NEW KENT C.H.
James River
RICHMOND
19
FAIR OAKS STA.
SAVAGE'S STA.
SEVEN PINES
Bottom's Bridge
ANDERSON
A.P. HILL
White Oak Swamp Creek
2
Long Bridge
Jones' Bridge
WARREN
12
3
18
NEW MARKET
MALVERN HILL
ST. MARY'S CHURCH
Chickahominy River
CHAPIN'S BLUFF
DREWRY'S BLUFF
DEEP BOTTOM
CHESTERFIELD C.H.
BEAUREGARD
BUTLER
BERMUDA HUNDRED
6
CHARLES CITY C.H.
4
W.F. SMITH
8
7
5
6
Appomattox River
PETERSBURG
10
9
W.F. SMITH
James River
FREDERICKSBURG and POTOMAC R.R.
RICHMOND and DANVILLE R.R.
RICHMOND & PETERSBURG R.R.
PETERSBURG & LYNCHBURG R.R.
NORFOLK & PETERSBURG R.R.
N
5 4 3 2 1 0 5 Miles
SCALE

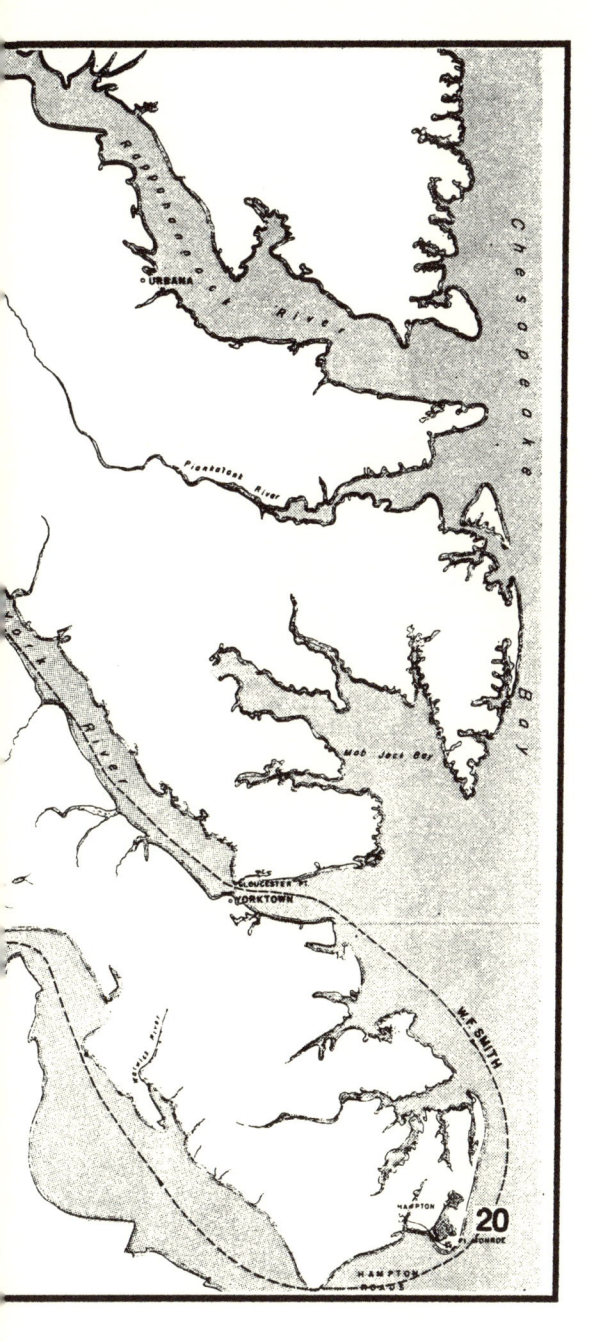

Crossing the James
June 14, 15, 16, 1864

(for details of these movements, see pages 121-124)

- **General Warren's** Fifth Corps moved from points 1, 2 & 3 blocking Lee from the crossing
- **General Lee** moved the Confederate Army from point 11 to point 12 to shield Richmond
- **General Smith** moved the Eighteenth Corps from point 15 to point 17, boards ships which move the troops to Bermuda Hundred, point 8
- **General Hancock** moved the Second Corps from point 13 to points 2, 6 and 9
- **General Burnside** moved the Ninth Corps from point 16 to points 17, 5 and 9
- **General Wright** moved the Sixth Corps from points 14, 5 and 9
- The Wagon Train swung far to the East to point 17, 4 and on to 9

Detail—Crossing of James

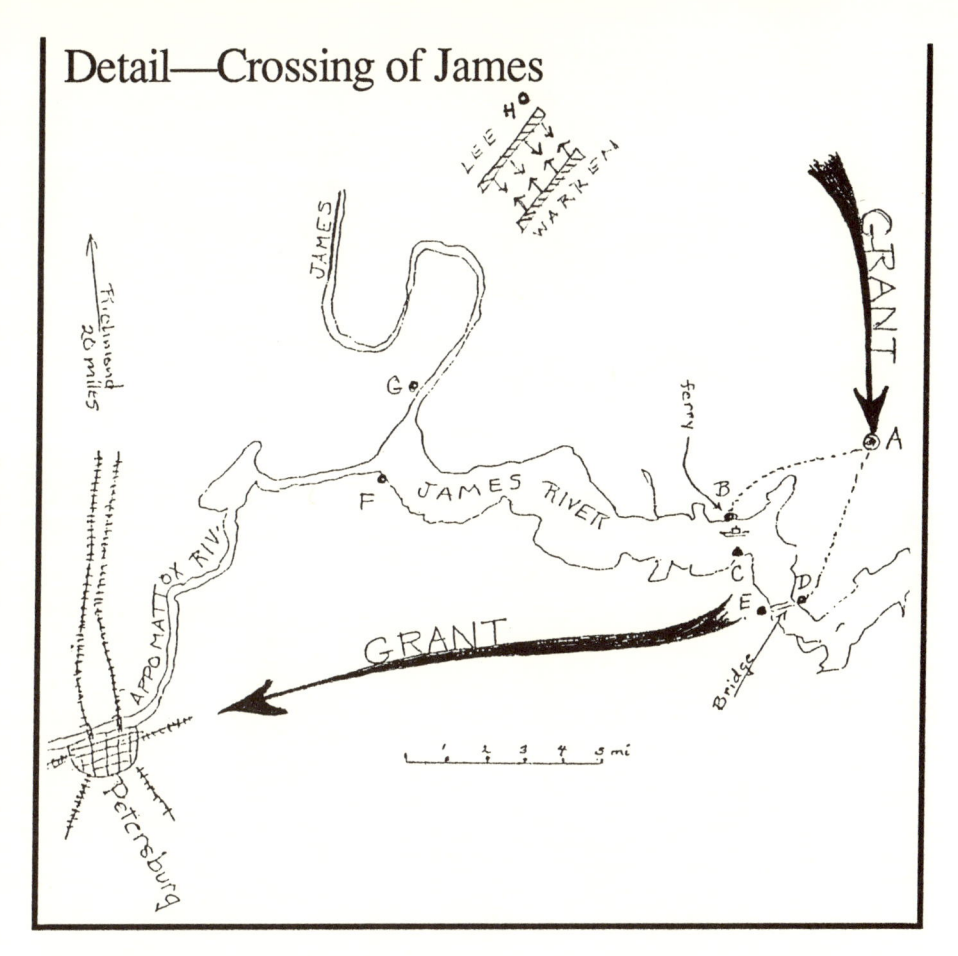

A. Charles City Courthouse (point at which army was concentrated)

B. Wilcox Landing (point of loading for ferry operation)

C. Windmill Point (site of discharge for ferry operation)

D. Weyanoke Neck (north end of the half mile Great Bridge)

E. Fort Powhatan (south end of the half mile Great Bridge)

F. City Point (headquarters of the Union army for the remainder of the war. Site of enormous Union supply base)

G. Bermuda Hundred (headquarters of General Butler's Army of the James)

H. Riddell's Shop (position of Lee's army during the crossing of the James by the Army of the Potomac)

GENERAL GRANT'S CAMPAIGN—TRANSPORTATION OF HANCOCK'S CORPS ACRO

ES AT WILCOX'S LANDING.—Sketched by William Waud.—[See Page 442.]

GENERAL GRANT'S CAMPAIGN—THE PONTOON BRIDGE OVER TH

GENERAL GRANT'S CAMPAIGN—FORT POWHATA

...IVER, ABOVE FORT POWHATAN.—Sketched by A. R. Waud.—[See Page 419.]

JAMES RIVER.—Sketched by A. R. Waud.—[See Page 419.]

Pontoon bridge over the James River at Weyanoke Point, view from the north bank looking southwest. O'Sullivan 6/15/64.

Crossing the James

Crossing Points of the James River

Wilcox Landing and Weyanoke Neck

General Hancock drove the men of the 2nd Corps thirty miles south by forced marches, and on the evening of June 13, 1864, the 2nd Corps bivouacked at Wilcox Landing on the north bank of the mighty James River.

Now the second phase, the crossing of the James River, would be the test of the careful planning and coordination of General Grant's staff, the logistical capability of the army in assembling the ships and bridging equipment and the professional skills of the U.S. Army Corps of Engineers in putting all of the pieces together.

Two crossing operations would be utilized. The first troops to arrive, General Hancock's 2nd Corps, would be ferried across the James River from Wilcox Landing to Windmill Point. This operation began immediately at daylight on June 14th:

The second operation three miles east at Weyanoke Neck required the construction of the half mile pontoon bridge. The bridge would carry the bulk of the troops, the wagon train, the artillery, cattle and cavalry.

During the crossing General Grant remained in the center of the operation, orchestrating, directing, controlling. This was the critical point. If the crossing failed, the army was in great danger:

HDQRS. ARMY OF THE UNITED STATES
Clarke's House, two miles west of Charles City Court House,
June 13, 1864-4:30 p.m.

Maj. Gen. B.F. BUTLER,
Bermuda Hundred, Va.,

Head of column has just reached this place. Will be at Fort Powhatan to commence crossing by 10 a.m. tomorrow. Communicate with me if infantry can be transferred rapidly from Wilcox's Wharf. If so, please direct quartermaster to make all necessary preparations immediately.

U.S. GRANT,
Lieutenant General.[4]

---

4 Official Records, Vol. XL, Part 11, Ser. No. 81, p. 12.

Crossing the James

HDQRS. DEPT. OF VIRGINIA AND NORTH CAROLINA,
In the Field, June 13, 1864.

Lieutenant-General GRANT,
Commanding Armies of the United States:

GENERAL: Major Babcock has reported to me with your dispatch. Owing to the burning of the wharves it may take a little time to be ready to transfer troops from Wilcox's Wharf to Wind Mill point, which is directly opposite; but I have ordered barges, landing material, and water transportation down there. You will then land about fourteen miles from Petersburg. <u>There were this morning but about 2,000 men in Petersburg, partly militia.</u> I can, by 3 o'clock tomorrow, have 3,000 well mounted cavalry ready to cooperate with you against Petersburg. General Weitzel is at Fort Powhatan, and will have a bridge ready there, I think, by 10 a.m. tomorrow. General Benham's pontoon train will also be at Fort Powhatan tonight. I should be very happy to meet you at my headquarters.

I have the honor to be, very respectfully, your obedient servant,
BENJ. F. BUTLER,
Major General, Commanding.[5]

FORT MONROE,
June 13, 1864.

Colonel Shaffer, Chief of Staff:

By order of General Grant I send all ferryboats and bridging material to Fort Powhatan, to remain there subject to orders of General Grant, through General Butler or General Meade. I have placed the boats in charge of Captain Lubey, Fifteenth New York Engineers, and Captain Robbins, Fiftieth New York Engineers. Am sending nails, spikes, rope, and lumber. Of the latter hope to get about 200,000 feet off today.
HERMAN BIGGS,
Lieutenant-Colonel and Quartermaster.[6]

---

[5] Official Records, Vol. XL, Part 11, Ser. No. 81, p. 12.
[6] Official Records, Vol. XL, Part 11, Ser. No. 81, p. 13.

Crossing the James

Bermuda,
June 13, 1864.

Colonel SHAFFER:

We have ready dispatch boats Winants and Hancox, mailboat Thomas Powell, steamer Emily, and at City Point Lady Lincoln and Sylvan Shore. Everything else has gone. We have only the barges that make the docks.

C.E. FULLER,
Lieutenant-Colonel, &c.[7]

CHARLES CITY COURT-HOUSE,
June 13, 1864-9 p.m.
(Received 5:15 a.m. 14th.)

Brigadier-General BENHAM:

The major-general commanding directs that all pontoons and other bridge material in your possession be brought immediately to Fort Powhatan.

A.A. HUMPHREYS,
Major-General and Chief of Staff.[8]

GENERAL BUTLER'S HEADQUARTERS
June 13, 1864-3:40 p.m.
(Received 10:10 a.m. 14th)

GENERAL BENHAM, *Of Engineers*:

Send all your pontoons and bridge material to Fort Powhatan in the quickest possible form and time, and come to that point yourself.

B.F. BUTLER,[9]
Major-General, Commanding

---

[7] Official Records, Vol. XL, Part 11, Ser. No. 81, p. 13.
[8] Official Records, Vol. XL, Part 11, Ser. No. 81, p. 4.
[9] Official Records, Vol. XL, Part 11, Ser. No. 81, p. 5.

Crossing the James

WILCOX'S WHARF, Va.,
June 14, 1864-9:30 a.m.

Major General MEADE,
Commanding Army of the Potomac:

GENERAL; There are three boats here for immediate use in crossing troops, and the officer in charge reports several others in the vicinity of Fort Powhatan. Expedition in crossing is what is wanted, and to secure this you can cross from different points or all from one place, as you deem best. One corps should remain on this side until artillery wagons are well over.

U.S. GRANT,
Lieutenant-General[10]

HEADQUARTERS ARMY OF THE POTOMAC,
June 14, 1864-8:30 a.m.

Maj. Gen. W.S. Hancock,
Commanding Second Corps:

SIR: The commanding general directs that you at once move your corps to the south side of the James River upon transports to be furnished by the quartermaster's department, and encamp upon suitable ground after crossing the river. You will cross at Wilcox's Wharf.

I am, very respectfully, your obedient servant,

S. WILLIAMS,
Assistant Adjutant-General.[11]

FORT MONROE,
June 14, 1864.

General A.A. HUMPHREYS,
Chief of Staff, Army of the Potomac, Charles City Court-House:

Yours received at 5:15 a.m. today. I sent pontoon bridging according to orders yesterday, as I advised you at 9 a.m. At 10:15 today I received orders from General Butler to send them and go myself. Presuming that this must be by authority of General

---

10 Official Records, Vol. XL, Part 11, Ser. No. 81, p. 19.
11 Official Records, Vol. XL, Part 11, Ser. No, 81, p. 24.

Crossing the James

Grant, I am now starting at 11, and will communicate with you as soon as possible.

H.W. BENHAM,
Brigadier-General.[12]

CHARLES CITY COURT-HOUSE
June 14, 1864-10:45 a.m.
(Received 3:30 p.m.)

Brigadier-General BENHAM:

The commanding general directs that immediately upon the receipt of this communication you bring all the bridge material you have, or that may be at Old Point Comfort, to Powhatan with all the expedition possible, and report the arrival. Similar orders were sent to you last night, telegraphed through the White House.

A.A. HUMPHREYS,
Major-General and Chief of Staff.[13]

HEADQUARTERS SECOND ARMY CORPS,
Wilcox's Landing, *June 14, 1864-6:10 p.m.*

Major-General HUMPHREYS,
Chief of Staff, Army of the Potomac:

GENERAL; I have the honor to state with the aid of four or five pontoon boats on the south side of the river we can make two landings instead of one, as is now the case. There are steamboats enough here to use both landings. There are two wharves on this side.

I am sir, very respectfully, your obedient servant,

WINF'D S. HANCOCK,
Major General, Commanding[14]

The first wave of troops General Grant sent up the James River to assail Petersburg were the 15,000 troops of General Smith's 18th Corps. They had been spared the long march. They had been transported 140 miles by ship from White House to Bermuda Hundred and were rested.

---

12 Official Records, Vol. XL Part 11 Ser. No. 81, p. 22.
13 Official Records, Vol. XL Part 11 Ser. No. 81, p. 22.
14 Official Records, Vol. XL Part 11 Ser. No. 81, p. 26.

Crossing the James

HEADQUARTERS ARMIES OF THE UNITED STATES,
Near Dispatch Station, Va., *June 13, 1864.*
Maj. Gen. W.F. SMITH,
Commanding Eighteenth Corps;
GENERAL: Send forward your troops to Bermuda Hundred as fast as they embark without waiting for division, the object being to get them to Bermuda Hundred at the earliest possible moment.
By command of Lieutenant-General Grant:
JNO. A. RAWLINS,
Brigadier-General and Chief of Staff.[15]

General W.F. Smith would be operating under General Butler's orders in his assault on Petersburg.

The second wave of troops Grant would throw against Petersburg were the 28, 000 troops of General Hancock's 2nd Corps:

HEADQUARTERS ARMY OF THE POTOMAC,
June 14, 1864-10 p.m.
Major-General HANCOCK:
General Butler has been ordered to send to you at Wind-Mill Point 60,000 rations. Soon as these are received and issued you will move your corps by most direct route to Petersburg, taking up a position where the City point railroad crosses Harrison's Creek at the crossroads indicated on the map at this point, and extend your right toward the mouth of Harrison's Creek* where we now have a work. After Barlow has crossed, you will cross as much of your artillery and ammunition train as possible up to the moment you are ready to move, and if all is quiet at that time the ferriage of the rest can be continued, and they can join you.
GEO. G. MEADE,
Major-General.[16]

By daylight of June 15, 1864 the 2nd Corps was across the James River and ready to move to Petersburg. The distance from Wilcox Landing to Petersburg is 15 miles as the crow flies.

*Federal maps were wrong. Harrison's Creek was behind Confederate lines.

---

15 Official Records, Vol. XL, Part 11, Ser. No. 81, p. 17.
16 Official Records, Vol. XL, Part 11, Ser. No. 81, p. 29.

Crossing the James

The Great Bridge

General Benham well understood that the Great Bridge was his responsibility and immediately pushed the construction: he has never received the recognition his magnificent performance deserved:

HEADQUARTERS ARMY OF THE POTOMAC
June 14, 1864-11:15 a.m. (Received 3:30 p.m.)
Brigadier-General BENHAM:
Commanding Engineer Brigade:
The commanding general directs that immediately upon the arrival of the bridge material at Fort Powhatan you construct the bridge across the James River at the point selected by General Weitzel, and the approaches to which are now being prepared.
A.A. HUMPHREYS,
Major-General and Chief of Staff.[17]

HEADQUARTERS ENGINEERS BRIGADE
On board Steamer J.A. Warner, near Wilson's Landing.
June 14, 1864-4 p.m.
Maj. Gen. A.A. HUMPHREYS,
Chief of Staff, Army of the Potomac:
SIR: I have just received your order of 11:15 a.m. today, and every exertion will be used by me to have the bridges down at the earliest moment. I left Fort Monroe today soon after 11, and within some forty minutes after I received an order from General Butler to send my pontoons and to come up myself. Your order of 9 p.m. last night was received at 5:15 p.m. today, but the pontoons had been sent up, as reported at 9 a.m. yesterday, with three companies and my best officers, yesterday afternoon, upon the instructions of General Grant through Lieutenant-Colonel Biggs, quartermaster. I have three companies with the siege material, &c., in six barges, and the most of my headquarters property, tents, & still at Fort Monroe, awaiting directions, according to previous orders, and the moment such bridge is completed, I will advise you as well as the nearer generals, as I suppose would be desired.
H.W. BENHAM,
Brigadier-General.[18]

---

17 Official Records, Vol. XL Part 11 Ser. No. 81, p. 22.
18 Official Records, Vol. XL Part 11 Ser. No. 81, p. 23.

Crossing the James

HEADQUARTERS ARMY OF THE POTOMAC,
June 14, 1864-9:30 p.m.

Brigadier-General BENHAM:

What progress in throwing the bridge, and at what time can you complete it, so far as you can now tell? I desire the work to be continued all night, if practicable.

GEO. G. MEADE,
Major-General.[19]

HEADQUARTERS ENGINEER BRIGADE,
June 14, 1864-10:50 [p.m.]

Major-General MEADE:

The bridge has now the last boat in position and the raft is ready to close the gap completely whenever it is safe to do so with reference to boats below, about which I am greatly in doubt. The bridge can be completed in fifteen minutes if you so order it. If it is important for the troops here to cross at once it can be done by closing the gap and holding the troop steamers, and quartermaster's boats below and let them pass in a body afterward, if you so order it.

H.W. BENHAM,
Brigadier-General.[20]

HEADQUARTERS ARMY OF THE POTOMAC,
June 14, 1864-11:30 p.m. (Received 12:45 a.m. 15th.)

Brigadier-General BENHAM:

Complete the bridge. General Burnside, with the Ninth Corps, will be ordered to cross at once. Request, in my name, the officer in command of the Atlanta to stop all boats below the bridge, and tomorrow a time will be fixed and a selection made of such as it is important to pass through. Take charge of the bridge. General Burnside will be directed to refer to you in passing over his command. Acknowledge receipt.

GEO. G. MEADE,
Major-General, Commanding.[21]

---

19 Official Records, Vol. XL Part 11 Ser. No. 81, p. 23.
20 Official Records, Vol. XL Part 11 Ser. No. 81, p. 23.
21 Official Records, Vol. XL Part 11 Ser. No. 81, p. 24.

Crossing the James

HEADQUARTERS ARMY OF THE POTOMAC,
June 14, 1864-11:50 p.m.

Brigadier-General Benham:
   I have changed the orders, and now have directed Burnside, Wright and Warren to send over their trains and surplus artillery with guards. I don't like to cross any troops till the big train gets nearer to us.

GEO. G. MEADE,
Major-General.[22]

Work on the great bridge began at 4:00 p.m. on June 14, 1864. 450 engineers under the direction of Brigadier General Benham worked steadily. The site for the enormous pontoon bridge was Weyanoke Point, three miles downstream (East) of Wilcox's Landing and five miles South of Charles City Court House.

William F. Frassanito describes the construction:

> Working from both sides of the river simultaneously, Union engineers eventually set 101 pontoons into position, spanning a total distance of seven hundred yards. The river at this point was exceptionally deep and the current treacherously swift, necessitating the support of several schooners midstream to provide firm anchorage. The bridge was constructed in such a way that the center portion could be opened at any time to permit the passage of transports. At eleven o'clock on the night of June 14, or roughly seven hours after the commencement of construction, the James River pontoon bridge was completed.[23]

The heavy wooden pontoons were 25 feet long and five feet wide with a 2'4" depth. They were clumsy and difficult to maneuver in place, but provided the buoyancy necessary to support the crossing of heavy supply trains, artillery, cavalry, as well as infantry. Lighter canvas frame pontoons were also carried in the train to supplement the wooden pontoons when needed in construction.

---

22 Official Records, Vol. XL Part 11 Ser. No. 81, p. 24.
23 Frassanito, William A., "Grant and Lee," Scribners, 1983, p. 207.

Crossing the James

Wooden pontoon on wagon

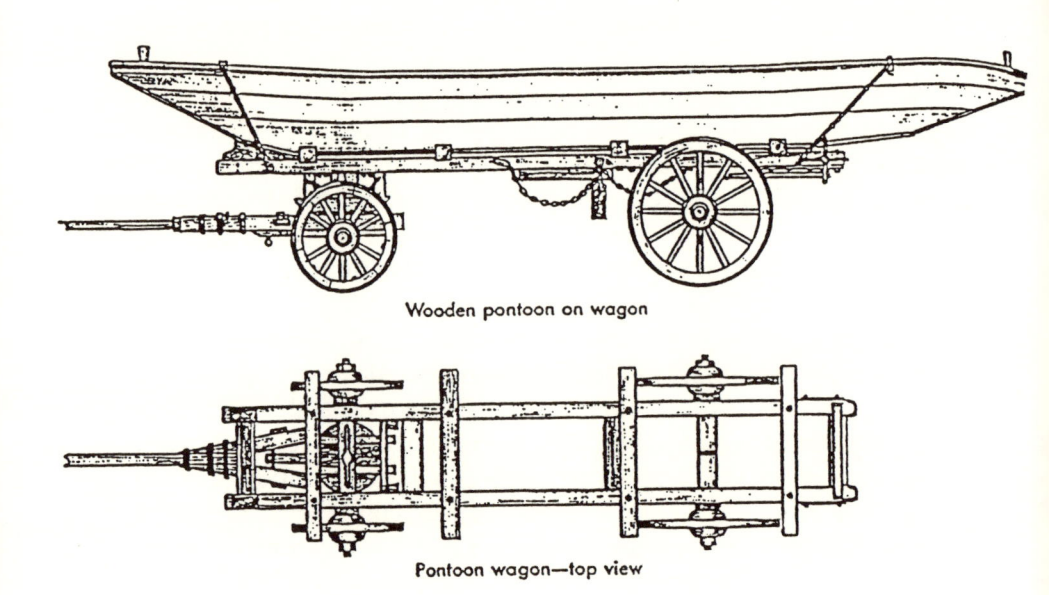

Pontoon wagon—top view

Besides the pontoons, the essential parts of the 1864 military bridge were:

    balks - the heavy timbers of the bridge were stretched between pontoons through cleats and held them in position (27" long, 5" x 5")

    chesses - the actual flooring planks of the bridge were nailed to the balks. (13' long, 12" wide, 4" thick)

---

24 Coggins, J. "Arms and Equipment of the Civil War", Broadfoot Publishing, Wilmington, N.C., 1987, p. 104.

Crossing the James

<u>side rails</u> - these heavy timbers were laid on top of the chesses, on either side of the bridge for its full length and lashed through the chesses to the balks to give the bridge stability and strength. (27' long, 5" x 5")[24]

Note these were interchangeable with the balks.

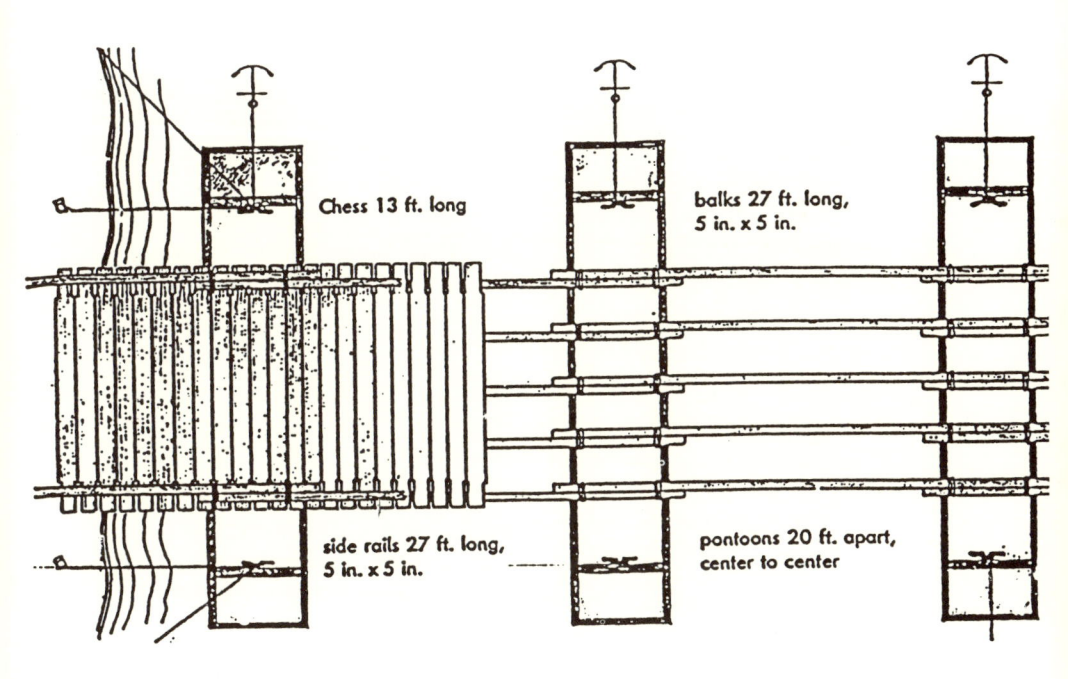

25

---

25 Coggins, J., "Arms and Equipment of the Civil War," Broadfoot Publishing, Wilmington N.C., 1987, p. 105

Crossing the James

General Weitzel was the chief engineering officer in General Butler's army that was sent by Butler to aid Gen. Benham. General Weitzel arrived at the bridge site first and immediately put his men to work constructing the important approaches for the bridge over the swampy ground on either bank. General Weitzel describes the work:

.....June 12, in anticipation of the crossing of the James River by the Army of the Potomac, I sent Lieutenant Michie, U.S. Engineers, to examine the river in the vicinity of Fort Powhatan to get all the information on the subject. He reported the width of the river at the three points (A, B, C) to be, respectively 1,250 feet, 1,570 feet, 1,992 feet; that the two approaches on the east bank at A would be from an old field across a marsh 1,000 yards wide; at B over a marsh about 800 yards wide; from these a spit of sand and gravel bordering the river from the bridgehead, averaging about forty feet wide and easily made into a good roadway sufficient for the passage of two columns of troops. On the west bank the approaches to the two first were already prepared, leading by gradual ascent to the bluff on which Fort Powhatan is situated. It would require, to make approaches to the third, the clearing away of trees, making a ramp of one-third leading to the field above, the filling up of ruts and gullies and making a roadway to the Petersburg and City Point road. In consequences of these facts, I telegraphed to Lieutenant-Colonel Comstock, senior aide to General Grant, that if the passage was to be made here I would only require, at the farthest, previous notice of thirty-six hours to have the approaches for the bridge ready.

June 13, without waiting for a reply, I directed Lieutenant Michie to proceed to the place and prepare the timber necessary for the corduroy across the marsh, as it seemed probable that it would be wanted. With 150 axman, 1,200 feet of timber, in sticks averaging 6 inches in diameter and 20 feet long, was cut and prepared before dark, and over 3,000 feet was brought down to the creek above Fort Powhatan ready to be rafted across. At about 3 p.m. I received a dispatch from General Grant informing me that the head of his column would be at the bridgehead at 10 a.m. the next day, and directing me to build approaches to the bridge at once at the point designated. An officer was immediately

Crossing the James

dispatched to Lieutenant Michie, with instructions to begin at once, using the detail that he had with him, and that I would join him, as soon as possible with a heavy detail to carry on the work. With the greatest exertion on the part of both officers and the men the approaches on both sides of the river, with a pier 150 feet long over the soft marsh on the east bank, was completed at 9:45 a.m. a quarter of an hour before the time indicated by General Grant; and the bridge would have been built, ready for the passage of the troops, at or before 10 a.m. on the 14th if the pontoon train had arrived, as it should, at this time. Through inexcusable tardiness, and more that culpable neglect of duty, Captain Robbins, of the Fiftieth New York Volunteer Engineers, did not appear in sight with his pontoons until after 12 o'clock at noon on the 14th, although he had but eighty miles to come from Fort Monroe, and received his orders to go as fast as he could at 2 p.m. on the 13th. So anxious was I that there should be no delay that I sent a dispatch boat to look for the pontoons down the river, with orders to go until they were found and hurry them up. Fifteen miles below Jamestown Island they were found at anchor, the captain being asleep. Owing to the strength of the current and tide, and depth of water, it was deemed necessary to moor three schooners each above and below to steady the bridge. These had been brought down the night before with a view to this disposition, were anchored by us, and used by General Benham for that purpose.

June 15, in obedience to instructions from General Grant, I superintended this day the obstruction of the channel of James River, about 800 yards above Alken's landing. Four schooners were sunk in the main left channel, first being moored fore and aft and connected with strong chains, and one schooner in the smaller right channel, thus leaving no aperture that a vessel of more that ten feet drought could pass through. The shallow water between the channels was obstructed by booms made from the masts of the vessels, connected by anchor chains.

June 16, owing to the strong attack of General Smith upon Petersburg, the enemy were compelled to withdraw all of their troops from our front to go to its relief. Over 1, 200 were sent out immediately to demolish the line of works erected by the enemy and to cut timber in our immediate front, heretofore

Crossing the James

impossible to reach on account of the enemy's sharpshooters. A rapid survey was also made of the enemy's works, the main line of which is shown in the accompanying tracing, with its position in reference to ours.

G. WEITZEL,
Brig. Gen. and Chief Engineers,
Dept. of Va. and N.C.[26]

A further report on the construction of the Great Bridge came from Capt. George H. Mendell of the Corps of Engineers:

HEADQUARTERS U.S. ENGINEER BATTALION,
Camp near Petersburg, Va.,
August 5, 1864,

.....The battalion was engaged in and did a great part of the work of throwing the bridge over the James, containing 101 wooden pontoons. In the channel the depth of water was twelve to fifteen fathoms, the tidal current strong, rising and falling about four feet. In the channel pontoons were anchored to vessels above and below moored for that purpose. The bridge was commenced from each end, and built by successive pontoons and by rafts. It was commenced about 4 p.m. on 15th* of June, two companies at each end, under the direction of Major Duane, chief engineer. Later in the afternoon and after considerable progress had been made, General Benham took command. The bridge was completed except a passage-way of 100 feet left for vessels, and the raft constructed to fill this gap by 11 p.m. The greater part of the infantry and artillery, all the wagon trains, and droves of beef-cattle of the army passed this bridge safely and without interruption, except such as resulted from a vessel moored above slipping her anchor, thereby carrying away a part of the bridge, which, however was promptly restored.....[27]

*Error - The correct date is June 14, 1864

---

26 Official Records, Vol. XL Part 1 Ser. No. 80, p. 675.
27 Official Records, Vol. XL Part 1 Ser. No. 80, p. 300.

Crossing the James

With the completion of the Great bridge at midnight June 14, the Army of the Potomac began to pour across. As General Meade put it, "I wish to keep the bridge occupied."[28] In addition to responsibility for the construction of the bridge, Brigadier General Benham was put in charge of the operation of the bridge. In his orders to General Burnside, General Meade stated:

> "Please direct the commanding officers to report their arrival to Brigadier General Benham, in charge of the bridge, and defer to his wishes in their movement across."[29]

General Benham specified when, where and how each unit should cross the great bridge. Officers were required to dismount and walk their horses across.

The actual crossing of the James river by the Union army was the greatest opportunity of the entire campaign for Lee to destroy Grant. The Army of the Potomac was strung out in long columns. The artillery was not in place and was some distance from the infantry.

For a 48 hour period, the 100,000 man Army of the Potomac was astride the James river, half on one side, half on the other. None of the units were in battle formation. If Confederate rams up river near Richmond had descended the James river from their bases and smashed the Great Bridge to pieces, they would have succeeded in dividing the Union army in two, isolating the two halves, dividing the infantry from its artillery and supply trains, isolating the cavalry, and separating commanders from their commands.

The success of the crossing of the James was in no small measure due to General Meade's administrative skills:

> HEADQUARTERS ARMY OF THE POTOMAC,
> *June 15, 1864-10:30 p.m.*
>
> Brig. Gen. John A. Rawlins, *Chief of Staff:*
> GENERAL: I have the honor to inclose, for the information of the lieutenant-general commanding, an order, just issued, for the movement of this army. At the present moment the Ninth Corps, artillery, and trains have crossed the river, and will move

---

28 Official Records, Vol. XL Part 11 Ser. No. 81, p. 30.
29 Official Records, Vol. XL Part 11 Ser. No. 81, p. 33.

Crossing the James

promptly to the front. I expect by 12 m. tomorrow the whole of the Fifth Corps will be across and in motion for the front. It will probably take till daylight of the 17th before the whole supply train will have crossed, and, during that day and night, the cavalry and Sixth Corps should be over and the bridge taken up. <u>Every effort will be made to push troops to the front</u>. I send a dispatch just received from General Wilson. It confirms my view that the enemy took first a position from White Oak Swamp to Malvern Hill, and, on discerning our movement, probably Hancock's crossing, at once commenced moving to the south side. They undoubtedly have a bridge above Drewry's Bluff, which, with their railroads, will give them an advantage. I will hurry up the troops all I can consistently with securing our long train, which I do not like to have outside of our entrenched line.

I shall leave here about 9 or 10 tomorrow, and will proceed at once to the vicinity of Burnside's position.

Respectfully, yours,

GEO. G. MEADE,
Major-General, Commanding.

Burnside will move all night.

[Enclosure]

[ORDERS]   HEADQUARTERS ARMY OF THE POTOMAC,
June 15, 1864-9:30 p.m.

The following movements of troops are ordered:

1. The Ninth Corps, Major-General Burnside, will immediately cross at the pontoon bridge, and with its train proceed on the road to Petersburg, via Court-House, and take position on the left of the Second Corps.

2. At 4 a.m. tomorrow morning the two divisions of the Fifth Corps, now at Clarke's will be ferried across at Wilcox's Wharf and the upper landing on the right bank. The two divisions of the Fifth Corps, now at Charles City Court-House, will move so as to commence, at 4 a.m., ferrying from the wharf near the pontoon bridge on this side and Wind Mill Point on the right bank. The artillery and trains of this corps will cross the pontoon bridge. The two divisions to cross at the bridge ferry and the trains will move by the most western of the two approaches to

Crossing the James

the bridge or in such manner as not to interfere with the movement of the general supply train. After the Fifth Corps is assembled on the right bank of the James Major-General Warren will move toward Petersburg, taking position on the left of the Ninth Corps, and in case that corps has not cleared the road he will look for a more southern road to move on.

3. The bridge will be given to the Ninth Corps and to the trains and artillery of the Fifth Corps whenever the latter are assembled in a body near the bridge. When not occupied as above the general supply train will continue to move across the bridge day and night until it is all over.

4. Brigadier-General Wilson, with the cavalry, will continue to watch the movements of the enemy in his advanced position until all the trains are across the bridge, when he will be withdrawn by Major-General Wright, commanding Sixth Corps, and passed across the bridge and join the army in front of Petersburg.

5. On the passage of the cavalry Major-General Wright will withdraw from the entrenched line he now holds; crossing the river and leaving sufficient guard till the bridge is taken up, will move with his corps and rejoin the army, taking position on the left of the Fifth Corps. Major-General Wright will call upon the commanding officers of the gunboats Atlanta and Mackinaw for cooperation in case the same is necessary.

6. On the passage of all the troops and trains as here indicated Brigadier-General Benham will take up the bridge and proceed with it to City Point, reporting his arrival there to these headquarters and to those of Lieutenant-General Grant. The bridge trains belonging to the army will be sent to their respective corps.

7. The chief quartermaster and chiefs of other departments will establish the depots of this army at City Point.

8. The supply train, as soon as it is all across the river, and the Ninth and Fifth Corps have moved forward, will be advanced to some suitable positions in rear of the center of the army, giving the road to the Sixth Corps when ready.

9. Headquarters will be moved tomorrow to the front in rear of the Ninth Corps.

Crossing the James

10. Should any demonstration of the enemy interfere with the above movements and threaten the security of the supply train Major-General Warren will cease crossing the river and, in conjunction with Major-General Wright, cover the movements of the supply train till it is within the entrenched line, when he will withdraw and cross the river by this bridge and bridge ferry.

By command of Major-General Meade:

S. WILLIAMS
Assistant Adjutant-General.[30]

General Meade makes clear that the various corps are to move promptly to Petersburg once they had crossed:

"At the present moment the Ninth Corps, artillery and trains have crossed the river, <u>and will move promptly to the front</u>."[31]

No one who was present at the crossing of the James ever forgot the magnificent sight. The most notable account is that of Charles Dana, Asst. Secretary of War:

HEADQUARTERS,
June 15, 1864-8 a.m. (Received 9:50 p.m.)

All goes on like a miracle. Pontoon bridge at Fort Powhatan finished at 2 a.m. Artillery trains instantly began crossing. Hancock's corps is nearly all landed by ferry at Wind-Mill Point; last of it will be over by 10 a.m. <u>Hancock moves out instantly for Petersburg to support Smith's attack on that place, which was to have been made at daylight</u>. General Warren will next be ferried, followed by Burnside and Wright. None of the boats sent by General Halleck, on General Grant's order, have arrived. The great wagon train has not yet begun to come up from the Windsor Shades, the pontoons sent back there having been delayed. Wilson's cavalry pickets now extend from White Oak Swamp bridge, on the right, to Malvern Hill, on the left. Wilson had constant sharp skirmishing on 13th, losing 50 men. He has taken

---

30 Official Records, Vol. XL, Part 11, Ser. No. 81 p. 49.
31 Official Records, Vol. XL, Part 11, Ser. No. 81, p. 49.

Crossing the James

prisoners who report that Hill and Ewell are entrenched on the line from White Oak Swamp to Malvern Hill. Lee appears to have had no idea of our crossing the James River. General Grant moves his headquarters to City Point this morning. Weather splendid.

C.A. DANA

Hon. E.M. STANTON,
Secretary of War.[32]

The newspapers at the time described the crossing triumphantly:

THE CROSSING OF THE JAMES

Our artist has contributed a sketch on (pages iv and v) of the pontoon bridge over the James, across which our army was in steady motions from Wednesday morning till Friday.

Says the *Times* correspondent: "As we approach the pontoon bridge we see distinctly the huge bodies of infantry, cavalry, horses, artillery, and wagons moving across the pontoon. They extend across the entire length of the bridge, and can be seen winding along from far away up the east bank of the James, enveloped in a dense cloud of dust, while on the western bank is a part of the great body which has already effected its crossing. The army has been steadily marching for fifty hours. A brigade of infantry with possibly a thousand cavalry horses and a battery of artillery has gotten over, and at this moment not more that twenty men are marching in units or couples across the bridge. Now comes a man leading a horse: now a cannon: now a dozen teamsters; now a battalion of Negro soldiers. But a heavy body of troops of all arms is passing out of the woods filing onto the bridge, and besides the column of infantry there are immense numbers of horses, long trains of wagons, numberless pieces of artillery and caissons.

"Now another body can be seen emerging from the woods on the river bank, and are passing on to the pontoons a long procession of beef cattle. They are in little detachments of four, five, or half a dozen each, every detachment preceded and followed by two or more Negro soldiers. Meridian is an hour gone, and about a mile up the river a heavy volume of dust is sweeping southward, Forward marches the long, long line of

---
32 Official Records, Vol. XL, Ser. No. 80, p. 19.

Crossing the James

cattle. All the afternoon they advance and pour over the river. The movement is slow. I am told that in this whole mass there are but 2500 head, or some six days' supply for the Army of the Potomac.

"Below the bridge may be seen a fleet of transports which have been accumulating, waiting for the bridge to be removed before they can pass up to City Point, the new base of supplies. It should be mentioned here that Warren's Corps protected the crossing of the trains."[33]

Some historians have questioned whether a second pontoon bridge across the James River had been constructed in the vicinity of Weyanoke Neck. Apparently the concept of a second bridge was considered but rejected because of a need for pontoons further east on the James, nearer Petersburg:

HEADQUARTERS,
Near Point of Rocks, Va.,
June 15, 1864-6 p.m.

Brigadier-General BENHAM,
Chief Engineer, Army of the Potomac, Fort Powhatan:
Can you spare us pontoons for 250 feet of bridge without detriment to the service? If so, please send them up at once by first boat. We can get along without them, but it would be very much more convenient with them.

BENJ. F. BUTLER,
Major-General.[34]

HEADQUARTERS ENGINEER BRIGADE,
Near Fort Powhatan,
June 15, 1864.

Major-General BUTLER:
GENERAL: I have only above the bridge the sixteen pontoons (320 feet), with their material, received from you this evening. I could send those up, but it may prevent the possibility of

---

33 Harper's Weekly July 2, 1864
34 Official Records, Vol. XL, Part 11, Ser. No. 81, p. 54.

Crossing the James

constructing another bridge tomorrow. I will send to General Meade, and if he authorizes it I will sent them up by the gunboat you sent me-the Parke.
Very respectfully, your obedient servant,

H.W. BENHAM,
Brigadier-General.[35]

HEADQUARTERS ARMY OF THE POTOMAC,
June 15, 1864-10 p.m.

Brigadier-General BENHAM:
You will furnish General Butler, on requisition, such bridging material as he requires. You will not open the bridge, however, for this purpose until all of the Ninth Corps has passed over.

Respectfully,
GEO. G. MEADE,
Major-General, Commanding[36]

Captain Kingsland will order the pontoon up at once, to be towed by the Parke, which is to return as soon as possible.

H.W. BENHAM,
Brigadier-General.[37]

The rapid movement of General Smith's 18th Corps up the James River to Bermuda Hundred was of utmost importance and its implementation received the highest priority. The 18th Corps was the spear point of the attack. The troops arrived at Bermuda Hundred well rested for the attack on Petersburg early on the morning of June 15th.

BERMUDA,
June 14, 1864

Colonel SHAFFER:
The steamers Webster, Albany, Nellie Pentz, and Claymont have arrived with troops. They draw too much water to go up the Appomattox. The troops are disembarking here and marching to

---

35 Official Records, Vol. XL, Part 11, Ser. No. 81, p. 54.
36 Official Records, Vol. XL, Part 11, Ser. No. 81, p. 55.
37 Official Records, Vol. XL, Part 11, Ser. No. 81, p. 55.

Crossing the James

the front. The General Hooker has arrived and has been ordered up the Appomattox. Will hurry up matters all I can.

C.E. FULLER,
Lieutenant-Colonel, &tc.[38]

WALKER'S POINT SIGNAL STATION,
June 14, 1864.

Lieutenant STRYKER:

Nine steamers have passed up the river laden with troops. Three vessels have passed down, one the S.R. Spaulding. The others a steamer and steam tug.

THOS. H. FEAREY,
Second Lieutenant,
Signal Corps, U.S. Army.[39]

BERMUDA,
June 14, 1864

General SMITH,
Commanding Eighteenth Corps:

The troops that came on steamers Nellie Pentz Eagle No. 2, Claymont, Webster and Albany were here before the orders to go to City Point were received. The General Hooker has gone to Point of Rocks. There have been no arrivals for an hour and a half. Six regiments started for General Butler's headquarters about an hour since. An officer should be sent to meet them to be sure that they do not miss the way.

C.E. FULLER,
Lieutenant-Colonel and Commander.[40]

General Meade was very clear at 7:30 a.m. in the morning as to the urgency of moving immediately on Petersburg:

---

38 Official Records, Vol. XL Part 11 Ser. No. 81, p. 37.
39 Official Records, Vol. XL Part 11 Ser. No. 81, p. 38.
40 Official Records, Vol. XL Part 11 Ser. No. 81, p. 43.

Crossing the James

HEADQUARTERS SECOND CORPS,
June 15, 1864-6:00 a.m.

Major General MEADE:
My infantry is all over but one regiment for fatigue. Four batteries are over, with horses, &c. I have now three ferryboats and shall make rapid progress with artillery and wagons. No rations received yet. The upper wharf on south side is just reported finished.

WIN'FD S. HANCOCK,
Major-General.[41]

HEADQUARTERS ARMY OF THE POTOMAC,
June 15, 1864-7:30 a.m.

Major-General HANCOCK:
You will not wait for the rations but move immediately to the position assigned you last evening. You will leave an officer to direct the boat with the rations to return to City Point or up the Appomattox to some more suitable point from whence you can draw them. The ferryboats will not be taken from you till all your artillery and wagons are over, you can then unload ammunition wagons to haul supplies.

Your dispatch just received. It is important you should move. Exercise your judgement as to which will be best to issue rations now or send them as directed in the foregoing.

GEO. G. MEADE,
Major-General.[42]

HEADQUARTERS SECOND CORPS,
June 15, 1864-3:30 p.m.

Major-General HUMPHREYS,
Chief of Staff:
GENERAL, Following my instructions to take the "nearest and most direct route to Petersburg," I have arrived at a point four miles from the Court House. The point marked Graysville or Gaysville [Garysville] on the map I cannot hear of, except

---

41 Official Records, Vol. XL Part 11 Ser. No. 81, p. 56.
42 Official Records, Vol. XL Part 11 Ser. No. 81, p. 57.

Crossing the James

that I am told that Gays or Gray's Tavern, which I find on this road, is meant. Bailey's Creek is much out of place on the map. To get to the position assigned me I turn to the right two miles this side of the Court-House and go by way of Old Court House. My rear division (General Barlow) I have turned to the right beyond Powell's Creek, to take the interior road and meet me at Old Court-House. My trains will also take this road. I have found some guides and have ceased traveling by the map. Firing of two or three hours' duration has been heard since we started. A Negro with us thinks it is on the Prince George Court-House road, one mile and a half this side. I hear of no enemy near Prince George Court-House or Old Court-House.

Your obedient servant,
WINF'D S. HANCOCK,
Major-General, Commanding.[43]

---

43 Official Records, Vol. XL Part 11 Ser. No. 81, p. 59.

Summary of Troop Movement Crossing of the James by the Army of the Potomac

Distances on Map 2 (p. 88, 89)

	Miles:
Cold Harbor to Long Bridge on the Chickahominy River (Point 11 to Point 2 on map)	15
Long Bridge on the Chickahominy River to Weyanoke Neck on the James River where the Great Bridge was constructed (Point 2 to 5 on map)	12
Wilcox Landing - site of ferry boat operation (The ferry boat operation was 3 miles west of Weyanoke Neck) (Point 6 to Point 6 on map)	
Wilcox Landing to Petersburg (Point 6 to Point 9 on map)	15
Bermuda Hundred to Petersburg (Point 8 to Point 9 on map)	5
Cold Harbor to Riddell's Shop (Lee's movement) (Point 11 to Point 12 on map)	12
Richmond to Petersburg (Point 19 to Point 10 on map)	20
Cold Harbor to White House (Point 11 to Point 17 on map)	15
Cold Harbor to Jones Bridge on the Chickahominy River (Point 11 to Point 18 on map)	25
Fortress Monroe to Weyanoke Neck (Point 20 to Point 5 on map)	60
From White House to Bermuda Hundred by boat, the route taken by General Smith and the 18th Corps (Point 17 to Point 8 on map)	140

Note: These mileages are given "as the crow flies." Actual distances on country roads could add 30%.

Crossing the James

General Warren's 5th Corps (Map 2, pages 88, 89)

Nightfall June 12, 1864	5th Corps left Cold Harbor marching South (See pt. 1)
1:30 AM June 13, 1864	5th Corps crossed Long Bridge on the Chickahominy River. (See pt. 2)
June 13, 1864	5th Corps established position at Riddell Shop. Skirmished with Confederate army. (See pt. 3)
Dawn - June 14, 1864	5th Corps evacuated Riddell Shop position and marched south.
Afternoon June 14, 1864	5th Corps arrived at North bank of James River. (See pt. 8)
June 15 & 16, 1864	5th Corps crossed the James River by the Great Bridge
June 17, 1864	5th Corps reached the Petersburg front. (See pt. 10)

General Smith's 18th Corps (Map 2, pages 88, 89)

Nightfall June 12, 1864	Left Cold Harbor marching east to White House. (See pt. 15)
Dawn June 13, 1864	Reached White House. Immediately boarded ships. (See pt. 17)
June 13 & 14, 1864	Transported by ship for 140 miles from White House (pt. 17) to Bermuda Hundred. (See pt. 8)
4:00 AM June 15, 1864	Marched for Petersburg, a distance of ten miles.
1:30 PM June 15, 1864	The 18th Corps arrives at the fortifications East of Petersburg. (See pt. 9)

Crossing the James

<u>General Hancock's 2nd Corps</u> (Map 2, pages 88, 89)

Nightfall June 12, 1864	Fell back to reserve line to cover army's withdrawal.
Nightfall June 12, 1864	Left Cold Harbor marching south. (See pt. 13)
Noon June 13, 1864	The head of the 2nd Corps reached Long Bridge on the Chickahominy River. (See pt. 2)
5:30 PM June 13, 1864	By forced marches the 2nd Corps reached Wilcox Landing on the North bank of the James River (See pt. 6)
June 14, 1864	General Hancock began moving the 2nd Corps across the James River by ferry boat between Wilcox Landing and Windmill Point (See pts. 6 & 6)
Dawn June 15, 1864	Before daylight on June 15th, 2nd Corps had completed its crossing of the James Rivers with four batteries of artillery.
Morning June 15, 1864	General Hancock holds up his advance waiting for rations.
6:30 PM June 15, 1864	Lead elements of General Hancock's 2nd Corps arrive at Petersburg. (See pt. 9)

(Note: Gen. Hancock's own report states that he made contact with Gen. Smith by 5:00 p.m.)

<u>General Burnside's 9th Corps</u> (Map 2, pages 88, 89)

Nightfall June 12, 1864	Left the extreme north end of the Union line at Cold Harbor and marched east. (See pt. 16)
Night June 13, 1864	Bivouacked on the north bank of Chickahominy River at Jones Bridge 20 miles from Cold Harbor. (See pt. 18)

Crossing the James

10:00 AM June 14, 1864	9th Corps completed crossing of the Chickahominy River at Jones Bridge and proceeded to the James River.
June 15 & 16, 1864	9th Corps crossed the James River by the Great Bridge. (See pt. 5)
June 16, 1864 afternoon	9th Corps arrived at the Petersburg front. (See pt. 9)

<u>General Wright's 6th Corps</u>   (Map 2, pages 88, 89)

Nightfall June 12, 1864	Fell back to reserve line to cover army's withdrawal. (See pt. 14)
Nightfall June 12, 1864	Left Cold Harbor marching East and then South.
Evening June 13, 1864	Reached Jones Bridge on the Chickahominy River and began crossing. (See pt. 18)
10:00 AM June 14, 1864	6th Corps completed crossing of Chickahominy River at Jones Bridge and proceeded to the James River.
June 16, 1864	6th Corps crossed the James River by the Great Bridge. (See pt. 5)
June 17th 1864	6th Corps arrived at the Petersburg front. (See pt. 9)

<u>Wagon Train</u>   (Map 2, pages 88, 89)

    The enormous Union wagon train (50 miles long) was swung far to the East so as to be well covered from attack and also so that it would not block the roads for the infantry. (See pt. 17 to pt. 4) It crossed the Chickahominy at Coles Landing.

    The wagon train was the last element to cross over the James River on the Great Bridge at Weyanoke Neck on June 16th. (Pt. 5)

Crossing the James

Confederate Reaction

General Lee entered a period of great uncertainty as to General Grant's intentions. General Lee had reported to Richmond:

June 13, 1864 10 p.m.

...At daybreak this morning it was discovered that the army of General Grant had left our front. Our skirmishers were advanced between 1 and 2 miles, but failing to discover the enemy were withdrawn, and the army was moved to conform to the route taken by him. He advanced a body of cavalry and some infantry from Long Bridge to Riddle's Shop, which were driven back this evening nearly 2 miles, after some sharp skirmishing.

Very respectfully, your obedient servant,

R. E. LEE,
General.[44]

Hon. SECRETARY OF WAR, Richmond.

On finding the Union army gone, Lee set the Army of Northern Virginia in motion. He did not pursue Grant. Most of Lee's cavalry had been sent North in pursuit of Sheridan. Lee had to move with great caution. Without his full complement of cavalry he could not penetrate the Union cavalry screen and find the Union army.

Lee moved the Confederate army away from the Union army. Lee moved 15 miles south of Cold Harbor to a position in Riddell's Shop area. Lee established a line between White Oak Swamp and Malvern Hill. By now Lee had reduced his army to only two Corps. A. P. Hill's 2nd Corps and Anderson's 1st Corps after sending Early to Charlottesville. Lee would remain in this position at Riddell's Shop, blocking Grant's anticipated advance on Richmond from the southwest for the next two days, June 14th and June 15th, the two most vital days of the entire campaign. General Lee's official report for June 14th was:

---

44 Dowdy, Clifford, Editor, "The Wartime Papers of R. E. Lee," Little Brown, 1961, p. 776.

Crossing the James

HEADQUARTERS ARMY OF NORTHERN VIRGINIA,
June 14, 1864-9 p.m.

SIR: The force of the enemy mentioned in my last dispatch as being on the Long Bridge road disappeared during the night. It was probably advanced to cover the movement of the main body, most of which as far as I can learn, crossed the Chickahominy at Long Bridge and below, and has reached James River at Westover and Wilcox's Landing. A portion of General Grant's army upon leaving our front at Cold Harbor is reported to have proceeded to the White House and embarked at that place. Everything is said to have been removed and the depot at the White House broken up. The cars, engine, railroad iron, and bridge timber that had been brought to that point have also been reshipped.

Very respectfully, your obedient servant

R. E. LEE,
General.[45]

Hon. SECRETARY OF WAR, Richmond, Va.

At noon on June 14th, Lee sent President Davis a personal letter in which he shared his thoughts on Grant's intentions.

Headquarters, Army of Northern Virginia
June 14, 1864, 12:10 p.m.

Mr. President:

I have just received your note of 11 1/2 p.m. yesterday. I regret very much that I did not see you yesterday afternoon, and especially after your having taken so long a ride. If the movement of Early meets with your approval, I am sure it is the best that can be made, though I know how difficult it is with my limited knowledge to perceive what is best.

I think the enemy must be preparing to move south of James River. Our scouts and pickets yesterday stated that Gen. Grant's whole army was in motion for the fords of the Chickahominy from Long Bridge down, from which I inferred that he was making his way to the James River as his new base. I cannot however learn positively that more than a small part of his army has crossed the Chickahominy. Our contest last evening, as far

---

45 Official Records, Vol. XXXVI Pt. 1, Ser. No. 67, p. 1035.

Crossing the James

as I am able to judge was with a heavy force of cavalry and the 5th Corps of his army. They were driven back until dark as I informed you by a part of Hill's corps. <u>Presuming that this force was either the advance of his army, or the cover behind which it would move to James River, I prepared to attack it again this morning, but it disappeared from before us during the night,</u> and a far as we can judge from the statements of prisoners, it has gone to Harrison's landing. The force of cavalry here was pressed forward early this morning, but as yet no satisfactory information has been obtained. It may be Gen. <u>Grant's intention to place his army within the fortifications around Harrison's landing, which I believe still stand, and where by the aid of his gunboats he could offer a strong defense</u>. I do not think it would be advantageous to attack him in that position. He could then either refresh it or transfer it to the other side of the river without our being able to molest it, unless our ironclads are stronger than his. It is reported by some of our scouts that a portion of his troops marched to the White House, and from information derived from citizens, were there embarked. I thought is probable that these might have been their discharged men, especially as a scout reported under date of the 9th instant that transports loaded with troops have been going up the Potomac for three days and nights, passing above Alexandria. On the night of the 8th, upwards of thirty steamers went up, supposed to be filled with troops, no doubt many of these were wounded and sick men. Still I apprehend that he may be sending troops up the James River with the view of getting possession of Petersburg before we can reinforce it. We ought therefore to be extremely watchful & guarded. Unless I hear something satisfactory by evening, I shall move Hoke's division back to the vicinity of the pontoon bridge across James River, in order that he may cross if necessary. The rest of this army can follow should circumstances require it.

The victories of Forrest [at Brice's Crossroads, Mississippi] and Hampton are very grateful at this time, and show that we are not forsaken by a gracious Providence. <u>We have only to do our whole duty, and everything will be well.</u> A scout in Prince William reports that the enemy are rebuilding the bridges on the Orange & Alexandria Railroad adjacent to Alexandria. This may be with

Crossing the James

the view of opening the Manassas Gap Railroad to communicate with the Valley, their tenure of which I trust will not be permanent.

Most respectfully, your obt servt
R. E. Lee
Gen.[46]

According to his June 14th letter, Lee was trying to figure out from scattered reports what Grant was up to:

a. "...I inferred that he was making his way to the James River as his new base..."

b. "...I cannot however learn positively that more than a small part of his army has crossed the Chickahominy..."

c. "...It may be Gen. Grant's intention to place his army within fortifications around Harrison's landing, which I believe still stands, and where by the aid of his gunboats, he could offer a strong defense..."

d. "...Still I apprehend that he may be sending troops up the James River with the view of getting possession of Petersburg before we can reinforce it..."

General Lee's uncertainty was reflected in the disposition of his army. Twenty-four hours later he again writes President Davis:

Headquarters, Army of Northern Virginia
June 15, 1864, 12:45 p.m.

Mr. President:

As I informed you last evening <u>I had intended to move the troops nearer the exterior lines of defences around Richmond,</u> but from the movements of the enemy's cavalry and the reports that have reached me this morning, his plans do not appear to be settled. Unless therefore I hear something more satisfactory, <u>they will remain where they are.</u> Should I move my camp, it will be somewhere on Cornelius Creek in the cleanest wood I can find near the New Market road or Osborne turnpike.

Most resply, your obt servt
R. E. Lee, Gen.[47]

---

46 Dowdey, Clifford, Editor, "The Wartime Papers of R. E. Lee," p. 777, Ltr. 773.
47 Dowdey, Clofford, editor, "The Wartime Papers of R. E. Lee," p. 780, Ltr. 777.

Crossing the James

The Confederate army remained on the Riddell's Shop line until June 17th. (See Map 2, pg. 88, 89, pt. 12) In the evening of June 15th General Lee explained his position more fully to the President.

>Riddell's Shop, Charles City Road
>*June 15, 1864 6:30 p.m.*

Mr. President:

Your note of 1:20 p.m. today has just been received. As soon as I heard of the enemy's crossing the Chickahominy at Long Bridge I moved Heth's division across the river to White Oak Swamp bridge, and prepared the other troops for motion. Our skirmishers at daylight were moved forward, and finding no enemy in front of our lines for between one and two miles were recalled, and the army moved over the Chickahominy. Gen. Heth's division holds the White Oak Swamp bridge, the rest of Hill's corps is at Riddell's Shop at the intersection of the Long Bridge and Charles City roads. Longstreet's corp is to his right on the Long Bridge road, and Hoke's division at the intersection of the Darbytown and Long Bridge roads. Our cavalry occupy the Willis Church road and Malvern Hill. The only enemy we have yet seen is that that has come up from the Long Bridge, and is opposed to Gen. Heth at White Oak Swamp bridge and extends to this point. We have driven him from this position down the Long Bridge road, but I have not yet heard that White Oak Swamp bridge is uncovered. <u>Gen. Early was in motion this morning at 3 o'clock</u> & by daylight was clear of our camps. He proceeded on the mountain road direct to Charlottesville, and arrangements have been made to give him 15 days supplies. <u>If you think it better to recall him, please send a trusty messenger to overtake him tonight.</u> I do not know that the necessity for his presence today is greater than it was yesterday. His troops would make us more secure here, <u>but success in the Valley would relieve our difficulties that at present press heavily upon us.</u> As I write, Wilcox's division is pressing the enemy down the Long Bridge road.

Most respectfully, you obt servt

R. E. LEE
Gen.[48]

---

48 Dowdey, Clofford, Editor, "The Wartime Papers of R. E. Lee," p. 782, Ltr. 780.

Crossing the James

Lee's ambiguity is very apparent in this letter. This is the final movement that could confine Lee to siege for the rest of the war. And yet he says to President Davis, "If you think it better to recall him (Gen. Early) please send a trusty messenger to overtake him tonight." He invites Davis to make the decision.

During this same period, June 14th and 15th, General Beauregard, commanding the forces defending Petersburg, had been bombarding the War Department in Richmond with reports of Union forces moving against him. Many contemporary historians tend to downgrade Beauregard's ability but on June 15, 1864, he had the clearest understanding of what was happening, more than any other Confederate leader:

(1)   DUNLOP'S HOUSE, *June 15, 1864-<u>7 a.m.</u>*

General BRAXTON BRAGG:

  Return of Butler's forces sent to Grant, and arrival of latter at Harrison's Landing renders my position more critical than ever; if not reinforced immediately, enemy could force my lines at Bermuda Hundred Neck, capture Battery Dantzler, now nearly ready, or take Petersburg, before any troops from Lee's army or Drewry's Bluff could arrive in time. Can anything be done in the matter?

                                                       G. T. BEAUREGARD.

(2)   SWIFT CREEK, *June 15, 1864-<u>9 a.m.</u>*

General BRAXTON BRAGG:

General Dearing reports at 7:35 a.m.:

  Enemy is still in our front in force; reported advancing in heavy force on Broadway road. A prisoner says some of Burnside's troops are there.

If so, it is very important.

                                                       G. T. BEAUREGARD.

(3)   SWIFT CREEK, *June 15, 1864-<u>9:30 a.m.</u>*

General BRAXTON BRAGG:

  Signal officer near Fort Clifton reports musketry and artillery heard on south side Appomatox. I have ordered Hoke's division from Drewry's Bluff to Petersburg, leaving one brigade at Port Walthall Junction until it can be relieved by another. Please order Ransoms, of Johnson's division to do so.

                                                      G. T. BEAUREGARD.

Crossing the James

(4)   SWIFT CREEK, *June 15, 1864-9:30 a.m.*

General BRAXTON BRAGG;

   General Dearing, from south side of Appomattox, reports enemy have attacked my outposts in force. Prisoners state there are four regiments of infantry and four of cavalry close behind. They say it is an "on to Petersburg" and more force behind.

                                             G. T. BEAUREGARD.

(5)   SWIFT CREEK, *June 15, 1864-10 a.m.*

General BRAXTON BRAGG:

   Two members of our signal corps captured at Coggins Point yesterday have escaped, and report that from 2 p.m. until sunset twelve transports of enemy had passed up crowded with troops.

                                             G. T. BEAUREGARD[49]

(6)   SWIFT CREEK, *June 15, 1864-11:45 a.m.*

General BRAXTON BRAGG:

   General: Wise reports General Dearing's cavalry driven back on Petersburg, with loss of one piece of artillery. Enemy reported three brigades of infantry and considerable force cavalry, apparently moving toward Baxter and Jerusalem plank roads. He calls for reinforcements on his whole line. We must now elect between lines of Bermuda Neck and Petersburg. We cannot hold both. Please answer at once.

                                             G. T. BEAUREGARD.

(7)   SWIFT CREEK, VA., *June 15, 1864-1 p.m.*

General BRAXTON BRAGG,
Richmond, Va.:

   Hoke's division is ordered to Petersburg; hope it will get there in time; I will hold lines of Bermuda Hundred Neck as long as practicable, but I may have to re-inforce Hoke with Johnson's division, when lines would be lost. I advise sending forthwith another strong division to intersection of turnpike and railroad near Port Walthall Junction.

                                             G. T. BEAUREGARD,
                                             General.

(Copy to General Lee)

---
49 Official Records, Vol. XL Part 11 Ser. No. 81, p. 655.

Crossing the James

(8)   SWIFT CREEK, *June 15, 1864-1:45 p.m.*

General BRAXTON BRAGG,
Richmond, Va.:

Your telegram of 12 m. received. I did not ask advice with regard to the movement of troops, but wished to know preference of War Department between Petersburg and lines across Bermuda Hundred Neck, for my guidance, as I fear my present force may prove unequal to hold both.

                                                     G. T. BEAUREGARD,
                                                         General.

(9)   PETERSBURG, VA., *June 15, 1864-9:11 p.m.*

General BRAXTON BRAGG,
Richmond, Va:

Reinforcements not having arrived in time, enemy penetrated lines from Battery 5 to 8 inclusive. Will endeavor to retake them by daybreak. I shall order Johnson to this point with all his forces. General Lee must look to the defenses of Drewry's Bluff and the lines across Bermuda Neck, if practicable.

                                                     G. T. BEAUREGARD,
                                                         General.

(Copy to General Lee.)

(10)   BEAUREGARD'S HEADQUARTERS,
                                            June 15, 1864-10:05 p.m.

General BRAXTON BRAGG:

The following just received from Lieutenant Woodley, at Fort Boykin: Since my dispatch of 7 a.m. three more steamers with troops have gone up, making thirteen in all today.

                                                     G. T. BEAUREGARD,
                                                         General.

Crossing the James

(11)   PETERSBURG, VA., *June 15, 1864-11:15 p.m.*

General R. E. Lee,
Headquarters Army of Northern Virginia:

    I have abandoned my lines on Bermuda Neck to concentrate all my forces here; skirmishers and pickets will leave there at daylight. Cannot these lines be occupied by your troops? The safety of our communication requires it. Five thousand or 6,000 men may do.
                           G. T. BEAUREGARD.[50]

General Beauregard's message of June 15, 1864 - 11:15 p.m. greatly alarmed General Lee. Petersburg was under attack and General Beauregard had abandoned the defense of the Bermuda Hundred Line to concentrate his troops at Petersburg. This created a gap between the two Confederate armies.

Lee, very upset, sprang into action. Now, he must accurately locate the position of General Grant's main army before committing his own army. Was Grant's main attack to be North of the James River toward Richmond or South of the James River towards Petersburg? Beauregard must be encouraged to do the best he could with what he had:

(1)   DREWRY'S BLUFF, *June 16, 1864-10:30 a.m.*

General BEAUREGARD:
Petersburg:

    Your dispatch of 9:45 received. It is the first that has come to hand. I do not know the position of Grant's army, and cannot strip north bank of James River. Have you not force sufficient?
                                    R. E. LEE.[51]

Lee was still blind as to Grant's intentions and movement:

(2)   *June 16, 1864-4 p.m.*

General BEAUREGARD,
Petersburg:

    The transports you mention have probably returned Butler's troops. Has Grant been seen crossing James River?
                                            R. E. LEE.[52]

---

50 Official Records, Vol. XL Part 11 Ser. No. 81, p. 656, 657.
51 Official Records, Vol XL Part 11 Ser. No. 81, p. 659.
52 Official Records, Vol. XL Part 11 Ser. No. 81, p. 659.

Crossing the James

At this late date in the war General Lee was placed in command of all military forces in Virginia by the Confederate War Dept. Heretofore General Lee and General Beauregard had exercised separate commands. Each had reported to the Secretary of War in Richmond. Now Lee was in charge.

SPECIAL ORDERS
No. 139.
       ADJT. AND INSP. GENERAL'S OFFICE,
            Richmond, June 15, 1864.

XX. All officers exercising separate commands in the States of Virginia and North Carolina will report to and receive orders from General R. E. Lee.

By command of Secretary of War:
           JNO WITHERS,
         Assistant Adjutant General.[53]

Because of this division of command it is very possible that many of General Beauregard's reports ended up in the files in Richmond and had not reached General Lee.

The Bermuda Hundred line had to be restored immediately, otherwise the Army of Northern Virginia could be cut off from Petersburg.

       DREWRYS BLUFF, *June 16, 1864-3 p.m.*
General BEAUREGARD:

GENERAL: Dispatch of 12:45 received. Pickett had passed this place at date of my first dispatch. I did not receive your notice of intended evacuation till 2 a.m. Troops were then at Malvern Hill, four miles from me. Am glad to hear you can hold Petersburg. Hope you will drive the enemy. <u>Have not heard of Grant's crossing James River.</u>
              R. E. LEE.[54]

When General Beauregard abandoned the Bermuda Hundred defense line, it had been immediately occupied by Union troops under General Butler who proceeded to tear up the railroads. Lee moved veteran 1st Corps troops under General Anderson back into the area and pushed the Union intruders out by midnight on June 16th:

---
53 Official Records, Vol. XL Part 11 Ser. No. 81, p. 654.
54 Official Records, Vol. XL Part 11 Ser. No. 81, p. 659.

Crossing the James

DREWRY'S BLUFF, *June 16, 1864-midnight.*

PRESIDENT OR SUPERINTENDENT
OF RICHMOND AND PETERSBURG RAILROAD,
Richmond Va.:
   The line of breastworks across Bermuda Neck is being reoccupied by our troops. General Anderson reports that the enemy tore up and burned about half a mile of the railroad below Walthall Junction. Preparations should be made to repair this portion of the track as soon as it is practicable.
R. E. LEE,
General.[55]

Having met the most immediate crisis at Bermuda Hundred, General Lee turned his attention to finding General Grant. Before committing his army, General Lee needed to know where the main body of the Union army was and where it was going. The Confederate cavalry was ordered to find the Union army.

CLAY'S HOUSE, *June 17, 1864-3:30 p.m.*

Maj. Gen. W. H. F. LEE,
Malvern Hill, via Meadow Station:
   Push after enemy and <u>endeavor to ascertain what has become of Grant's army</u>. Inform General Hill.
R. E. LEE.[56]

Although General Lee did not feel he could totally rely on reports from General Beauregard, he still moved one of his Corps closer to Petersburg.

CLAY'S HOUSE, *June 17, 1864-4:30 p.m.*

Lieut. Gen. A. P. HILL,
Riddell's Shop, via Meadow Station:
   General Beauregard reports large number of Grant's troops crossed James River above Fort Powhatan yesterday. If you have nothing contradictory of this move to Chaffin's Bluff.
R. E. LEE.[57]

---

55 Official Records, Vol. XL Part 11 Ser. No. 81, p. 660.
56 Official Records, Vol. XL Part 11 Ser. No. 81, p. 663.
57 Official Records, Vol. XL Part 11 Ser. No. 81, p. 662.

Crossing the James

CLAY'S HOUSE, *June 17, 1864-4:30 p.m.*

General G. T. BEAUREGARD,
Petersburg, Va.:

Have no information of Grant's crossing the James River, but upon your report have ordered troops up to Chaffin's Bluff.

R. E. LEE.[58]

Finally on the night of June 17, the doubt and uncertainty were removed. Douglas Southall Freeman provides the best account:

"Rooney" Lee, who commanded the cavalry advance in the vicinity of Malvern Hill, had been ordered on the afternoon of the 17th to ascertain, if possible, what had 'become of Grant's army,' but the son of the commanding general, had not let reconnaissance wait on orders. At the very time that instructions were being drafted for him, he had on the road to Chaffin's Bluff a courier with a detailed report. During the night this was placed in the hands of the senior Lee. It contained information that the enemy had a pontoon bridge across the James at Weyanoke Neck and that the rear of the enemy had left Dr. Wilcox's the previous night after posting a notice that Petersburg, with twenty-two guns and 3,000 prisoners, had been captured.*[59]

*Obviously a false report left by the Union army.

Rooney Lee's report galvanized the Confederate army into action. The great threat by the Union army was to Petersburg.

The fastest way for Gen. Lee to get troops to Petersburg was by rail.

DREWRY'S BLUFF, *June 18, 1864-3:30 a.m.*

SUPERINTENDENT RICHMOND
AND PETERSBURG RAILROAD, *Richmond*

Can trains run through to Petersburg? If so, send all cars available to Rice's Turnout. If they cannot run through, can any be sent from Petersburg to the point where the road is broken. It is important to get troops to Petersburg without delay.

R. E. LEE.[60]

---

58 Official Records, Vol. XL Part 11 Ser. No. 81, p. 665.
59 Freeman, Douglas Southall, "Lee's Lieutenants," Vol. 111, p. 536.
60 Official Records, Vol. XL Part 11 Ser. No. 81, p. 668.

Crossing the James

General Early, with an independent command consisting of 20% of the Confederate army must be notified of developments.

HEADQUARTERS ARMY OF NORTHERN VIRGINIA,
June 18, 1864

General J. S. EARLY, Lynchburg:
 Grant is in front of Petersburg. Will be opposed there. Strike as quick as you can, and, <u>if circumstances authorize, carry out the original plan, or move upon Petersburg without delay.</u>
R. E. LEE.[61]

General Lee's message to General Early on June 18, 1864 was again very revealing. Lee's ambiguity is apparent. He leaves the final decision to his subordinate. He gave Early the option of going to the Valley or to Petersburg. At this critical stage of the war, either move was of vital importance. Lee left it up to Early which bet he would take.

On June 18, 1864, Lee rushed his entire army to the trenches of Petersburg. The siege that he had dreaded was upon him. Lee was committed now to a no-win defense position from which he could not break out. Petersburg would become the "mere question of time"[62] until the end of the Confederacy.

On June 16th, as the fate of the Confederacy was being sealed, a request for leave was forwarded from General Longstreet, Lee's "Warhorse", who had been severely wounded in the Wilderness:

BUREKEVILLE, June 16, 1864.

General S. COOPER;
 My wound is healed, but my right arm is still paralyzed. I desire to visit my friends in Georgia until it recovers. Please answer at Danville.
J. LONGSTREET.[63]

---

61 Official Records, Vol. XL Part 11 Ser. No. 81, p. 667.
62 Jones, J. Williams, <u>Personal Reminiscences of General Robert E. Lee,</u> p. 40.
63 Official Records, Vol. XL Part 11 Ser. No. 81, p. 661.

IV
ASSAULT ON PETERSBURG JUNE 15, 1864 TO JUNE 18, 1864

Everything now depended on General W. F. Smith and his 18th Corps. Smith's troops were well rested from a 140 mile boat ride from White House to Bermuda Hundred.

At 1:30 p.m. on June 15, 1864 General Smith arrived at the defense line surrounding Petersburg. (See Map 2, p. 88, 89, point 9). The Union force, augmented by units from the Army of the James totaled 15,000 men. The Confederate force to oppose them were a scant 2,000 men, hardly enough to delay an aggressive attack. Petersburg lay wide open for the Union army to walk in.

General Beauregard, the Confederate commander, later wrote that the city "at that hour was clearly at the mercy of the Federal commander, who had all but captured it."[1]

General Smith at this point halted. His army did absolutely nothing for five and one-half hours while he personally conducted his reconnaissance of the Confederate line. The slave-built fortifications around Petersburg were indeed impressive. There were many cannon.

Any competent general could have quickly evaluated the situation. If the defenses of Petersburg were manned, they were impregnable. If the defenses of Petersburg were held by a skeleton force, they could be taken. The opportunity would vanish with delay. The only way to find out was to send forward a skirmish line. An immediate answer could be had.

General Smith's five and one-half hour personal reconnaissance was one of the most expensive blunders of the war. General Smith was a West Point graduate. He had performed extremely well at Chattanooga

---

1 Life/Time Series, William C. Davis, editor, "The Civil War, Death in the Trenches," p. 43.

Assault on Petersburg

in helping to relieve the Confederate siege in November 1863. He had shown daring and imagination. The fact that he was expected to move quickly and aggressively was well understood. At this critical point, General Smith's resolve failed him:

> HEADQUARTERS EIGHTEENTH CORPS,
> *June 15, 1864.*
>
> Major-General HANCOCK or GIBBON:
> GENERAL: General Grant has authorized me to call on you to hurry forward to Petersburg to aid in its capture. I do not suppose at present there is much infantry over there, but the wide open spaces along my entire front, and the heavy artillery fire of the enemy, have prevented me from attempting any assault and also preventing me from getting any artillery into position to do any service. If the Second Corps can come up in time to make an assault tonight after dark in vicinity of Norfolk and Petersburg Railroad I think we may be successful. But tonight is the last night, as General Lee is reported crossing at Chaffin's Bluff. Please inform me by bearer when the head of your column may be expected here. My left is on the Jordan's Point road.
> Respectfully,
> WM. F. SMITH,
> *Major-General, Commanding*[2]

General Butler at Bermuda Hundred, Smith's commanding officer, did all that he could to urge General Smith forward to attack Petersburg. General Butler made it perfectly clear to General Smith that immediate action was expected of him. An aggressive assault on Petersburg was the reason for the 140 mile boat ride. General Smith had not been sent to Petersburg as an observer:

---

2 Official Records, Vol. XL Part 11 Ser. No. 81, p. 59.

Assault on Petersburg

June 15, 1864-7:20 p.m.

General SMITH:

I grieve for the delays, Time is the essence of this movement. I doubt not the delays were necessary, but now push and get the Appomattox between you and Lee. Nothing has passed down the railroad to harm you yet.

BENJ. F. BUTLER,
Major-General, Commanding.[3]

June 15, 1864-9 p.m.

General BUTLER:

I must have the Army of the Potomac re-enforcements immediately.

SMITH,
General.[4]

COBB'S HILL SIGNAL STATION,
June 15, 1864. (Received 9:30 p.m.)

General SMITH:

Hancock has been ordered up by General Grant's and my orders. Another army corps will reach you by 10 a.m. tomorrow. It is crossing. They have not got 10,000 men down yet. Push on to the Appomattox.

B.F. BUTLER,
Major-General, Commanding.[5]

General Butler was authorized by General Grant to also urge General Hancock and his 2nd Corps forward.

HEADQUARTERS,
Near Point of Rocks, *June 15, 1864-8:30 p.m.*

Major-General HANCOCK:

General Smith has carried the outer line of works and the only defensive line of Petersburg. They are crowding down troops from

---

3 Official Records, Vol. XL Part 11 Ser. No. 81, p. 83.
4 Official Records, Vol. XL Part 11 Ser. No. 81, p. 83.
5 Official Records, Vol. XL Part 11 Ser. No. 81, p. 83.

Assault on Petersburg

Richmond. General Grant supposes that you will move out and aid General Smith. Please move up at once to the aid of Smith and put the Appomattox between you and Lee's army. This is important. I have already forwarded you the same suggestion by Major Ludlow. Provisions are on the way to you. More will be started during the night. I will see you supplied. I can send you if needed a couple of batteries of artillery.

BENJ. F. BUTLER,
Major-General, Commanding.

P.S.-While writing the above have received the following dispatch from General Grant which is enclosed. General Grant directs me to order you up.

Respectfully,
BENJ. F. BUTLER,
Major-General, Commanding.[6]

When General Smith finally did go forward at 7:00 p.m., his attack was an immediate success. He took the first Confederate line in 20 minutes. The 2,000 Confederates could not begin to cover their defense line or work the cannon. As a result, the massive fortifications were an illusion. The Union army easily took a mile wide section of the line including Redans 3 through 11. Even with the five and one-half hour delay, Petersburg could have been taken with ease. At this point General Smith's judgment again failed:

June 15, 1864 12 midnight.

General BUTLER:

It is impossible for me to go farther tonight, but, unless I misapprehend the topography, I hold the key to Petersburg. General Hancock not yet up. General Amos not here. General Brooks has three batteries, General Martindale one, and General Hinks ten light guns.

W. F. SMITH,
Major-General.[7]

Lee's army was at Riddell's Shop, 15 miles north of the Petersburg battlefield, on June 15, 1864. Lee was still north of the James River. Lee still expected an attack on Richmond.

---

6 Official Records, Vol. XL Part 11 Ser. No. 81, p. 60.
7 Official Records, Vol. XL Part 11 Ser. No. 81, p. 83.

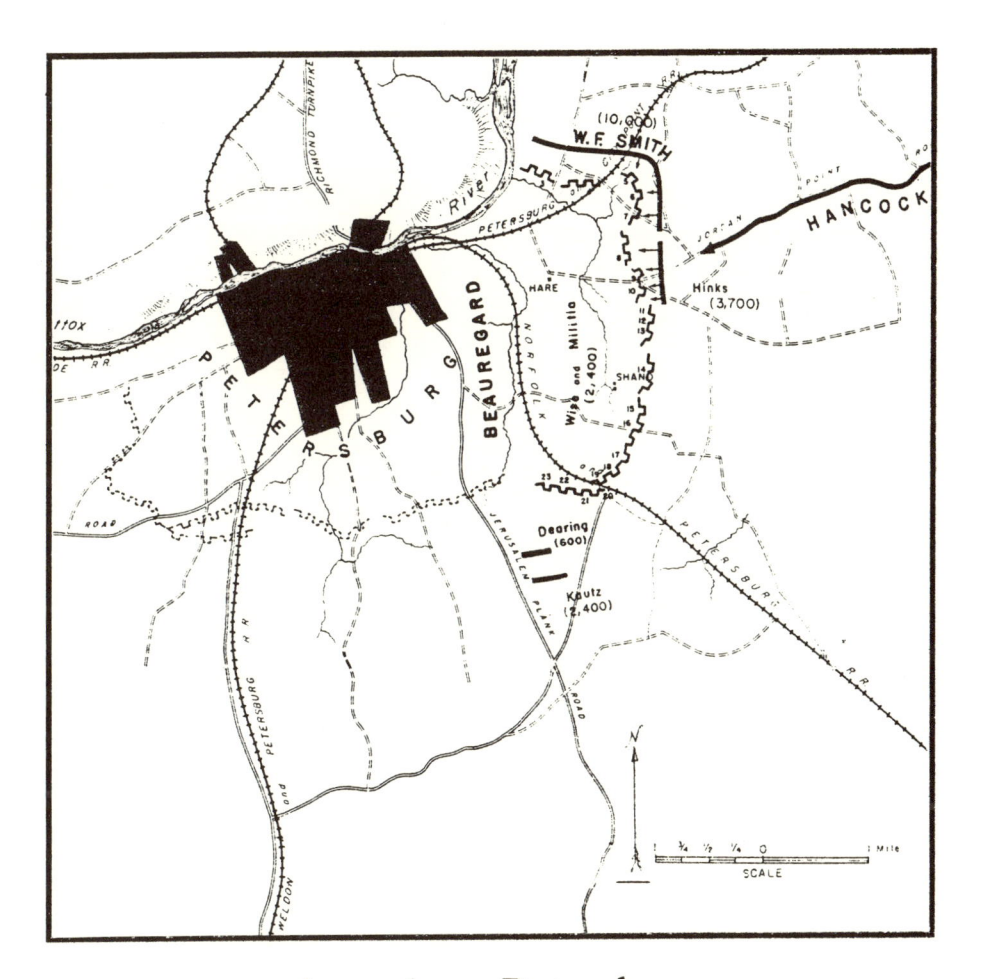

Assault on Petersburg

June 15, 1864

Assault on Petersburg

Not only that, but General Hancock had arrived with the 2nd Corps, 28,000 men, more than enough to keep the offensive rolling. There was a full moon.

"...it was, as one of Hancock's artillerymen declared, a night 'made to fight on'."[8]

Grant urged coordinated movement forward.

>   HEADQUARTERS ARMIES OF THE UNITED STATES,
>   City Point, Va., *June 15, 1864-8:30 p.m.*
>   (Received 11. 12 p.m.)
>
> Major-General HANCOCK,
> Commanding Second Army Corps:
>   GENERAL: If requested by General Butler or Smith to move up to where Smith now is do so. The enemy are not seen to be reinforcing Petersburg by rail and by troops marching. So far, however, but two regiments and eleven carloads have been reported. Your rations have gone up. Hope they have reached you by this time. General Butler says he understands you have halted at a creek short of the one (Harrison's Creek) to which you were to go.
>
>   Respectfully, U. S. GRANT,
>   *Lieutenant-General.*

However, Hancock, confirms that he had already arrived by 5:00 p.m. on June 15:

>   HEADQUARTERS SECOND ARMY CORPS,
>   *June 15, 1864*
>
> Maj. Gen. B. F. BUTLER, Commanding, &c.:
>   GENERAL: My leading division connected with General Smith about 5 p.m. I now have two divisions in line. They are now formed on his left. I have another division to place in reserve as soon as it arrives, it having found difficulty in finding its way on account of the darkness. The night is of that nature, and my having arrived at this point after dark, I can determine little about the features of the country, and I cannot tell what the morning

---

8 Life/Time Series, William C. Davis, editor, "The Civil War - Death in the Trenches," p. 44.

Assault on Petersburg

will bring forth; but I think we cover all of the commanding points in front of Petersburg. I am now at the Bryant house, but am going to move to the vicinity of General Smith's headquarters in a short time. I will be glad if the provisions arrive early in the morning. I am much obliged for your offer of artillery, and if my reserve artillery does not come up I may apply to you for some; but at present I think I have enough to place in position, as I know the country. I received a communication from General Grant this afternoon, but have not had time to reply to it. You will oblige me by sending a copy of this communication to him. General Smith and myself have examined the country, but cannot determine the exact position of the enemy.

> Your obedient servant,
> WINF'D S. HANCOCK,
> *Major-General, Commanding.*

Forwarded to General Grant, by request of General Hancock, by telegraph.[9]

At Hancock's confirmed arrival at the front by 5:00 p.m. on June 15, 1864, the Confederates still had only 2,000 troops defending Petersburg. General Smith's letter of June 15, 1864 (page 146) is misleading. Perhaps it is an attempt to cover his blunder?

Although Hancock was the senior officer at Petersburg, he waived rank to General Smith: there would be no night attack. Hancock did not grasp the urgency of the situation and the need for immediate action.

General Beauregard had been given back Petersburg by the Union commanders responsible for taking it. They gave Beauregard the thing that he needed most - time. General Smith delayed the first attack on the city for five and one-half hours. After the first successful attack, General Smith, and ultimately, General Hancock, gave the Confederates the entire night to reinforce and fortify.

By dawn of June 16, 1864, Beauregard had a newly dug line and 14,000 men along the eastern edge of Petersburg.

General Smith's explanation of his blunder is as difficult to accept today as it was at the time:

---

9   Official Records, Vol. XL Part 11 Ser. No. 81, p. 60.

Assault on Petersburg

Report of Maj. Gen. William F. Smith, U.S. Army, commanding Eighteenth Army Corps, of operations, June 15.
HEADQUARTERS EIGHTEENTH CORPS,
June 16, 1864.

GENERAL. I have the honor to make the following report of my operations of yesterday:

About 4 a.m. the head of my column left Broadway. Near Baylor's farm our cavalry came upon the enemy's artillery and infantry. General Kautz being unable to dislodge them, General Hinks was ordered to make an attack. The rifle-pits we gallantly carried by General Hinks' command and one piece of artillery captured. My command was then ordered to move forward according to the original orders of the day, and got into position around the enemy's works at Jordan's house about 1:30 p.m. I found the enemy's artillery so arranged as to have a cross-fire on most of my entire front, and some batteries which I had ordered into position were immediately driven out by enemy's fire. As no engineer officer was ordered to report to me I was obliged to make the reconnaissance in person, and some time was unnecessarily wasted on that account, but not till about 7 p.m. were the final preparations completed for the assault. In about twenty minutes the works at Jordan's house and on the left were carried by the divisions of General Brooks and Hinks, capturing guns, caissons, horses, ammunition, colors, camp and garrison equipage, and entrenching tools and prisoners. Some heavy profile works in rear of the line captured still keeping up a galling artillery fire I ordered the colored troops to carry them by assault. This was gallantly done. About this time I learned that General Martindale, on my right, with Stannard's brigade in advance, had carried the enemy's works between Jordan's house and the Appomattox, capturing two pieces of artillery, with teams, caissons, &c., complete. By this time darkness had set in, and having learned some time before that reinforcements were rapidly coming in from Richmond, and deeming that I held important points of the enemy lines of works, I thought it prudent to make no further advance, and made my dispositions to hold what I already had. About midnight Gibbon's division of the Second Corps, came up to relieve the part of my too extended lines.

Assault on Petersburg

Too much praise cannot be awarded to the troops for their gallantry of yesterday, and the colored troops are deserving of special mention.

I am, general, very respectfully, your obedient servant,

WM. F. SMITH,
Major-General, Commanding.[10]

Major-General BUTLER,
Commanding Department of Virginia, &c.

After his dismissal from the army, an embittered Smith blamed his failure on Grant and did what he could to undermine Grant's reputation.

Grant summoned General Meade from his location at the James River crossing to take personal charge of the attacking forces at Petersburg:

Near Petersburg June 16th, 1864.
10:15 a.m.

MAJ. GEN. MEADE
COMD. G. A. P.
GEN.

Gen. Smith carried very strongly located and well constructed works forming the left of the enemy's defences of Petersburg taking some prisoners and sixteen pieces of Artillery. The enemy still hold their right works and are massing heavily in that direction. Hurry Warren up by the nearest road to reach the Jerusalem plank road about three miles out from Petersburg. As soon as you receive this and give the necessary directions start yourself, by steamer, and get here to take command in person. Leave your Hd Qts. train to follow by land. Put Wright in charge of all left behind with directions to get the trains over as rapidly as possible to be followed by the Cavalry, to cut in as soon as the last wagon gets within his, Wrights, lines.

U.S. GRANT
Lt. Gen.[11]

General Meade arrived at Petersburg the afternoon of June 16th. An attack was organized for 6:00 p.m. Some units attacked with great vigor

---

10 Official Records, Vol. XL Part 1 Ser. No. 80, p. 705.
11 Official Records, Vol. XL Part 11 Ser. No. 81, p. 86.

Assault on Petersburg

and made good progress. Other units and commanders hung back and did not press the fighting. Meade had great difficulty controlling the whole front in the confusion of a new and strange battlefield. Meade reports the next morning:

June 17, 1864 6:00 a.m.

Lt. Gen. U. S. Grant

    The attack was made at 6 p.m. yesterday, as ordered, on the whole of the front of the Second Corps and by that corps. Birney made considerable progress, taking some of the advanced works of the enemy and one of their main works of their first line. About 8 p.m. I directed Burnside to form a strong column of attack to move from Barlow's left. This column was organized and the attack made about 4 a.m. Burnside carried the enemy's works, capturing 21 guns, 400 prisoners, and, he reports, two redoubts. This advantage will be pushed. There has been continuous fighting all along the line since the attack commenced at 6 p.m. yesterday. <u>Advantage was taken of the fine moonlight to press the enemy all night.</u> The loss has not been great. A rough estimate would make it under 2000 killed & wounded-I regret to say many valuable officers are among this number - Col. Kelly comd. Irish brigade Lt. Col McCreary 146,[145] Pa Vols are reported killed - Col. Egan 40th NY, Lt. Col. McGee 69. N.Y. Col Hopgood 6th N.H. wounded, The 5th Corps reached the ground about 11 p.m. & will be placed in position this morning - Two brigades of the 18th were taken to support & take part in the attack of the 2d Corps-I cannot ascertain from prisoners that any considerable part of Lee's army is in our front - They report Hokes command, Bushrod Johnston Division, Wise legion & some say Longstreet or part of his corps are present. - Their men are tired, and the attacks have not been made with the vigor & force which characterized our fighting in the Wilderness - If they had been I think, we should have been more successful - I will continue to press. - ALS (incomplete), DNA, RG 108, Letters Received. O.R., I, xi, part 2, 117.

                                  G. G. Meade,
                                  Maj. Gen.[12]

---

12 John Y. Simon, "The Papers of Ulysses S. Grant," Vol. 11, p. 63.

Assault on Petersburg

Despite the efforts of the Army of the Potomac, Petersburg could not be taken on June 16th, 17th or 18th. As more and more units of Lee's army arrived the resistance of the besieged town stiffened. The advantage of the defense became decisive. By June 18th it was obvious to all that Petersburg could not be taken, and that further attacks would be bloody and futile.

The final communication of the 46 day campaign was sent by General Grant on the night of June 18, 1864.

By telegraph from Grant's HD. QTRS. 10 p.m.
June 18th 1864.

To Maj. Gen. George G. Meade

To MAJ GENL MEADE

I am perfectly satisfied that all has been done that could be done and that the assaults today were called for by all the appearances and information that could be obtained. Now we will rest the men and use the shade for their protection until a new vein can be [s]truck. As soon as Wilsons Cavalry [i]s rested we must try & cut the Enemy's lines of communication. In view of a temporary blockade of the river being possible I think it advisable that supplies in depot should be kept up to full twenty days besides ten 10 days in wagons & haversacks. If nothing occurs to prevent I shall be absent tomorrow from ten 10 a.m. to about three 3 p.m. up the river near the Naval Fleet.

U.S. GRANT
Lt. Gen.[13]

With this letter General Grant brought the 46 day campaign to a close and initiated the siege of Richmond/Petersburg. General Grant now occupied the key position he had proposed in his letter of January 19th. By occupying this key position South and East of Petersburg the Union army held General Lee firmly in place in the trenches of Petersburg. Grant had his "line further South". General Lee could not advance or retreat or maneuver. He was immobilized. He could only sit and wait for the next move by the enemy.

From this key position, Grant spread Union fortifications south and west of Petersburg and north to Richmond for a distance of thirty-five

---

13 John Y. Simon, "The Papers of Ulysses S. Grant," Vol. 11 p. 78.

Assault on Petersburg

miles. City Point now supplied the Union army by means of a newly built railroad. Lee's army was stretched spread eagle over this thirty-five mile front he had to defend. At no place was he strong. At all places he was weak.

From this key position Grant immediately launched a series of attacks against vulnerable Confederate supply lines, destroying and occupying railroads, bridges, roads and depots. After a few months only one railroad remained in Confederate hands. With the broad area he had to defend, Lee was forced to rush his inadequate reserves from one area of attack to another. Often when he reached his destination the Union army had attacked the area he had vacated.

All Confederate resources in the Eastern theater were poured into the single industry of maintaining supply lines into Richmond/ Petersburg. There were no resources for anything else. There was no assistance available for crumbling armies in the rest of the Confederacy.

As summer merged into fall and fall merged into winter, General Lee's letters to President Jefferson Davis reflected the growing misery and desperation of the Confederate army. The problem of food was uppermost. Lack of manpower was a close second. These problems were followed by desertion, lack of arms, lack of soap, lack of slaves to dig fortifications and lack of a mobile strike force to meet federal attacks.

Confederate General Porter Alexander described the situation in June 1864 as the siege began:

> The position which he (Grant) had now secured, & the character of the military operations he now contemplated, removed all risk of any serious future catastrophe, however bold we might be, or however desperately we might fight. We were sure to be soon worn out. It was now only a question of a few moves more or less.
>
> Of this period the future historian will doubtless write that by all the rules of war & of statecraft the time had now fully arrived for President Davis to open negotiations for peace. Now was the time to save his people the most of blood, of treasure, & of political rights. The last chance of winning independence, if it ever existed, had now expired, & all rules must condemn the hopeless shedding of blood.[14]

---

14 Alesander, General Edward Porter, Editor Gary W. Gallagher, "Fighting for the Confederacy," p. 433, published by University of North Carolina press.

Assault on Petersburg

By December, 1864, all hope for the existence of the Confederacy was gone. In December, Grant wrote his friend and subordinate, General Sherman, congratulating him on the completion of his successful march across Georgia from Atlanta to Savannah.

To Maj. Gen. William T. Sherman
Washington D. C. Dec. 18th 1864

Confidential
MY DEAR GENERAL,

I have just received and read, I need not tell you with how much gratification your letter to Gen. Halleck. I congratulate you, and the brave officers and men under your command, on the successful termination of your most brilliant campaign. I never had a doubt of the result. When apprehensions for your safety were expressed by the President I assured him with the Army you had, and you in command of it, there was no danger but you would strike bottom on Salt Water some place. That I would not feel the same security, in fact would not have entrusted the expedition to any other living commander.

It has been very hard work to get Thomas to attack Hood. I gave him the most preemptory orders and had started to go there myself before he got off. He has done magnificently however since he started. Up to last night 5000 prisoners and 49 pieces of Captured Artillery, besides many wagons and innumerable small Arms, had been received in Nashville. This is exclusive of the enemy's loss at Franklin which amounted to Thirteen (13) General officers killed, wounded and captured. The enemy probably lost 5000 men at Franklin and 10,000 in the last three days operations. Breckeridge is said to be making for Murphreesboro. If so he is in a most excellent place. Stoneman has nearly wiped out John Morgan's old command and five days ago entered Bristol. I did think the best thing to do was to bring the greater part of your Army here and wipe out Lee. The turn affairs things now seem to be taking has shaken me in that opinion. I doubt whether you may not accomplish more towards that result where you are than if brought here, especially as I am informed since my arrival in the City that it would take about two months to get you here with all the other calls there is for ocean transportation.

Assault on Petersburg

I want to get your views about what ought to be done and what can be done. If you capture the garrison of Savannah it certainly will compel Lee to detach from Richmond or give us nearly the whole South. <u>My own opinion is that Lee is averse to going out of Va. and if the cause of the South is lost he wants Richmond to be the last place surrendered. If he has such views it may be well to indulge him until we get everything else in our hands.</u>

Congratulating you and the Army again upon the splendid results of your campaign, the like of which is not read of in past history, I subscribe myself, more than ever, if possible,

Your Friend
U. S. GRANT
Lt. Gen. [15]

Grant's letter to Sherman reflects his near perfect understanding of Robert E. Lee.

"My own opinion is that Lee is averse to going out of Va. and if the cause of the South is lost he wants Richmond to be the last place surrendered. If he has such views it may be well to indulge him until we get everything else in our hands."

And that was exactly what Grant ordered his generals to do: "get everything else in our hands". Once the Army of Northern Virginia had been immobilized by siege the Confederacy crumbled. Isolated Confederate armies were disposed of one by one. The Confederate government became less and less effective. It would be almost a disaster a month until the end of the war:

---

[15] Simon, John Y., editor, "The Papers of Ulysses S. Grant," Vol. 13, page 129.

Assault on Petersburg

A Disaster A Month

Aug. 5, 1864 — Mobile, Alabama fell to Admiral Farragut.

Sept. 1-2, 1864 — Atlanta, Georgia fell to General Sherman.

Oct. 19, 1864 — Battle of Cedar Creek-General Sheridan (U.S.) defeated General Early (CSA) ending Confederate resistance in the Shenandoah Valley.

Nov. 12, 1864 — In the state of Georgia. General Sherman began his destructive march from Atlanta to the sea.

Dec. 15, 1864 — Nashville, Tennessee. General Thomas destroyed General Hood (the last Rebel army in the Western Theater)

Dec. 21, 1864 — Savannah, Georgia fell to General Sherman.

January 1865 — The States of Alabama and Georgia. General Wilson led a cavalry army of 17,000 troopers through the deep South with minimal resistance.

January 15, 1865 — Fort Fischer, Willmington, N.C. fell to a joint army/navy task force similar to WW 11 operations. This sealed off supplies from Europe.

February 17, 1865 — Charleston, S. C. surrendered by Confederate forces after being cut off by General Sherman.

February 17, 1865 — Columbia, S. C. the capital of South Carolina, caught fire as Sherman's army entered.

March 25, 1865 — In desperation Lee attacked the Union line at Fort Stedman opposite Petersburg. He was repelled with a loss of 3500 casualties.

April 9, 1865 — Lee surrendered.

V
AFTER JUNE
JUNE 19, 1864 TO APRIL 1865

Some historians take the view that, when General Lee arrived at Petersburg June 18, 1864, and put his troops into trenches to defend the city, he had won the 46 day campaign. They cite as evidence of this the fact that Grant failed to take Richmond. Winston Churchill and Liddell Hart took this view.

> " Yet by the end of the summer of 1864 the ripe fruit of victory had withered in his hands.* The Union forces had almost reached the end of their endurance, and Lincoln despaired of re-election- a sorry repayment for the blank cheque he had given his military executant. It is an ironical reflection that the determination with which Grant had wielded his superior masses, now fearfully shrunk after the fierce battles of the Wilderness and Cold Harbor, had utterly failed to crush the enemy's army, while the chief result-the geographical advantage of having worked round close to the rear of Richmond-was gained by the bloodless maneuvers which had punctuated his advance. He had thus the modified satisfaction of being back, after immense loss, in the position which McClellan had occupied in 1862."
>
> — Liddell Hart[1]

*Grant's hands.

"(Grant) established a new base on the south bank (of the James) He set himself to attack Richmond by the "back-door," as

---
1 Liddell Hart, "Strategy," p. 149.

After June

McClellan had wished to do. Repulsed at Petersburg, he laid siege with an army now reinforced to a hundred and forty thousand men to the trench lines covering that stronghold and the lines east of Richmond. He failed again to turn Lee's right flank by movements south of the James, and at the end of June resigned himself to trench warfare attack by spade, mine, and cannon. There was no investment, for Lee's western flank remained open. There static conditions lasted till April 1865. These performances, although they eventually gained their purpose, must be regarded as the negation of generalship."
~ Winston Churchill[2]

There is an interesting contradiction between Liddell Hart and Winston Churchill. Liddell Hart describes the Union army as "now fearfully shrunk after the fierce battles." Winston Churchill describes the Union army as "now reinforced to a hundred and forty thousand men." In this case Churchill is correct. The Union army had been heavily reinforced. 100,000 Union troops crossed the James River. Additional Union forces were pouring in.

The conclusions reached by Winston Churchill and Liddell Hart may be emotionally satisfying to partisans or the old South but they are terrible military history. Both Churchill and Hart neglected to perform any responsible research and instead simply repeated the approved Confederate claptrap.

One can tolerate this nonsense from Englishmen. But to read this rubbish from a current American author is very disturbing.

Noah Andre Trudeau wrote a current best seller called "Bloody Roads South" in which he described "The Wilderness to Cold Harbor May-June 1864." Although Mr. Trudeau has presented many interesting facts and amusing anecdotes, he has failed completely to grasp the significance of the 46 day campaign. Mr. Trudeau has spent his time counting trees and missed the forest:

> In the loneliness of his White House office, Abraham Lincoln sat holding a War Department telegram. It had arrived yesterday from Grant, who, in typical understatement, was reporting that his army would be crossing the James shortly and that he had hopes of quickly capturing Petersburg. Grant closed with the

---
2 Winston Churchill, "History of the English Speaking People" Vol. IV, p. 254.

After June

comment that his movement to the James "has been made with great celerity and so far without loss or accident."

Forty-seven days before, Lincoln had wished Grant well and asked "that any great disaster, or the capture of our men in great numbers, shall be avoided." What Grant had provided for Lincoln was a succession of nightmares: the Wilderness, Spotsylvania, Cold Harbor. His strategy had resulted in massive casualty lists, and the piteously groaning evidence of the slaughter wheeled almost daily through the streets of the capital. No longer was Grant hailed as the savior of the Union. The tag applied to him more and more often now was "butcher."

In the deepest, darkest part of his heart, Lincoln knew that the war had had to come to this-a mutual butchery in which the strongest would live and the weakest die. The Confederacy could not be defeated in a normal sense-no loss of arms or land could make it recant its defiant secession. Defeat would have to be total, overwhelming. More men would have to die, more wives would have to be widowed, and more mothers would have to mourn their lost sons. Lincoln and the country had traveled too far down the bloody path of war to stop now that the end was in sight.[3]

Mr. Trudeau is mixing his facts. In paragraph one he says,

> "Grant closed with the comment that his movement to the James 'has been made with great celerity and so far without loss or accident'."

The movement of the 100,000 man Union army from Cold Harbor to Petersburg on June 12, 13, 14, 15, 1864 was a military miracle without significant casualties. Grant was reporting honestly.

In the next paragraph Mr. Trudeau refers to the large scale fighting in Northern Virginia, Wilderness and Spotsylvania, in which both sides lost heavily, and the Confederate army lost any offensive capability. Grant's description was of the movement to and the crossing of the James. (June 12-June 17) Grant was not describing the heavy fighting of May 4-May 21st. Mr. Trudeau tries to imply that Grant was dishonest in his report to Lincoln.

---

[3] Trudeau, Noah Andre, "Bloody Roads South," p. 321.

After June

The Union army reported all of its casualties accurately throughout the campaign. It was the Confederate army that did not report casualties and covered up its losses to hide the fact that Lee lost an immense portion of his army fighting Grant.

Mr. Trudeau again does us an historical disservice in his depiction of Lincoln's role.

> "What Grant had provided for Lincoln was a succession of nightmares: the Wilderness, Spotsylvania, Cold Harbor."

Mr. Trudeau gives the impression that naive, tender hearted Lincoln was surprised and shocked by the big battles. This is ridiculous. Abraham Lincoln understood war.

President Lincoln had been searching three years for a general who would take the magnificent Army of the Potomac that he had created and attack and destroy Lee. Lincoln's extensive writings to this effect are discussed at length in Appendix "A". General Grant did exactly what President Lincoln had wanted. In 46 days Grant drove Lee to siege and out of action, out as an influence in the war. The military technology of the time did not provide the means for storming fortified cities. Lincoln knew the price of breaking Lee would be high, but he was willing to pay the price. The relationship between Lincoln and Grant was one of complete understanding and support.

Mr. Trudeau then plays the final card that suddenly, after three years of bloody Civil War, Grant in his Virginia campaign, turned what must have been heretofore a romantic, pleasant affair into:

> "...a mutual butchery in which the strongest would live and the weakest die."

War is butchery. In the first three months of assuming command of the Army of Virginia, General Lee rolled up 50,000 Confederate casualties in constant offensive fighting. At Gettysburg, Lee rolled up 28,000 Confederate casualties in three days. The Civil War was butchery from beginning to end. In the Virginia campaign, Grant obtained something for the butchery: the destruction of Lee as an offensive force.

Mr. Trudeau is an excellent gatherer of selected facts, but, like some historians, he is unable to sort them out and come up with the significant conclusions.

After June

In the "Notes" of his book, Mr. Trudeau provides a table of casualties for the 46 day campaign. This table reports:

> Union Forces: May 5-June 5, 1864
> Grand Total— 54,259 casualties
> Confederate Forces: May 5-June 12, 1864
> Grand Total — 31,763 casualties.[4]

Many historians have concluded that because Grant lost more men than Lee, Grant lost the campaign. This conclusion is pitifully naive. Eisenhower lost more men than the Germans at Normandy, but he established his beachhead. Grant suffered heavy casualties in 1864 but, in 46 days he had trapped Lee.

In modern warfare (accurate rifles and cannon) the defense enjoys a 5-to-1 advantage over the offense. In World War II, the American marines had terrible casualties attacking the Japanese defenses on Iwo Jima and Okinawa. In the Civil War, Union soldiers had terrible casualties attacking Confederate defenses at Spotsylvania and Cold Harbor. In all instances the American casualties were high. Anytime Confederate troops attacked entrenched Union troops, the Confederates suffered heavily.

Sound military analysis requires that we look at campaigns as a whole and judge them by whether or not they achieved valid military objectives. Grant's Virginia campaign of 1864 reversed three years of Union defeat in the Eastern theater, destroyed much of the Army of Northern Virginia, drove Lee south 80 miles through the heart of Virginia and trapped Lee in a siege from which Lee was never able to maneuver. After June 1864, all of Lee's efforts were devoted to trying to maintain his supply lines. The battles Lee fought were reactive, defensive battles driving off a Union thrust on a railroad, a road, a bridge or a depot. Grant's army did not remain stationary in the 35 miles of trenches. Grant's army constantly attacked Lee in the north, in the south and in the center. As Lee wrote President Davis on December 14, 1864:

> "I do not know what may be General Grant's next move"[5]

---

4 Trudeau, Noah Andre, "Bloody Roads South," p. 341.
5 Jones, Rev. J. W., editor, "Life and Letters of Robert Edward Lee" Sprinkle Publications, 1978, p. 345.

After June

Lee did not achieve a single military objective. He did well to survive. Grant achieved every strategic military objective he had planned during his 46 day Virginia campaign.

To imply, as some historians do, that Robert E. Lee could be defeated without the extensive killing of men on both sides is to deny three years of Civil War history. <u>Robert E., Lee was a fighting general</u>. He lost more men in a single day than any other general (Antietam). He lost more men in a single battle than any other general (Gettysburg). Robert E. Lee fought hard, and, in fighting, killed a lot of Yankees and killed a lot of Confederates.

To imply that Robert E. Lee could be taken without large casualties is contrary to Lee's character and code of honor. Lee loved the state of Virginia. He was protecting his beloved country and its citizens. Lee fought hard at the Wilderness. Lee fought hard at Spotsylvania. The only reason he was unable to fight hard in Southern Virginia was that he had run out of manpower.

Robert E. Lee's determination to fight Grant with everything he had is borne out by the long months of siege. Almost surrounded, with no realistic hope of ultimate success, Lee fought on through a desperate winter as his men starved. In his final flight to Appomattox, it was clear that if Lee had escaped with his army to the mountains, he would have continued to fight.

Without hesitation, Lee withdrew west in April, 1865, so that he could fight again with an army that was starving.

To say that Lee, driven into siege, was a winner, is historical nonsense. When Lee reached the trenches of Petersburg he knew that he had lost the campaign and lost the war. The disaster that befell the Army of Virginia on June 18, 1864, when the Army of the Potomac succeeded in capturing its rear, is told most eloquently and accurately by **Robert E. Lee** himself in his letters to President Davis and the Confederate Secretary of War; Robert E. Lee understood his position better than any other man at the time with the exception of Ulysses S. Grant:

After June

Outline-Letters of General Robert E. Lee
Describing the Siege of Richmond/Petersburg
from June 1864 - April 1865,

1. June 19, 1864 — "My greatest apprehension at present is the maintenance of our communications south."

2. June 21, 1864 — "I hope your (Excellency) will put no reliance in what I can do individually for I feel that will be very little."

3. June 26, 1864 — "Lee is reluctant to "attack General Grant in his entrenchments" because of the fearful losses he would incur. Plan to seize Federal prison."

4. Sept. 2, 1864 — "Increase the strength of our armies. The enemy's position enables him to move his troops right or left."

5. Oct. 21, 1864 — "The amount of subsistence issued to the army is not sufficient."

6. Oct. 27, 1864 — "I had supposed that General Grant would make some movement simultaneously."

7. Dec. 5, 1864 — "Small contingent of troops available for Georgia. All we want to resist them is men."

8. Dec. 11, 1864 — "Retention of our present slave work force until Christmas......."

9. Dec. 14, 1864 — "Threats from all directions."

10. Jan. 11, 1865 — "We have but two days' supply."

11. Jan. 16, 1865 — "Informed of the break in our railroad connection. Appeal to the farmers for food."

12. Jan. 19, 1865 — "Troops suffering for want of soap."

13. Jan. 25, 1865 — "The need for civilians to surrender arms to the army."

14. Feb. 8, 1865 — "Troops suffering from reduced rations. The strength of the men....must fail."

15. Feb. 14, 1865 — "Pardon to deserters, to those who have abandoned their comrades in the hour of peril."

16. Feb. 19, 1865 — "I do not see how Sherman can make the march anticipated by General Beauregard"

After June

17. Feb. 21, 1865   "Destroy everything in the enemy's route."
18. Feb. 22, 1865   "The Valley force is under 1,800. (Grant) may anticipate my withdrawal."
19. Feb. 22, 1865   "Move to improve the discipline of your troops."
20. Feb. 24. 1865   "A state of despondency exists among the people."
21. March 9, 1865   "Arrest deserters."
22. March 17, 1865   "The cotton in Mobile will be burned. Supplies which Sheridan has destroyed...."
23. March 27, 1865   "Plans for organizing the colored troops."
24. April 1, 1865   "Gen. Pickett's battle at Five Forks."
25. April 2, 1865   "It is absolutely necessary that we abandon our position tonight...."

Letter # 1:

On June 19, 1864 as the siege began, General Lee told President Davis that...

"it would be impossible for the Confederate army to maintain uninterrupted railroad communication to the South."

As the months of siege went by this would prove fatal to the Confederacy.

HEADQTRS ARMY NO. VA.
NEAR PETERSBURG VA
June 19th 1864.

His Excellency JEFFERSON DAVIS
President Confed. States
MR. PRESIDENT

I have received your letter of the 18th. I was able to leave with General G. W. C. Lee only the forces which belong to Richmond. I placed at his disposal two battalions of artillery under Colonel Carter in addition to what he originally had, which I thought might be advantageously employed in connection with [M. M?] Gary's cavalry and such infantry support as General Lee could furnish, in operating on the James River against any parties that might be

After June

landed, or in embarrassing its navigation. I wished him to display as much force as possible, and to be active and vigilant in warding off any threatened blow. His force is not more than sufficient for this purpose, but if we can get early intelligence, and especially maintain the road from Petersburg to Richmond in running order, I think we shall be able to meet any attack the enemy may make upon the latter place. Night before last he apparently reduced the force on his lines in front of Bermuda Hundred, and from the reports received during the night, matters seemed to be so threatening in Petersburg, that I directed General Anderson to march at once with Kershaw's and Field's divisions, Pickett's division being left to guard our lines from Howlett's to Ashton Creek. I halted one division of Hill's on the north side of the Appomattox, in supporting distance of both places. General Beauregard had felt constrained to contract his lines on the east side of Petersburg before my arrival, and I found his troops in their new position. I am unable to judge of the comparative strength of the two lines, but as far as I can see, the only disadvantage is the proximity of the new line to the city. No attack has been made by the enemy since my arrival, though sharp skirmishing and cannonading has been kept up. <u>My greatest apprehension at present is the maintenance of our communications south. It will be difficult, and I fear impracticable to preserve it uninterrupted. The enemy's left now rests on the Jerusalem road, and I fear it would be impossible to arrest a sudden attack aimed at a distant point, in addition, the enemy's cavalry in spite of all our efforts, can burn the bridges over the Nottoway and its branches, the Meherrin & even the South side road is very much exposed, and our only dependence seems to me to be on the Danville.</u> Every effort should be made to secure to that road sufficient rolling stock by transferring that of other roads, and to accumulate supplies of all kinds in Richmond in anticipation of temporary interruptions. <u>When roads are broken every aid should be given to the companies to enable them to restore them immediately.</u> Duplicate timbers for all the bridges should be prepared in safe places to be used in an emergency, and every other arrangement made to keep the roads in running order.

Most respectfully and truly yours

R. E. LEE, Genl.[6]

---

6 Freeman, Douglas Southall, editor, "Lee's Dispatches," G. P. Putnam's Sons, 1957, p. 250.

After June

Letter #2:

On June 21, 1864 General Lee told President Davis that -

General Grant has the strongest position the Union army has had in the entire war.

General Grant can do Confederate forces great injury from that position.

There is very little that he, General Lee, could do about it.

Of some interest is Lee's analysis of General Pendleton's abilities. General Pendleton was a great admirer of Lee and eulogized Lee as "the perfect man"

PETERSBURG 21 June '64

Mr. PRESIDENT

I have recd your letter of the 20th Inst: enclosing one from the Pres: of the Petersburg & Richmond R.R. It is stated the road will be in operation this morg-Genl. Grant will concentrate all the troops here he can raise, from every section of the U. S. I saw it stated some days since in one of their papers. That A. T. Smith's corps, which had returned from the Red River, had embarked at Vicksburg in a number of transports & ascended the Missp-I have not heard of it since. Its destination may have been Memphis. I hope Early will be able to demolish Hunter, but I doubt whether Hampton will be able to injure Sheridan. His force is small in comparison with the enemy's & he seems to be looking to reinforcements more than to what he can accomplish himself. <u>I hope your Excy will put no reliance in what I can do individually, for I feel that will be very little. The enemy has a strong position, & is able to deal us more injury than from any other point he has ever taken. Still we must try & defeat them. I fear he will not attack us but advance by regular approaches. He is so situated that I cannot attack him.</u>* The battery at Howlett's will open today at 12 M-The Navy & G. W. C. Lee cooperating as far as they can-I very much regret to learn that my reply to your confidential note has not reached you- It was sent the night I recd it by the messenger (one of Genl. Bragg's I think) who brought your note.

164

After June

I stated that notwithstanding my esteem & admiration for Genl. Pendleton-his truthfulness, sincerity & devotion to the country, I had never thought of recommending him for the command of a corps in this army. You must not understand that I think him incapable for such a command, but I had never seen anything that caused me to select him, & therefore was unable to recommend him. I can spare him if you think he is the best available. I do not know the officers in Genl. J's army whom you enumerate. Genl. Stuart may be the best. Genl. Johnston had a high opinion of Genl. Ewell & I can bear testimony to his soldierly qualities. But I think his health & nervous system has been shaken by his great injury & though active & attentive that he cannot without breaking himself down undergo the arduous duties of a Corps Commdr. I can spare him if Genl. Johnson desires. I should think he would require a commander at once as I understand Genl. Loring is the Senior present

Praying that you may enjoy all health & happiness,

I remain most respy & truly
R. E. LEE
Genl.

His Excy JEFF DAVIS
Pres: C States.[7]

*This is the first reference in this correspondence to the probable outcome of the campaign,-the first time Lee admitted that he could not expect victory.[7]

Letter #3:

On June 26, 1864 General Lee told President Davis that -

he, General Lee, is apprehensive-about "our ability to procure supplies for the army." He, General Lee is reluctant to "attack General Grant in his entrenchments" because of the fearful losses he would incur.

---

[7] Freeman, Douglas Southall, editor, "Lee's Dispatches," G. P. Putnam's Sons, 1957, p. 253.

After June

It is interesting that Lee acknowledges the great advantage of fighting defensively from trenches, an advantage he enjoyed for most of the campaign.

From his entrenched position south and east of Petersburg, Grant can easily defend his army while at the same time launch attacks on the Southern railroads.

General Lee proposes a commando raid on a prison camp, Point Lockout, "to release Confederate prisoners who might then march around" Washington. Lee is desperate to find a way out of the trap he has fallen into. He lacks the manpower to break out.

HEADQUARTERS ARMY NORTHERN VIRGINIA
June 26, 1864.

HIS EXCELLENCY JEFFERSON DAVIS,
President Confederate States.

MR. PRESIDENT, I have the honor to acknowledge the receipt of your letter of the 25th instant. General Hunter has escaped Early, and will make good his retreat, as far as I can understand, to Lewisburg. Although his expedition has been partially interrupted, I fear he has not been much punished except by the demoralization of his troops and the loss of some artillery. From his present position he can easily be reorganized and re-equipped, and unless we have sufficient force to resist him, will repeat his expedition. This would necessitate the return of Early to Staunton. I think it better that he should move down the Valley if he can obtain provisions, which would draw Hunter after him, and may enable him to strike Lew Wallace before he can effect a junction with Hunter. If circumstances favor, I should also recommend his crossing the Potomac. <u>I think I can maintain our lines here against General Grant. He does not seem disposed to attack, and has thrown himself strictly on the defensive. I am less uneasy about holding our position than about our ability to procure supplies for the army. I fear the latter difficulty will oblige me to attack General Grant in his entrenchments, which I should not hesitate to do, but for the loss it will inevitably entail. A want of success would, in my opinion, be almost fatal and this causes me to hesitate, in the hope that some relief may be procured without running such great hazard.</u>

I should like much to have the benefit of your Excellency's good judgment and views upon this subject.

After June

    Great benefit might be drawn from the release of our prisoners at Point Lookout if it can be accomplished. The number of men employed for this purpose would necessarily be small, as the whole would have to be transported secretly across the Potomac where it is very broad, the means of doing which must first be procured. I can devote to this purpose the whole of the Marylanders of this army, which would afford a sufficient number of men of excellent material and much experience, but I am at a loss where to find a proper leader. As he would command Maryland troops and operate upon the Maryland soil, it would be well that he should be a Marylander. Of those connected with this army, I consider Col. Bradley Johnson the most suitable. He is bold and intelligent, ardent and true, and yet I am unable to say whether he possesses all the requisite qualities. Everything in an expedition of this kind would depend upon the leader. <u>I have understood that most of the garrison at Point Lookout is composed of Negroes. I should suppose that the commander of such troops would be poor and feeble. A stubborn resistance, therefore, may not reasonably be expected</u>. By taking a company of the Maryland artillery armed as infantry, the dismounted cavalry, and their infantry organization, as many men would be supplied as transportation could be procured for. By throwing them suddenly on the beach with some concert of action among the prisoners, I think the guard might be overpowered, the prisoners liberated and organized, and marched immediately on the route to Washington.

    The artillery company could operate the guns captured at the Point. The dismounted cavalry with the released prisoners of that arm could mount themselves on the march, and the infantry would form a respectable force. Such a body of men, under an able leader, though they might not be able without assistance to capture Washington, could march around it and cross the upper Potomac where fordable. I do not think they could cross the river in a body at any point below Washington, unless possibly at Alexandria. Provisions, etc., would have to be collected in the country through which they pass. The operations on the river must be confined to an able naval officer, who I know will be found in Colonel Wood. The subject is one worthy of consideration, and can only be matured by reflection.

After June

The sooner it is put in execution the better if it is deemed practicable. At this time, as far as I can learn, all the troops in the control of the United States are being sent to Grant, and little or no opposition could be made by those at Washington.

With relation to the project of Marshal Kane, if the matter can be kept secret, which I fear is impossible, should General Early cross the Potomac he might be sent to join him.

Very respectfully, your Excellency's obedient servant,

R. E. LEE,
General.[8]

General Lee's contempt for black soldiers could hardly be clearer.

Letter #4:

On September 2, 1864, two months later, General Lee told President Davis that -

--Grant is able to move troops freely and attack the long Confederate line at unexpected points of weakness.

--Reserve troops must be raised at once from the civilian population.

--"....the time has come when no man capable of bearing arms should be excluded... "

--This must be done "to prevent disaster..."

HEADQUARTERS ARMY OF NORTHERN VIRGINIA,
September 2, 1864.

HIS EXCELLENCY JEFFERSON DAVIS,
President Confederate States.

MR. PRESIDENT: I beg leave to call your attention to the importance of immediate and vigorous measures to increase the strength of our armies, and to some suggestions as to the mode of doing it. The necessity is now great, and will soon be augmented by the results of the coming draft in the United States. As matters now stand, we have no troops disposable to meet movements of the enemy or strike when opportunity presents,

---

8 Jones, Rev. J. W., editor, "Life and Letters of Robert Edward Lee," Sprinkle Publications, 1978, p. 333.

After June

without taking them from the trenches and exposing some important point. <u>The enemy's position enables him to move his troops to the right or left without our knowledge until he has reached the point at which he aims, and we are then compelled to hurry our men to meet him, incurring the risk of being too late to check his progress, and the additional risk of the advantage he may derive from their absence. This was fully illustrated in the late demonstration north of the James River, which called troops from their lines here who, if present, might have prevented the occupation of the Weldon Railroad.</u> These rapid and distant movements also fatigue and exhaust our men, greatly impairing their efficiency in battle. It is not necessary, however, to enumerate all the reasons for recruiting our ranks. The necessity is as well known to your Excellency as to myself, and as much the object of your solicitude.

The means of obtaining men for field duty, as far as I can see, are only three: A considerable number could be placed in the ranks by relieving all able-bodied white men employed as teamsters, cooks, mechanics, and laborers, and supplying their places with Negroes. I think measures should be taken at once to substitute Negroes for whites in every place in the army or connected with it where the former can be used. It seems to me that we must choose between employing Negroes ourselves and having them employed against us. <u>A thorough and vigorous inspection of the rolls of exempted and detailed men is in my opinion of immediate importance</u>. I think you will agree with me that no man should be excused from service for any reason not deemed sufficient to entitle one already in service to his discharge. I do not think that the decision of such questions can be made so well by any as by those whose experience with troops has made them acquainted with the urgent claims to relief which are constantly brought to the attention of commanding officers, but which they are forced to deny. For this reason I would recommend that the rolls of exempts and details in each State be inspected by officers of character and influence who have had nothing to do with exemptions and details. If all that I have heard be true, I think it will be found that very different rules of action have been pursued toward men in service and those liable to it in the matter of exemptions and details, and I respectfully

After June

recommend that your Excellency cause reports to be made by the enrolling bureau of the number of men enrolled in each State, the number sent to the field, and the number exempted or detailed. I regard this matter as of the utmost moment. <u>Our ranks are constantly diminishing by battle and disease, and few recruits are received.</u> <u>The consequences are inevitable</u>, and I feel confident that the time has come when no man capable of bearing arms should be excused unless it be for some controlling reason of public necessity. The safety of the country requires this, in my judgment, and hardship to individuals must be disregarded in view of the calamity that would follow to the whole people if our armies meet with disaster. No detail of an arms-bearing man should be continued or granted except for the performance of duty that is indispensable to the army, and that cannot be performed by one not liable to or fit for service. Agricultural details take numbers from the army without any corresponding advantage. I think that the interest of landowners and cultivators may be relied upon to induce them to provide means for saving their crops if they be sent to the field. If they remain at home, their produce will only benefit the enemy, as our armies will be insufficient to defend them. If the officers and men detailed in the conscript bureau have performed their duties faithfully, they must have already brought out the chief part of those liable to duty, and have nothing to do now except to get such as from time to time reach military age. If this be true, many of these officers and men can be spared to the army. If not, they have been derelict, and should be sent back to the ranks, and their places supplied by others who will be more active. Such a policy will stimulate the energy of this class of men. The last resource is the reserve force. Men of this class can render great service in connection with regular troops by taking their places in trenches, forts, etc., and leaving them free for active operations. I think no time should be lost in bringing out the entire strength of this class, particularly in Virginia and North Carolina. If I had the reserves of Virginia to hold the trenches here, or even to man those below Richmond on the north side of the river, they would render greater service than they can in any other way. They would give me force to act with on the offensive or defensive, as might be necessary, without weakening any part of our lines. Their mere

After June

presence in the works below Richmond would prevent the enemy from making feints in that quarter to draw troops from here, except in such force as to endanger his own lines around Petersburg. But I feel confident that with vigorous effort, and an understanding on the part of the people of the necessity of the case, we could get more of this class than enough for the purpose last indicated. We could make our regular troops here available in the field. The same remarks are applicable to the reserves of North Carolina, who could render similar services at Wilmington, and allow the regular troops to take the field against any force that might land there. <u>I need not remind your Excellency that the reserves are of great value in connection with our regular troops to prevent disaster, but would be of little avail to retrieve it. For this reason they should be put in service before the numerical superiority of the enemy enables him to inflict a damaging blow upon the regular forces opposed to him.</u> In my opinion the necessity for them will never be more urgent or their services of greater value than now. And I entertain the same views as to the importance of immediately bringing into the regular service every man liable to military duty. <u>It will be too late to do so after our armies meet with disaster, should such unfortunately be the case.</u>

I trust your Excellency will excuse the length and earnestness of this letter in view of the vital importance of its subject, and am confident that you will do all in your power to accomplish the objects I have in view.

With great respect, your obedient servant,

R. E. LEE,
General.[9]

General Lee is convinced that many men have been exempted from military service who should not have been.

<u>Letter #5</u>

On Oct. 21, 1864 General Lee told President Davis that,

"The amount of subsistence issued to the army in Virginia and North Carolina is not sufficient to enable us to retain what is required..."

---

9 Jones, Rev. J. W., editor, "Life and Letters of Robert Edward Lee," Sprinkle Publications, 1978, p. 338

After June

HEADQUARTERS ARMY OF NORTHERN VIRGINIA,
October 21, 1864.

HON. SEC. OF WAR Richmond.

SIR: I consider it very important to supply the garrisons in the forts below Wilmington with thirty days' provisions, in case the enemy should succeed in cutting them off from the city. I directed General Whiting to endeavor to obtain provisions for the purpose in North Carolina, but he has not succeeded in doing so, nor do I know that it is in his power. <u>The amount of subsistence issued to the army in Virginia and North Carolina is not sufficient to enable us to retain what is required for these garrisons for the time indicated. We now get bacon for the troops only once in four days, and the Commissary Department informed Colonel Cole, chief C.S. of the army, that we must rely on cattle.</u> As the collection of supplies is in the hands of the officers of the C. S. Department, Colonel Cole does not know what number of cattle or what amount of provisions he can count upon, so as to make any arrangements to provide for those garrisons from stores that may come into their hands. I think that it would be better that the C. S. Department should provide the desired supplies if practicable, and I respectfully ask that you will direct that it be done if it be in the power of that department to accomplish it.

Very respectfully, your obedient servant,

R. E. LEE,
General.[10]

<u>Letter #6</u>

On Oct. 27, 1864 General Lee told the Sec. of War of the Confederacy in Richmond that:

>--General Grant may attack Willmington, N.C. or Charleston, S.C. or some other point.

>--and that whoever is not attacked should send reinforcements to the point attacked.

---

10 Jones, Rev. J. W. editor, "Life and Letters of Robert Edward Lee, "Sprinkle Publications, 1978, p. 341.

After June

In other words, General Lee is only certain of one thing: Grant will attack.

> HEADQUARTERS ARMY OF NORTHERN VIRGINIA
> October 7, 1864.
>
> HON. SEC. OF WAR Richmond.
>
> SIR: I have the honor to acknowledge the receipt of the signal message sent me by your order yesterday. <u>I had supposed that General Grant would make some movement simultaneously with any attack on Wilmington to prevent reinforcements being sent from here,</u> and in that view I consider it important that in such an event General Hardee should reinforce General Bragg with all his available troops, or <u>on the other hand, should Charleston and not Wilmington be the real point of attack, a demonstration will be made against the others to detain the troops at either from the real point.</u> The officers in command must judge which is the true movement and act accordingly.
>
> I think it would be well that the policy which they are to pursue should be made the subject of an order from the Department directing the one not attacked to reinforce the one who is with all the troops he can spare.
>
> Very respectfully, your obedient servant,
>
> R. E. LEE,
> General.[11]

<u>Letter #7</u>

On Dec. 5, 1864 Lee told President Davis what Confederate troops had been sent to Georgia to oppose General Sherman's army of 60,000 seasoned troops which was cutting a path 50 miles wide through the heart of the state. Lee sent 400 cavalrymen (without horses). As Union forces are closing in on him Lee expected attack from any direction:

> HEADQUARTERS, TURNBULL'S, December 5, 1864.
> HIS EX. JEFFERSON DAVIS,
> President C. States, Richmond.
>
> MR. PRESIDENT: I have received the dispatch from General Bragg of the 4th inst., forwarded to me by Mr. B. N. Harrison,

---
11 Jones, Rev. J W., editor, "Life and Letters of Robert Edward Lee," Sprinkle Puboications, 1978, p. 343.

After June

stating that there is still time for him to receive any assistance that can be spared. On the 27th ult. General Whiting informed me that General Bragg had carried with him 2,700 of the best troops from Wilmington. Since that he has ordered to Charleston a regiment of the North Carolina reserves. and I do not think, so far as I can judge, that more troops can be taken with propriety unless we were certain that all danger of an attack was removed from that point. In addition, <u>I sent General Young with about 400 cavalrymen (without horses), and ordered all those previously sent to Georgia and South Carolina to report to him at Augusta;</u> which Hampton thinks will give him about 800 mounted men. which I thought would strengthen the cavalry very much in that department. General Baker has also gone to General Bragg, so that he will have another good cavalry commander.

I fear I can do nothing more under present circumstances. General Early reports that his scouts stated the Sixth Corps had broken camp on the 2d, and taken the cars at Stevenson's Depot- said to be going to City Point. From reports received from Longstreet and Ewell last night, I think this corps or a part of it may have reached the north side of James River last night. My last report from scouts on the James River was to the 2d. There had been great activity on the river in transportation of supplies, but no troops had passed in any numbers since the 17th ult. <u>Reports of Early and Longstreet have not yet been corroborated but the whole preparations of the enemy indicate some movement against us. All we want to resist them is men.</u>

With great respect, your obedient servant.

R. E. LEE,
General.[12]

Letter #8

On Dec. 11, 1864 General Lee told Confederate Sec of War Seddon that the 2,200 slaves sent to him for digging fortifications fell short of the 5,000 promised and that he would be unable to accomplish all that he wished:

---

[12] Jones, Rev. J.W., editor, "Life and Letters of Robert Edward Lee," Sprinkle Publications, 1978, p. 344.

After June

HEADQUARTERS ARMY OF NORTHERN VIRGINIA.
December 11, 1864.

HON. JAMES A. SEDDON,
Secretary of War, Richmond.

SIR: I have been informed by General Stevens that you have consented to the retention of our present negro force until Christmas. This will prove to be some relief, but not sufficient for our wants. My original request was for 5,000 laborers: 2,200 is the greatest number which ever reported, and those in small bodies at different intervals. The period for which they were first called was thirty days, and subsequently extended to sixty days. <u>A large number of them have deserted, many not serving the first thirty days. Since the expiration of this period the desertions have greatly increased.</u> I cannot state the present strength of the force, but think it cannot exceed 1,200. I consequently have not been able to accomplish half I desired. <u>In our present extended line, requiring the troops to be always on duty and prepared for any movements of the enemy, I cannot use them, as formerly, for any work requiring them to leave their trenches.</u> This is the reason why a laboring force is necessary, and unless I can get it for the completion of interior lines of defense, construction of roads, and other work necessary to the existence of an army, I shall be unable to hold my position. Of the negroes called for under the act of February 17, 1864, I have not yet received enough to replace the white teamsters in the army. In fact, we have not received more than sufficient to supply teamsters for the Third Corps and a portion of one division. Not one has yet been received for laboring purposes, and to any inquiries on the subject I get no satisfactory reply. I beg, therefore, to call your attention to this matter, which I deem of the greatest importance. and request that prompt measures may be taken to supply this demand.

I am, with great respect, your obedient servant,

R. E. LEE.
General[13]

In his 35 miles of trenches Lee was everywhere weak and nowhere strong.

---

13 Jones, Rev. J. W., editor, "Life and Letters of Robert Edward Lee," Sprinkle Publications, 1978, p. 345.

After June

<u>Letter #9</u>

On Dec. 14, 1864 General Lee told President Davis that--

he did not know "what may be Grant's next move." Savannah may fall. There is a tone of urgency in Lee's letter, He is beset with more problems than he has either the time or the resources with which to deal. The world is crumbling around him. General Early's small army in the Shenandoah Valley was crushed at the Battle of Cedar Creek on Oct. 19, 1864 and by this time largely existed only on paper:

Near Petersburg, *DECEMBER 14, 1864.*

MR. PRESIDENT:
After sending my dispatch to you yesterday, knowing that the snow in the Valley was six inches deep and the weather very cold, and presuming that active operations would necessarily be suspended, I directed Rodes's division to march for Staunton and requested the quartermaster-general to send cars to convey it to Richmond. It is now on the road, and should reach Staunton tomorrow evening. If the quartermaster's department is active, it should arrive in Richmond Friday morning. A dispatch received from General Early last night stated that the scouts just in report that the Nineteenth Corps of the enemy had left the Valley, and that the Eighth was under marching orders. The latter might be preparing to move nearer the Baltimore and Ohio Railroad, for I do not think they will strip it of all defense, or both corps may be coming to General Grant. Colonel Wither's scouts report that a New York regiment of infantry and part of the Seventh Regiment of cavalry had left the Kanawha for the valley; but I suppose they might have been intended to replace the garrison at New Creek. <u>I do not know what may be General Grant's next move; his last against the Weldon Railroad and our right flank failed.</u> The expeditions from Plymouth and New Berne against Fort Branch on the Roanoke, and Kinston. N. C., have both retreated, before the forces moved against them, back to their former positions. Everything at this time is quiet in the departments of Virginia and North Carolina. If the reports of the prisoners and the statements of Federal officers to the citizens of the country

After June

are true, the object of the last expedition was to make a permanent lodgment at Weldon, draw supplies by the Roanoke and Seaboard Railroad and thence operate against the railroad in North Carolina. <u>General Grant may not now be prepared to break through our center, as the canal at Dutch Gap is reported nearly completed.</u> As long as he holds so large an army around Richmond, I think it very hazardous to diminish our force. <u>We now can oppose about a division to one of his corps. I fear Savannah is in great danger, and unless our operations there are bold and energetic I am apprehensive of its fall.</u> I hope, though, if all our troops are united Sherman may be repulsed. But there is no time to lose. If the Nineteenth Corps does not come to Grant we might spare a division; but if the Nineteenth and Eighth are both drawn to him, we shall require more than we have. I ordered Gen. J. A. Walker with the Virginia reserves from Weldon to Kinston to oppose the movement against that place. He is now on his return to his position on the Danville and Southside Roads.

With a firm reliance on our merciful God that He will cause all things to work together for our good, I remain, with great respect,

Your obedient servant.
R. E. LEE,
General.[14]

Lee's statement, "We now can oppose a division to one of his corps," tells everything about the condition of his army.

<u>Letter #10</u>

Letter #10 speaks for itself. After six months of siege Confederate forces in the Petersberg/Richmond enclave have exhausted their resources. Their efforts to retain control of the railroads south have proven to be fruitless. The Danville is all that is left:

---

[14] Jones, Rev. J. W., editor, "Life and Letters of Robert Edward Lee," Sprinkle Publications, 1978, p. 345.

After June

(Telegram from Headquarters A. N. Va.)
HEADQUARTERS ARMY OF NORTHERN VIRGINIA,
January 11, 1865

HON. J. A. SEDDON:
There is nothing within reach of this army to be impressed. The country is swept clear; our only reliance is upon the railroads. We have but two days' supplies.

R. E. LEE.[15]
General

Letter #11:

On Jan. 12, 1865 General Lee appealed to the farmers of the area for food. A temporary break in the last railroad gave grave evidence of what was to come:

HEADQUARTERS ARMY OF NORTHERN VIRGINIA,
January 16, 1865.

HON. SEC. OF WAR, RICHMOND,
SIR: I have the honor to acknowledge the receipt of your letter of the 12th inst., with its enclosures. I thank you for your prompt, energetic measures for the relief of the army. As soon as I was informed of the break in our railroad connections I issued the enclosed appeal to the farmers and others in the country accessible by our remaining communications, and sent Major Tannahill to them to obtain all the supplies that could be procured. I am glad to say that, as far as I know, the crisis in relation to this matter is now past.

Very respectfully, your obedient servant,

R. E. LEE,
General.

(Endorsement)
Noted with pleasure. It was the most effectual mode of obtaining supplies-more effective, I doubt not, than coercive action of the Department.

J.A S.

---

[15] Jones, Rev. J. W., editor, "Life and Letters of Robert Edward Lee," Sprinkle Publications, 1978, p. 348.

After June

(Enclosure)

HEADQUARTERS ARMY OF NORTHERN VIRGINIA,
January 12, 1865.

TO THE FARMERS EAST OF THE BLUE RIDGE AND SOUTH OF JAMES RIVER:

The recent heavy freshet having destroyed a portion of the railroad from Danville to Goldsboro, and thereby cut off temporarily necessary supplies for the Army of Northern Virginia, an appeal is respectfully made to the farmers, millers, and other citizens to furnish with all possible promptness whatever breadstuffs, meats (fresh or salt), and molasses they can spare. Such citizens as Major Robert Tannahill may select are asked to act as agents in purchasing and collecting supplies through the various officers connected with the commissary department on the lines of railroad.

Arrangements have been made to pay promptly for all supplies delivered under this appeal, or to return the same in kind as soon as practicable.

R. E. LEE.[16]

Letter #12

The condition of the Confederate army is pitiful. The troops are held together by a personal loyalty to Lee, not by any hope of victory.

HEADQUARTERS ARMY OF NORTHERN VIRGINIA,
January 19, 1865.

HON. SEC. OF WAR, RICHMOND.

SIR: <u>There is great suffering in the army for want of soap. The neglect of personal cleanliness has occasioned cutaneous diseases to a great extent in many commands.</u> The Commissary Department has been applied to, but the supply received from it is entirely inadequate. Soap is an article of home manufacture in every family almost. The materials for making it are found in every household, and the art is familiar to all well-trained domestics. I cannot but think that by proper efforts a plan might

---

[16] Jones, Rev. J. W., editor, "Life and Letters of Robert Edward Lee," Sprinkle Publications, 1978, p. 349.

be devised to meet this want of our soldiers. All that is necessary, I think, is to employ or contract with some intelligent and practical business men in the different States to insure a supply. I do not suppose that agents or officers of the C. S. Department can succeed as well as private individuals, if it be made to the interest of the latter to procure what we need. I beg that you will endeavor to make arrangement by which the suffering of the men in this particular can be relieved.

Very respectfully, your obedient servant,

R. E. LEE,
General.[17]

Letter #13

On January 25, 1855 General Lee appealed to private citizens to turn over their arms to the Confederate army.

On January 15, 1865 Fort Fischer fell and with it the blockade running port of Wilmington. Supplies from Europe were now completely cut off and the Confederates were totally dependent on the resources they had in hand.

(Circular)

HEADQUARTERS ARMY OF NORTHERN VIRGINIA,
January 25, 1865

To arm and equip an additional force of cavalry there is need of carbines, revolvers, pistols, saddles, and other accouterments of mounted men. Arms and equipments of the kind desired are believed to be held by citizens in sufficient numbers to supply our wants. Many keep them as trophies, and some with the expectation of using them in their own defense. But it should be remembered that arms are now required for use, and that they cannot be made so effectual for the defense of the country in any way as in the hands of organized troops. They are needed to enable our cavalry to cope with the well-armed and equipped cavalry of the enemy, not only in the general service, but in

---

[17] Jones, Rev. J. W., editor, "Life and Letters of Robert Edward Lee," Sprinkle Publications, 1978, p. 349.

After June

resisting those predatory expeditions which have inflicted so much loss upon the people of the interior. To the patriotic I need make no other appeal than the wants of the service; but I beg to remind those who are reluctant to part with the arms and equipments in their possession that by keeping them they diminish the ability of the army to defend their property, without themselves receiving any benefit from them <u>I therefore urge all persons not in the service to deliver promptly to some of the officers designated below such arms and equipments (especially those suitable for cavalry) as they may have, and to report to those officers the names of such persons as neglect to surrender those in their possession.</u> Every citizen who prevents a carbine or pistol from remaining unused will render a service to his country. Those who think to retain arms for their own defense should remember that if the army cannot protect them, the arms will be of little use.

While no valid title can be acquired to public arms and equipments except from the Government, it is reported that many persons have ignorantly purchased them from private parties. A fair compensation will, therefore, be made to all who deliver such arms and equipments to any ordinance officers, officer commanding at a post, officers and agents of the Quartermaster and Commissary Departments at any station, or officers in the enrolling service or connected with the nitre and mining bureau. All these officers are requested, and those connected with this army are directed, to receive and receipt for all arms and equipments, whatever their condition, and forward the same, with a duplicate receipt, to the Ordinance Department at Richmond, and report their proceedings to these headquarters. The persons holding the receipt will be compensated upon presenting it to the ordnance bureau.

<u>While it is hoped that no one will disregard this appeal, all officers connected wuth the Army are required, and all others are requested, to take possession of any public arms and equipments they may find in the hands of persons unwilling to surrender them to the service of the country</u> and to give receipts therefor. A reasonable allowance for their expenses and trouble will be made to such patriotic citizens as will collect and deliver to any of the officers above designated such arms and equipments

After June

as they may find in the hands of persons not in the service, or who will report the same to those officers. A prompt compliance with this call will greatly promote the efficiency and strength of the Army, particularly of the cavalry, and render it better able to protect the homes and property of the people from outrage.

R. E. LEE.
General.[18]

Apparently Lee's need for additional arms is desperate.

<u>Letter #14</u>

On Feb. 8, 1865 General Lee told Confederate Sec. of War Seddon and President Davis of the condition of his soldiers. This is one of the most heart rending eloquent letters of the Civil War. There is now no hope whatever of a Confederate victory. Yet Confederate leaders stubbornly fought on completing the destruction of the South, adding to the death, desolation and misery of the Southern people.

(Telegram)

HEADQUARTERS ARMY OF NORTHERN VIRGINIA,
February 8, 1865.

HON. JAS. A. SEDDON,
Sec. of War, Richmond, Va.

SIR: All the disposable force of the right wing of the army has been operating against the enemy beyond Hatcher's Run since Sunday. Yesterday, the most inclement day of the winter, they had to be retained in line of battle, having been in the same condition the two previous days and nights. I regret to be obliged to state that under these circumstances, heightened by assaults and fire of the enemy, some of the men had been without meat for three days, and all were suffering from reduced rations and scant clothing, exposed to battle, cold, hail, and sleet. I have directed Colonel Cole, chief commissary, who reports that he has not a pound of meat at his disposal, to visit Richmond and

---

[18] James, Rev J. W., editor, "Life and Letters of Robert Edward Lee," Sprinkle Publications, 1978, p. 350.

After June

see if nothing can be done. If some change is not made and the Commissary Department reorganized, I apprehend dire results. The physical strength of the men, if their courage survives, must fail under this treatment. <u>Our cavalry has to be dispersed for want of forage. Fitz Lee's and Lomax's divisions are scattered because supplies cannot be transported where their services are required. I had to bring Wm. H. F. Lee's division forty miles Sunday night to get him in position.</u> Taking these facts in connection wish the paucity of our members you must not be surprised if calamity befalls us. According to reports of prisoners, we were opposed on Hatcher's Run by the Second and Fifth Corps, part of the Ninth, one division of the Sixth, Gregg's division (Third Brigade of cavalry). It was also reported that the Twenty-third Corps (Schofield's) reached City Point on the 5th, and that it was present. But this is not confirmed by other reports. At last accounts it was stated to be on the Potomac, delayed by ice. A scout near Alexandria reports it is to march on Gordonsville, General Baker on Kinston. I think it more probable it will join Grant here.

With great respect, your obedient servant,

R. E. LEE,
General.

Respectfully sent to the President for perusal. Please return it.
JOHN C. BRECKINRIDGE,
Secretary of War.

(Endorsement)

This is too sad to be patiently considered, and cannot have occurred without criminal neglect or gross incapacity. Let supplies be had by purchase or borrowing or other possible mode. J.D.[19]*

This comment by Jefferson Davis was added to Lee's letter and forwarded to the Confederate Secretary of War.

One wonders what is in the minds of Southern leaders.

---

19 Jones, Rev. J. W., editor, "Life and Letters of Robert Edward Lee," Sprinkle Publications, 1978, p. 352.

After June

<u>Letter #15</u>

On Feb. 14 1865 General Lee attempted to deal with the growing problem of desertion by appealing to the soldiers absent without leave. Desertion was now on a wholesale basis with entire companies of troops leaving during the night. As usual, the common soldier was more intelligent than his government or his military leaders. If he stayed, all he had to look forward to was death. A steady stream of Confederate soldiers entered Union lines with the promise of food and a full pardon. Congress enacted a law that restored citizenship to Confederate soldiers who came to the Union lines, surrendered and took the oath of allegiance to the United States. The effect of this law was devastating to Confederate armies. Desertion became rampant:

HEADQUARTERS ARMIES OF THE CONFEDERATE STATES,
14th February, 1865

General Orders, No. 2.

In entering upon the campaign about to open the General-in-chief feels assured that the soldiers who have so long and so nobly borne the hardships and dangers of the war require no exhortation to respond to the calls of honor and duty.

With the liberty transmitted by their forefathers they have inherited the spirit to defend it.

The choice between war and abject submission is before them. To such a proposal brave men with arms in their hands can have but one answer. They cannot barter manhood for peace nor the right of self-government for life or property.

But justice to them requires a sterner admonition to those who have abandoned their comrades in the hour of peril.

A last opportunity is afforded them to wipe out the disgrace and escape the punishment of their crimes.

By authority of the President of the Confederate States a pardon is announced to such deserters and men improperly absent as shall return to the commands to which they belong within the shortest possible time, not exceeding twenty days from the publication of this order, at the headquarters of the department in which they may be.

After June

Those who may be prevented by interruption of communication may report within the time specified to the nearest enrolling officer or other officer on duty, to be forwarded as soon as practicable, and upon presenting a certificate from such officer showing compliance with the requirement will receive the pardon hereby offered.

Those who have deserted to the service of the enemy, or who have deserted after having been once pardoned for the same offense, and those who shall desert or absent themselves without authority after the publication of this order, are excluded from its benefits, Nor does the order of pardon extend to other offenses than desertion and absence without permission.

<u>By the same authority it is also declared that no general amnesty will again be granted, and those who refuse to accept the pardon now offered, or who shall hereafter desert or absent themselves without leave, shall suffer such punishment as the courts may impose, and no application for clemency will be entertained.</u>

Taking new resolution from the fate which our enemies intend for us, let every man devote all his energies to the common defense.

<u>Our resources, wisely and vigorously employed, are ample, and with a brave army, sustained by a determined and united people, success with God's assistance cannot be doubtful.</u>

The advantage of the enemy will have but little value if we do not permit them to impair our resolution. Let us then oppose constancy to adversity, fortitude to suffering, and courage to danger, with the firm assurance that He who gave freedom to our fathers will bless the efforts of their children to preserve it.

R. E. LEE,
General.[20]

Letter #16

On Feb. 19, 1865 General Lee describes to the new Confederate Secretary of War Breckinridge the encirclement of the Confederacy by Union forces that is taking place. Of particular interest is General Lee's statement:

"I fear it may be necessary to abandon all our cities, and preparation should be made for this contingency."

---

20 Jones, Rev. J. W., editor, "Life and Letters of Robert Edward Lee," Sprinkle Publications, 1978, p. 353.

After June

Apparently General Lee intends to just go on fighting, on and on:

> HEADQUARTERS, PETERSBURG, *February 19, 1865.*
> HIS EXCELLENCY J. C. BRECKINRIDGE,
> Secretary of War, Richmond, Va.
>
> SIR: The accounts received today from South and North Carolina are unfavorable. General Beauregard reports from Winnsborough that four corps of the enemy are advancing on that place, tearing up the Charlotte Railroad, and they will probably reach Charlotte by the 24th and before he can concentrate his troops there. He states that General Sherman will doubtless move thence on Greensboro, Danville, and Petersburg, or unite with General Schofield at Raleigh or Weldon.
>
> General Bragg reports that General Schofield is now preparing to advance from New Berne to Goldsboro, and that a strong expedition is moving against Weldon Railroad at Rocky Mount. <u>He says that little or no assistance can be received from the State of North Carolina-that exemptions and reorganizations under late laws have disbanded the State forces, and that they will not be ready for the field for some time.</u>
>
> I do not see how Sherman can make the march anticipated by General Beauregard, but he seems to have everything his own way, which is calculated to cause apprehension. General Beauregard does not say what he proposes or what he can do. I do not know where his troops are or on what lines they are moving. His dispatches only give movements of the enemy. He has a difficult task to perform under present circumstances, and one of his best officers, General Hardee, is incapacitated by sickness. I have also heard that his own health is indifferent, though he has never so stated. Should his strength give way, there is no one on duty in the department that could replace him, nor have I any one to send there. Gen. J. E. Johnston is the only officer whom I know who has the confidence of the army and people, and if he was ordered to report to me I would place him there on duty. It is necessary to bring out all our strength, and I fear, to unite our armies, as separately they do not seem able to make head against the enemy. <u>Everything should be destroyed that cannot be removed out of the reach of General Sherman and Schofield.</u> Provisions must be accumulated in Virginia, and every

After June

man in all the States must be brought off. <u>I fear it may be necessary to abandon all our cities, and preparation should be made for this contingency.</u>

I have the honor to be, your obedient servant,

R. E. LEE,
General[21]

<u>Letter #17</u>

On Feb. 21, 1865 Lee informed Secretary of War Breckinridge of the possibility of escaping from Petersburg to the west in order to continue fighting:

(Confidential)

HEADQUARTERS, PETERSBURG, February 21, 1865.
HON. J. C. BRECKINRIDGE,
Sec. of War, Richmond.

SIR: I have had the honor to receive your letter of yesterday's date. <u>I have repeated the orders to the commanding officers to remove and destroy everything in enemy's route</u>. In the event of the necessity of abandoning our position on the James River, I shall endeavor to unite the troops of the army about Burkeville (junction of Southside and Danville Railroad), so as to retain communication with the North and South as long as practicable, and also with the West.

I should think Lynchburg or some point west of the most advantageous place to which to remove stores from Richmond. This, however, is a most difficult point at this time to decide, and the place may have to be changed by circumstances.

It was my intention in my former letter to apply for Gen. J. E. Johnston, that I might assign him to duty should circumstances permit. I have had no official report of the condition of General Beauregard's health. It is stated from many sources to be bad; if he should break entirely down, it might be fatal. In that event I should have no one with whom to supply his place. I therefore

---

21 Jones, Rev. J. W. editor, "Life and Letters of Robert Edward Lee," Sprinkle Publications, 1978, p. 354.

After June

respectfully request that General Johnston may be ordered to report to me, and that I may be informed where he is.

With great respect, your obedient servant,

R. E. LEE,
General[22]

Letter #18

In his letter of Feb. 22, 1865 to Confederate Secretary of War Breckinridge, Lee is in a fantasy world:

"Everything of value should be removed from Richmond."

Removed to where? The Confederacy is gone. The pressing need is <u>to stop the killing</u>:

HEADQUARTERS, PETERSBURG, *February 22, 1865.*
HON. J. C. BRECKINRIDGE,
Sec. of War, Richmond, Va.

SIR: I have just received your letter of the 21st. I concur fully as to the necessity of defeating Sherman. I hope that General Beauregard will get his troops in hand at least before he can cross the Roanoke. If any additions can be given him, it cannot be south of that stream. <u>The troops in the Valley are scattered for subsistence, nor can they be concentrated for the want of it. The infantry force is very small. At the commencement of winter think it was reported under 1,800.</u> That in western Virginia you know more about than I do, and there are only two regiments in western North Carolina. These united would be of some assistance. At the rate that Beauregard supposes Sherman will march, they could not be collected at Greensboro in time, still, I hope to make some use of them. But you may expect Sheridan to move up the Valley and Stoneman from Knoxville as Sherman draws near Roanoke. What, then, will become of those sections of country? I know of no other troops that could be given to Beauregard. Bragg will be forced back by Schofield, I fear, and <u>until I abandon James River nothing can be sent from this army.</u>

---

22 Jones, Rev. J. W., editor, 'Life and Letters of Robert Edward Lee," Sprinkle Publications, 1978, p. 355.

After June

Grant, I think, is now preparing to draw out by his left with the intent of enveloping me. He may wait till his other columns approach nearer, or he may be preparing to anticipate my withdrawal. I cannot tell yet. I am endeavoring to collect supplies convenient to Burkeville. <u>Everything of value should be removed from Richmond. It is of the first importance to save all powder.</u> The cavalry and artillery of the army are still scattered for want of provender, and our supply and ammunition trains, which ought to be with the army in case of a sudden movement, are absent collecting provisions and forage, some in western Virginia and some in North Carolina. You will see to what straits we are reduced. But I trust to work out.

With great respect, your obedient servant,

R. E. LEE,
General.[23]

<u>Letter #19</u>

In the General Order dated Feb. 22, 1865, Lee's comment that <u>there will be more opportunity for promotion:</u>

"The recent law abolishing the system of elections and opening the way to promotion to all who distinguish themselves by the faithful discharge of duty affords a new incentive to officers and men."

(Circular)

HEADQUARTERS ARMIES OF THE CONFEDERATE STATES,

22d February, 1865.

GENERAL:

The spirit which animates our soldiers and the natural courage with which they are so liberally endowed have led to a reliance upon these good qualities to the neglect of those measures which would increase their efficiency and contribute to their safety. Many opportunities have been lost and hundreds of valuable lives uselessly sacrificed for want of a strict observance of discipline.

---

23 Jones, Rev. J. W., editor, "Life and Letters of Robert Edward Lee," Sprinkle Publications, 1978, p. 356.

After June

Its object is to enable an army to bring promptly into action the largest possible number of its men, in good order and under the control of their officers. Its effects are visible in all military history, which records the triumphs of discipline and courage far more frequently than those of numbers and resources.

At no time in the war has the necessity of close attention to this important subject been greater than at present, and at no time has its cultivation promised more valuable results. The proportion of experienced troops is larger in our army than in that of the enemy, while his numbers exceed our own. These are the circumstances most favorable for the display of the advantages of discipline, and in which the power it imparts will be most clearly perceived.

I desire therefore that you will direct every effort to improve the discipline of your troops. This will not only require your own unremitting attention, but also the zealous cooperation of your officers, commissioned and noncommissioned.

<u>The recent law abolishing the system of elections and opening the way to promotion to all who distinguish themselves by the faithful discharge of duty affords a new incentive to officers and men.</u> In addition to the usual and stated instructions, which must be given at all times as fully as circumstances will permit, the importance and utility of thorough discipline should be impressed on officers and men on all occasions by illustrations taken from the experience of the instructor or from other sources of information. They should be made to understand that discipline contributes no less to their safety than to their efficiency. Disastrous surprises and those sudden panics which lead to defeat and the greatest loss of life are of rare occurrence among disciplined troops. It is well known that the greatest number of casualties occur when men become scattered, and especially when they retreat in confusion, as the fire of the enemy is then more deliberate and fatal. The experience of every officer shows that those troops suffer least who attack most vigorously and that a few men retaining their organization and acting in concert accomplish far more with smaller loss than a larger number scattered and disorganized.

The appearance of a steady, unbroken line is more formidable to the enemy, and renders his aim less accurate and his fire less

After June

effective. Orders can be readily transmitted, advantage can be promptly taken of every opportunity, and, all efforts being directed to a common end, the contest will be briefer and success more certain.

Let officers and men be made to feel that they will most effectually secure their safety by remaining steadily at their posts, preserving order, and fighting with coolness and vigor.

Fully impressed with the truth of these views, I call your attention particularly to the accompanying order with reference to the duties of file-closers, which you will immediately carry into execution.

<u>Impress upon your officers that discipline cannot be attained without constant watchfulness on their part. They must attend to the smallest particulars of detail. Men must be habituated to obey or they cannot be controlled in battle, and the neglect of the least important order impairs the proper influence of the officer.</u>

In recommending officers or men for promotion you will always, where other qualifications are equal, give preference to those who show the highest appreciation of the importance of discipline and evince the greatest attention to its requirements.

Very respectfully, your obedient servant,

R. E. LEE[24]

<u>Letter #20</u>

In his letter to Gov. Vance on Feb. 24, 1865 General Lee concedes that a "state of despondency" exists in the South and that desertion is a growing problem. Lee asks Gov. Vance to enlist "influential citizens" to talk to people and tell them that

> "the cause is not hopeless, that the situation of affairs, though critical, is so to the enemy as well as ourselves..."

General Lee seems to be determined to go on fighting:

---

24 Jones, Rev. J. W., editor, "Life and Letters of Robert Edward Lee," Sprinkle Publications, 1978, p. 357.

After June

HEADQUARTERS CONFEDERATE STATES ARMIES.
February 24, 1865.

HIS EXCELLENCY Z. B. VANCE,
Governor of North Carolina, Raleigh.

GOVERNOR: <u>The state of despondency that now prevails among our people is producing a bad effect on the troops. Desertions are becoming very frequent and there is good reason to believe that they are occasioned to a considerable extent by letters written to the soldiers by their friends at home.</u> In the last two weeks several hundred have deserted from Hill's corps, and as the divisions from which the greatest number of desertions have taken place are composed chiefly of troops from North Carolina, they furnish a corresponding proportion of deserters. I think some good can be accomplished by the efforts of influential citizens to change public sentiment and cheer the spirits of the people. It has been discovered that despondent persons represent to their friends in the army that our cause is hopeless, and that they had better provide for themselves. They state that the number of deserters is so large in the several counties that there is no danger to be apprehended from the Home-guards. <u>The deserters generally take their arms with them.</u> The greater number are from regiments from the western part of the State. <u>So far as the despondency of the people occasions this sad conditions of affairs, I know of no other means of removing it then by the counsel and exhortation of prominent citizens. If they would explain to the people that the cause is not hopeless, that the situation of affairs, though critical, is so to the enemy as well as ourselves,</u> that he has drawn his troops from every other quarter to accomplish his designs against Richmond, and that his defeat now would result in leaving nearly our whole territory open to us; that this great result can be accomplished if all will work diligently, and that his successes are far less valuable in fact than in appearance, I think our sorely-tried people would be induced to make one more effort to bear their sufferings a little longer, and regain some of the spirit that marked the first two years of the war. If they will, I feel confident that with the blessing of God what seems to be our greatest danger will prove the means of deliverance and safety.

After June

Trusting that you will do all in your power to help us in this great emergency,

I remain, very respectfully, your obedient servant,

R. E. LEE.
General.[25]

Letter #21

In his letter of March 9, 1865 to Gov. Vance of North Carolina, Lee is very clear that there should be no mercy to deserters:

HEADQUARTERS CONFEDERATE STATES ARMIES,
March 9, 1865.

HIS EXCELLENCY Z.B. VANCE,
Governor of North Carolina, Raleigh,

GOVERNOR; I received your letter of the 2d inst. and return to you my sincere thanks for your zealous efforts in behalf of the Army and the cause. I have read with pleasure and attention your proclamation and appeal to the people, as also extracts from your address. I trust you will infuse into your fellow citizens the spirit of resolution and patriotism which inspires your own action. I have now no cavalry to spare for the purpose you mention, and regret that I did not receive the suggestion at an earlier period. I think it a very good one and would have been glad to adopt it. I have sent a force of infantry under Brigadier-General Johnston (R. D.) to guard the line of the Roanoke and operate as far as practicable in the adjacent counties to arrest deserters. Another detachment of 500 men under Colonel McAllister has been sent to Chatham and Moore counties, in which the bands of deserters were represented to be very numerous. They will, however, operate in other quarters as occasion may require. <u>They are instructed to take no prisoner among those deserters who resist with arms the civil or military authorities.</u> I hope you will raise as large a force of local troops to cooperate with them as you can, and think that the sternest course is the best with the class I have referred to. <u>The immunity which these lawless organizations afford is a great cause of desertion, and they cannot be too sternly</u>

---

25 Jones, Rev. J. W., editor, "Life and Letters of Robert Edward Lee," Sprinkle Publications, 1978, p. 359.

dealt with. I hope you will be able to aid General Johnston, who needs all the reinforcements you can give him. If he can check the progress of General Sherman, the effect would be of the greatest value. I hope the late success of General Bragg near Kinston will revive the spirits of the people and render your labors less arduous. The conduct of the widow lady whom you mention deserves the highest commendation. If all our people possessed her spirit, our success I should feel to be assured.

Very respectfully, your obedient servant,

R. E. LEE,
General.[26]

Letter #22

In his letter of March 17, 1865, to Confederate Secretary of War Breckinridge, Lee is admitting that General Sheridan's destruction of farms in the Shenandoah Valley had real military significance to the Confederate war effort:

HEADQUARTERS, PETERSBURG, VIRGINIA,
March 17, 1865.

HON. JOHN C. BRECKINRIDGE,
Sec. of War, Richmond, Va.

SIR: A dispatch from Lieutenant-General Taylor at Meridian on the 12th inst. states that he had returned that morning from West Point; that Thomas was reported to be moving with the Fourth Army Corps and about 12,000 cavalry; that General Maury reports enemy, some 30,000 strong, moving with fleet and by land from Pensacola on Mobile; that about 30,000 bales of cotton in Mobile will be burned as soon as the city is invested: that he has provided for these movements as fully as his resources permitted, but that he had received no aid from Mississippi or Alabama, yet hoped to embarrass the enemy in his efforts to take those States. If the estimate of the enemy's strength is correct, I see little prospect of preserving Mobile, and had previously informed him that he could not rely upon the return of the Army of Tennessee to relieve that city, and suggested the

---

26 Jones, Rev. J. W., editor, "Life and Letters of Robert Edward Lee," Sprinkle Publications, 1978, p. 360.

After June

propriety of withdrawing from it, and endeavor to beat the enemy in the field. I hope this course will meet with the approbation of the Department.

General Johnston on the 16th. from Smithfield, reports the Federal army south of the Cape Fear, but near Fayetteville. He had ordered 1,000 wagons of the Tennessee army to be used in filling gaps in railroads and 100 wagons to collect supplies in South Carolina for this army. I hope this will furnish some relief.

General Echols at Wytheville, on the 10th, reports that a portion of the troops in East Tennessee had removed south of Knoxville, destination not known, and that the engineer corps which had commenced to repair the Tennessee Railroad from Knoxville east had been withdrawn and sent to Chattanooga for the purpose, it was thought, of repairing the road toward Atlanta. He also states that an intelligent scout just from Kentucky reports Burbridge's force had been taken to Nashville, and that considerable bodies of troops were passing up the Ohio on their way to Grant. He believed all these reports may be relied on.

The enemy seems still to be collecting a force in the Shenandoah Valley, which indicates another movement as soon as the weather will permit. Rosser's scouts report that there is some cavalry and infantry now at Winchester, and that Hancock has a portion of his corps at Hall Town. I think these troops are intended to supply the place of those under General Sheridan, which it is plain General Grant has brought to his army. The addition of these three mounted divisions will give such strength to his cavalry, already numerically superior to ours, that it will enable him, I fear, to keep our communications to Richmond broken. <u>Had we been able to use the supplies which Sheridan has destroyed in his late expedition in maintaining our troops in the Valley in a body, if his march could not have been arrested it would at least have been rendered comparatively harmless, and we should have been spared the mortification that has attended it.</u> Now, I do not see how we can sustain even our small force of cavalry around Richmond. I have had this morning to send Gen. William H. F. Lee's division back to Stony Creek, whence I had called it in the last few days, because I cannot provide it with

---

27 Jones, Rev. J. W., editor, "Life and Letters of Robert Edward Lee," Sprinkle Publications, 1978, p. 360.

After June

forage. I regret to have to report these difficulties, but think you ought to be apprised of them, in order if there is any remedy it should be applied.

I have the honor to be, your obedient servant,

R. E. LEE,
General.[27]

Letter #23

In his letter of March 27, 1865 General Lee attests to the extreme desperation of the Confederate cause. By enlisting black troops in the Confederate army the Confederate government is undermining its own basic beliefs—if black men make good soldiers then the whole theory of slavery falls apart:

HEADQUARTERS CONFEDERATE STATES ARMIES,
March 27, 1865.

HON. SEC. OF WAR, Richmond.

SIR: I have been awaiting the receipt of the order from the Department for raising and organizing the colored troops before taking any action in the matter. I understand that orders have been published in the newspapers, but have not seen them. In the mean time, I have been informed that a number of recruits may be obtained in Petersburg if suitable persons be employed to get them to enlist.....

Very respectfully, your obedient servant,

R.E. Lee
General.[28]

Letter #24

In his letter of April 1, 1865 to Sec. of War Breckinridge, General Lee describes the Battle of Five Forks which sealed the doom of the Army of Northern Virginia. All of the Confederates and Union soldiers were needlessly sacrificed by Confederate leaders too willful and stubborn to make peace:

---

28 Jones, Rev. J. W. editor, "Life and Letters of Robert Edward Lee," Sprinkle Publications, 1978, p. 362.

After June

HEADQUARTERS ARMY OF NORTHERN VIRGINIA.
April 1, 1865.

HON SEC. OF WAR, Richmond.

SIR: After my dispatch of last night I received a report from General Pickett, who with three of his own brigades and two of General Johnston's supported the cavalry under Gen. Fitz Lee near Five Forks on the Road from Dinwiddie Court House to the Southside road. After considerable difficulty, and meeting resistance from the enemy at all points, General Pickett forced his way to within less than a mile of Dinwiddie Court House. By this time it was too dark for further operations, and General Pickett resolved to return to Five Forks to protect his communications with the railroad. He inflicted considerable damage upon the enemy, and took some prisoners. <u>His own loss was severe, including a good many officers.</u> General Terry had his horse killed by a shell, and was disabled himself. Gen. Fitz Lee's and Rosser's divisions were heavily engaged, but their loss was slight. <u>Gen. W. H. F. Lee lost some valuable officers.</u> General Pickett did not retire from the vicinity of Dinwiddie Court House until early this morning, when his left flank being threatened by a heavy force, he withdrew to Five Forks where he took position with Gen. W. H. F. Lee on his right, Fitz Lee and Rosser on his left, with Robert's brigade on the White Oak road, connecting with General Anderson.

The enemy attacked General Roberts with a large force of cavalry, and after being once repulsed drove him back across Hatcher's Run.

A large force of infantry, believed to be the Fifteenth Corps with other troops, turned General Pickett's left, and drove him back on the White Oak road, separating him from Gen. Fitz Lee, who was compelled to fall back across Hatcher's Run. General Pickett's present position is not known. Gen. Fitz Lee reports that the enemy is massing his infantry heavily behind the cavalry in his front. The infantry that engaged General Anderson yesterday has moved from his front toward our right, and is supposed to participate in the operations above described. Prisoners have been taken today from the Twenty-fourth Corps, and it is believed that most of the corps is now south of the James. Our loss today is not known. A report from Staunton represents

After June

that the Eighth Corps passed over the Baltimore and Ohio Railroad from the 20th to the 25th ult. General Hancock is at Harper's Ferry with 2,000 men. One division of the Tenth Corps is at Winchester with about 1,000 cavalry. The infantry at Winchester have marching orders, and all these troops are said to be destined for General Grant's army.

The enemy is also reported to have withdrawn all his troops from Wolf Run Shoals and Fairfax Station, and to have concentrated them at Winchester.

Very respectfully, your obedient servant,

R. E. Lee
General.[29]

Letter #25

In his letter of April 2, 1865 to Confederate Secretary of War Breckinridge, Lee announces his intention to continue fighting:

PETERSBURG, *April 2, 1865.*

GEN. J.C. BRECKINRIDGE, Sec. of War.

SIR: <u>It is absolutely necessary that we should abandon our position tonight or run the risk of being cut off in the morning.</u> I have given all the orders to officers on both sides of the river, and have taken every precaution that I can to make the movement successful. It will be a difficult operation, but I hope not impracticable. Please give all orders that you find necessary in and about Richmond. The troops will all be directed to Amelia Court House.

R. E. LEE.[30]

Lee would needlessly kill a few thousand more men. What is Lee "being cut off" from? He is a man living in a dream. Lee's world— the Confederacy— no longer exists.

End

---

29 Jones, Rev. J. W., editor, 'Life and Letters of Robert Edward Lee," Sprinkle Publications, 1978, p. 362.
30 Jones, Rev. J. W., editor, Life and Letters of Robert Edward Lee," Sprinkle Publications, 1978, p. 363.

Appendix A
GRANT'S PLAN/LINCOLN'S PLAN

General Halleck's Correspondence

To understand Union military correspondence in the Civil War it is essential to know the status of the various officials, especially General Halleck. His name appears on numerous letters and directives. Although General Halleck appeared to be a man of importance and signed a lot of orders, he was in reality only President Lincoln's military secretary. By his own admission, in his Feb. 16, 1864 letter, all of General Halleck's communications must be considered as having been cleared and approved by Lincoln. President Lincoln, the consummate politician, preferred to let Halleck do a lot of the "dirty work", and all of the routine administration. Halleck understood his position well and did not question it. In a letter to his good friend, General Sherman, Halleck explains his position within the Lincoln administration:

HEADQUARTERS OF THE ARMY,
Washington, *February 16, 1864.*

Maj. Gen. W. T. SHERMAN,
Vicksburg, Miss.:

MY DEAR GENERAL: Yours of January 29, dated on board the Juliet, is received and I thank you for the kind allusions to me in your Memphis speech. I saw some notice of it in the newspapers, but not so full as in your letter. You have probably seen the attempt in the newspapers to create difficulties and jealousies between me and General Grant. This is all for political

Appendix A: Grant's Plan/Lincoln's Plan

effect. There is not the slightest ground for any such assertions. There cannot and will not be any differences between us. If he is made lieutenant-general, as I presume he will be, I shall most cordially welcome him to the command, glad to be relieved from so thankless and disagreeable a position. I took it against my will, and shall be most happy to leave it as soon as another is designated to fill it. The great difficulty in the office of General-in-Chief is, that it is not understood by the country. The responsibility and odium thrown upon it does not belong to it. <u>I am simply a military adviser of the Secretary of War and the President, and must obey and carry out what they decide upon, whether I concur in their decisions or not.</u> As a good soldier I obey the orders of my superiors. If I disagree with them in opinion I say so, but when they decide it is my duty faithfully to carry out their decision. Moreover, I cannot say to the public I approve this and I disapprove that. I have no right to say this, as it might embarrass the execution of a measure fully decided on. <u>My mouth is closed except when officially called on to give such opinion.</u> It is my duty to strengthen the hands of the President as Commander-in-Chief, not to weaken them by factious opposition. I have, therefore, cordially cooperated with him in every plan decided upon, although I have never hesitated to differ in opinion. I must leave it to history to vindicate or condemn my own opinions and plans. They will be found at some future time on record. What we now have to do is to put down this rebellion. We have not time to quibble and contend for the pride of personal opinion. On this subject there seems to be a better feeling among the officers in the West than here. There is less jealousy and backbiting, and a greater disposition to assist each other. Here we have too much party politics and wire-pulling. Everybody wants you to turn a grindstone to grind his particular ax, and if you decline he regards you as an enemy and takes revenge by newspaper abuse.

The rebels will give us much trouble in the spring, and I fear we will not be fully prepared for them. The country does not seem to fully appreciate the vast importance of military operations for the next six months. In my opinion, they will be the most important of the war.

Appendix A: Grant's Plan/Lincoln's Plan

Give my kind regards to McPherson and Hurlbut if they are with you. Yours, truly,

H. W. HALLECK.[1]

Halleck's position had at one time been one of considerable importance. In 1862, after a series of victories in the Western theater by Grant, General Pope and others, President Lincoln had brought Halleck East in the belief that Halleck, as Western theater commander, had been responsible for the victories of his subordinates. President Lincoln had made General Halleck General in Chief, and expected that he would take overall charge of military affairs.

But after the disastrous Peninsula campaign, and the debacle of Second Manassas, Halleck lost his nerve and refused to make any military decisions. President Lincoln again had to assume the burden of running the war.[2] President Lincoln kept Halleck in the capacity of "military advisor," and used him in an administrative capacity to issue orders and to communicate with generals.

With a clear understanding that all of Halleck's official letters were reviewed and approved by President Lincoln, the correspondence becomes a great deal more interesting. Lincoln is speaking through Halleck. Lincoln is telling his generals what they can and cannot do. It is Lincoln who is establishing policy and approving military actions. Lincoln as Commander in Chief was in full control of the Northern war effort and allocated the country's war resources to those generals who proved that they could apply them effectively. Lincoln made and broke generals, and through control of war resources, decided which campaigns would be pushed forward. Grant quickly grasped the power structure in Washington and his ability to work with Lincoln was a major factor in the eventual Union victory.

Grant's Plan

The Virginia campaign began January 19, 1864 with a letter to Washington from General Grant:

---

1 Official Records, Vol. 32, Series 1. Part 11. Ser. No. 58, p. 407.
2 Tyler Dennett, editor, "Lincoln and the Civil War in the Diaries and Letters of John Hay" p. 176.

Appendix A: Grant's Plan/Lincoln's Plan

[CONFIDENTIAL]

HDQRS MIL. DIV.
OF THE MISSISSIPPI,
Nashville, Tenn., *January 19, 1864.*

Maj. Gen. H. W. HALLECK,
General-in-Chief-of the, Army, Washington, D. C.:

<u>GENERAL: I would respectfully suggest whether an abandonment of all previously attempted lines to Richmond is not advisable, and in lieu of these one be taken farther south. I would suggest Raleigh, N. C. as the objective point and Suffolk as the starting point. Raleigh once secured, I would make New Berne the base of supplies until Wilmington is secured.</u>

<u>A moving force of 60,000 men would probably be required to start</u> on such an expedition. This force would not have to be increased unless Lee should withdraw from his present position. In that case the necessity for so large a force on the Potomac would not exist. <u>A force moving from Suffolk would destroy first all the roads about Weldon, or even as far north as Hicksford. From Weldon to Raleigh they would scarcely meet with serious opposition.</u> Once there, the most interior line of railway still left to the enemy, in fact the only one they would then have, would be so threatened as to force him to use a large portion of his army in guarding it. <u>This would virtually force an evacuation of Virginia and indirectly of East Tennessee. It would throw our armies into new fields, where they could partially live upon the country and would reduce the stores of the enemy.</u> It would cause thousands of the North Carolina troops to desert and return to their homes, it would give us possession of many negroes who are now indirectly aiding the rebellion. It would draw the enemy from campaigns of their own choosing, and for which they are prepared, to new lines of operations never expected to become necessary. <u>It would effectually blockade Wilmington, the port now of more value to the enemy than all the balance of their seacoast. It would enable operations to commence at once by removing the war to a more southern climate, instead of months of inactivity in winter quarters.</u> Other advantages might be cited which would be likely to grow out of this plan, but these are enough. From your better opportunities of studying the country and the armies that would be involved in this plan, you will be better able to judge of the

Appendix A: Grant's Plan/Lincoln's Plan

practicability of it than I possibly can. I have written this in accordance with what I understand to be an invitation from you to express my views about military operations, and not to insist that any plan of mine should be carried out. Whatever course is agreed upon, I shall always believe is at least intended for the best, and until fully tested will hope to have it prove so.

I am, general, very respectfully, your obedient servant,

U. S. GRANT,
Major-General.[3]

Note: Map on p. xvi shows location of Grant's proposed attack.

General Grant's letter of January 19, 1864 has never received the attention it deserves. Historians have avoided it because this letter of Grant's is totally inconsistent with the conventional thought of most Civil War historians. This is one of the important letters of the Civil War lying buried and unappreciated in the Official Records. It is clear, concise and brilliant.

The January 19th, 1864 letter reveals Grant's military genius; he understood what the North needed to do to win the war. The January 19th letter explains how the Civil War was eventually won by the Union. Once Grant got south of Lee, he destroyed his railroads. Lee was finished. The lack of attention to this letter is one of the major oversights by previous Civil War historians.

The January 19th letter is all Grant. At first glance the letter is deceptively simple. But what Grant is saying is rather complex. In essence, Grant is making a commentary on the conduct of the war in the Eastern theater for the last three years. Even more, Grant is explaining how this new creation of science and industry--Modern War--really works. Grant is saying:

> Modern armies are not destroyed in the field.
> Modern armies are too large and complex.
> Modern armies, when defeated, retreat into siege positions.
> Modern armies must be driven to capitulate by destroying the logistical base of the society that supports them.

Grant had not learned this at West Point. It was a concept Grant had discovered as a very astute observer of the Civil War.

---
3 Official Records, Vol. XXXIII, Series 1, Ser. No. 60, p. 395.

Appendix A: Grant's Plan/Lincoln's Plan

General Robert E. Lee had won a series of victories over the Army of the Potomac but he never destroyed that army in the field. After each defeat, the Army of the Potomac, retreated, rebuilt, and came back to fight.

In the Civil War, only one general destroyed armies. General Grant destroyed three armies by capturing them in their entirety:

> Ft. Donelson - 12,000 prisoners
> Vicksburg - 30,000 prisoners
> Appomattox - 25,000 prisoners

By analyzing his experience, Grant developed the science of modern warfare. Subsequent wars fought by the United States have followed Grant's pattern. Armies are confronted in the field by American armed forces, but enormous attention is given to destroying the logistical base of the society that supports them. In World War II, rather than attacking every island in the South Pacific, the Americans island-hopped to Okinawa and Iwo Jima from which heavy bombers could reach Japan. Lessons from the Civil War have had a profound effect.

Grant shared the contents of his January 19th letter with his two principal associates in the Western theater, General Sherman and General Thomas. These were men Grant respected greatly. They were collaborators. Grant had sought their counsel on many occasions regarding strategy. Sherman approved the North Carolina invasion heartily.

In his letter to Grant, Sherman is discussing his forthcoming raid from Vicksburg, Miss. eastward to destroy a Confederate base at Meridian, Alabama:

HEADQUARTERS DEPARTMENT OF THE TENNESSEE,
Steamboat Silver Cloud. *January 19, 1864.*

Maj. Gen. U. S. GRANT,
Via Nashville:

DEAR GENERAL: I am now on my return to Memphis, which we shall reach tomorrow, the 20th, and if I find all things as I expect shall start all hands by the 25th. The river is now clear of ice thus far up and we hope to find none this side of Memphis, but the water is from 19 to 20 feet lower than it was at same period last year and therefore to ascend Red River will be impossible. But the other trip will do most for our department and your army: therefore I do not regret it. The guerrillas seem to let the boats pass unmolested, and so long as they do we can

Appendix A: Grant's Plan/Lincoln's Plan

afford to encourage the people to reoccupy their lands and resume their industrial pursuits. I found General McPherson in fine health: his troops in like condition, only 4 percent, on the sick report. He has 21,000 effective men, so that he can take with him 10,000 and leave Vicksburg and Natchez, the only points in his district fitted with stationary artillery, safe against any probable danger. As near as I can ascertain, General Polk's command at Meridian, with Loring at Canton; his division has not over 8,000. Conscripts at Brandon and Enterprise, Forrest has North Mississippi, and not over 2,500 irregular cavalry, Cosby's and Whitfield's brigades are still watching on their old ground from Yazoo City via Brownsville, Canton, Jackson, Brandon, and Port Gibson, a thin line of guard to prevent intercourse with Vicksburg. Logan's old command, now commanded by Wirt Adams, is down behind Port Hudson and Baton Rouge, doubtless to prevent the people from becoming too familiar with the Yankees. I have one of my best Memphis private spies out, who will be back in time to let me know all we want. I observe you were right in your calculation that Longstreet would be re-enforced in East Tennessee and make a struggle for that mountain region. <u>Halleck should compel a movement in North Carolina on Weldon and Raleigh, if possible, which would, in connection with active demonstrations against the Alabama border, force the enemy to call back the re-enforcements or to allow these valuable districts to be overrun by us.</u> If we could draw all of Lee's army into East Tennessee they would be bound to go ahead or fall back. The mountains on either flank will restrict their line to the railroad, and the army which is on the defensive has the advantage. I will write to Logan and Dodge to hurry the railroad and try and be there in all [sic] February. The fortifications of Vicksburg are nearly done, the redoubt at Mrs. Lane's house being the only one incomplete. McPherson tells me those of Natchez are equally advanced.

I am, with great respect,

W. T. SHERMAN,
Major-General.[4]

Boat trembles, and my writing is more illegible than ever.

---

4 Official Records, Vol. XXXII, Series 1, Part 11, Ser. No. 58, p. 146.

Appendix A: Grant's Plan/Lincoln's Plan

General Thomas went even further in approving Grant's plan, adding suggestions as to the route of the invading army so that it could take advantage of certain rivers in North Carolina.

HEADQUARTERS DEPARTMENT
OF THE CUMBERLAND,
Chattanooga, Tenn., *January 30, 1864.*

Maj. Gen. U. S. GRANT.
Comdg. Mil. Division of the Mississippi, Nashville, Tenn.:

GENERAL: As I have seen you since the receipt of your letter of the 29th instant, I deem it of but little consequence to make any reply to that portion referring to the movements of this army and the Army of the Tennessee this spring, as I fully concur with you in the view you take of the best moves for them to make.

In reply to the latter portion of your letter,* I would suggest the landing of the column at Smithfield and vicinity, marching from that point to Sussex Court-House, thence to Hicksford, on the Petersburg and Roanoke Railroad, and thence to Raleigh. By this route the column would experience but little difficulty in crossing the Notoway, Meherrin, and Roanoke Rivers, and would also find large plantations well supplied with forage and cattle. The roads are also good and well watered. By the lower route or the one you propose the column would encounter great difficulties in crossing all three of the above-named streams, because they are bordered by extensive and boggy swamps. I will also suggest another route, which perhaps might be better for a smaller force than either of the other two (say 20,000 infantry and 10,000 cavalry). I would land at Winton, on Chowan River, march thence to Northampton Court-House, and thence to Weldon. This is the shortest practicable route, and only presents one difficulty-that of crossing Roanoke River. There is still another route. Land at Washington, march thence to Raleigh, and from Raleigh to Weldon. The Roanoke is one of the finest streams in the country to cover the movements of an army.

I am, general, very respectfully, your obedient servant,

GEO. H. THOMAS,
Major-General, U S. Volunteers, Commanding. [5]

*Invasion of North Carolina

---

[5] Official Records, Vol. XXX11, Series 1, Part 11, Ser. No. 58, p. 264.

Appendix A: Grant's Plan/Lincoln's Plan

General Thomas, a Virginian, was familiar with the territory.

Grant's letter of January 19, 1864 requires further analysis.

First of all Grant calls for the "abandonment of all previously attempted lines to Richmond." This is an enormous statement. Grant is saying that three years of warfare in the Eastern theater at enormous cost, has been a waste of time and resources. All previous commanders of the Army of the Potomac and Lincoln have been wrong. Grant, obviously, was not seeking favors from the Lincoln administration.

Secondly, Grant proposes "a moving force of sixty thousand men" to be transported by sea to New Bern, North Carolina. Of all Civil War generals, Grant was the most familiar with amphibious operations. Grant liked them. You could move men quickly and easily deep into the enemy's rear if you had control of rivers, or in this case, the ocean. Not only was the sea a good way to move large bodies of troops long distances in a way that the enemy could not oppose, but the sea was also an excellent supply line, safe from Confederate cavalry.

Thirdly, Grant suggests Raleigh North Carolina as the objective point and Suffolk as the starting point. "Raleigh once secured I would make New Bern the base of supplies until Wilmington is secured." Grant is proposing the attack be made where the enemy is absent. The forces to oppose this move in North Carolina were so small that they would not even delay operations. Grant recognized Raleigh as a strategic rail center and the railroads running North to Richmond as the jugular vein of the Confederacy. Without these railroads and the supplies they carried from the South, Richmond could not be held by the Confederates. General Grant had correctly identified the most sensitive spot in the Eastern theater, the key position the Confederates had to hold to survive and a position that was free for the taking by a bold commander because it was virtually unguarded.

The Army of Northern Virginia was concentrated along the Rapidan in winter quarters, prepared to counter any move by General Meade and the Army of the Potomac at Culpepper. There is no way the Confederate army could move quickly enough over one hundred miles to block Grant's move into North Carolina before Grant reached Raleigh. The Union striking force would be well into the enemy's rear before the Confederate army could react.

Appendix A: Grant's Plan/Lincoln's Plan

The proposal by Grant to move into North Carolina was in no way similar to General McClellan's Peninsula Campaign. General McClellan landed his army on a narrow peninsula opposite Richmond. Slowly, with much deliberation McClellan advanced on Richmond, to attack or to lay siege to the town. He was allowed to get as far as he did by cautious General Joe Johnston. McClellan confined his enormous army to a very narrow area, the Peninsula. McClellan would have been easily stopped and bottled up by a vigorous, aggressive General Robert E. Lee. McClellan did not conceive of the idea of attacking south of Richmond and seizing the railroads feeding the city. McClellan's siege would have been endless. With McClellan's lack of will to engage the enemy, it is hard to see how the Union army could have been successful

By contrast, Grant's plan for the invasion of North Carolina was to cut the vital railroads feeding the Richmond/Petersburg enclave. Without these railroads, General Lee could not remain in Virginia. The soundness of Grant's strategy is attested to by General Robert E. Lee himself:

> HEADQUARTERS, *April 12, 1864,*
>
> MR. PRESIDENT: My anxiety on the subject of provisions for the army is so great that I cannot refrain from expressing it to Your Excellency. I cannot see how we can operate with our present supplies. <u>Any derangement in their arrival or disaster to the railroad would render it impossible for me to keep the army together, and might force a retreat into North Carolina.</u> There is nothing to be had in this section for man or animals. We have rations for the troops today and tomorrow. I hope a new supply arrived last night, but I have not yet had a report. Every exertion should be made to supply the depots at Richmond and at other points. All pleasure travel should cease, and everything be devoted to necessary wants.
>
> I am, with great respect, your obedient servant.
>
> R. E. LEE,
> General.[6]

Driven into siege in Petersburg in June 1864, General Lee fought desperately to keep control of the railroads running South. Once the last Southern railroad was lost at the Battle of Five Forks, Lee immediately

---
6 Official Records, Vol. XXX111, Series 1, Ser. No. 60, p. 1275.

Appendix A: Grant's Plan/Lincoln's Plan

evacuated the Richmond/Petersburg complex and was ultimately forced into surrender. History proved that Grant was completely right.

It is necessary to point out one of the things that Grant did not say in his January 19th letter. There was no mention of an assault on Richmond.

Lincoln's Plan

Beneath Lincoln's jokes, kindness, and patience, was a very hard man. Lincoln knew well the price of victory. The armies of the South had to be destroyed. To destroy these armies, thousands of men would have to be killed. There would be enormous bloodshed and suffering.

The North would have to pay a price in thousands of its finest young men. Lincoln had sent for Grant because he believed Grant was strong enough to do the bloody job that had to be done.

President Lincoln did not want an amphibious invasion of North Carolina. The Peninsula Campaign of 1862 had been a bitter defeat. Lincoln wanted the Army of the Potomac concentrated in one powerful force that would attack Lee's army and destroy or cripple it. Once Lee's army was broken, the Civil War would be won.

Abraham Lincoln defined the role of Commander in Chief for all time. He took an unarmed, civilian society and turned it into the greatest military power in the world. Lincoln evaluated his generals and gave the country's precious resources to the men who demonstrated the competence to use them. Charles Dana, Assistant Secretary of War, recalled Lincoln's mastery of the art of war:

> Another interesting fact about Abraham Lincoln is that he developed into a great military man; that is to say, a man of supreme military judgment. I do not risk anything in saying that if one will study the records of the war and study the writings relating to it, he will agree with me that the greatest general we had, greater than Grant or Thomas, was Abraham Lincoln. It was not so at the beginning; but after three or four years of constant practice in the science and art of war, he arrived at this extraordinary knowledge of it, so that Von Moltke was not a better general or an abler planner of or expounder of a campaign, than was President Lincoln. To sum it up, he was a born leader of men. He knew human nature; he knew what chord to strike, and was never afraid to strike it when he believed that the time had arrived.[7]

---

7 Charles A. Dana, Asst. Sec. of War 1863 to 1865, article "Reminiscences of Men and Events of the Civil War," Missouri Historical Society, St. Louis.

Appendix A: Grant's Plan/Lincoln's Plan

Out of confusion and defeat, Lincoln brought order and strength. Out of hopelessness and despair, Lincoln brought overwhelming, dazzling victory. At no point in the war did Lincoln release his control over military affairs. President Lincoln would continue to make the major military decisions.

General Halleck's Letter of February 17, 1864

General Halleck's letter to Grant dated Feb. 17, 1864 is again one of the important and neglected letters of the Civil War. It is a clear statement of the military policy of the Lincoln administration in 1864. It clearly enunciates Lincoln's primary military objective: destroy Lee's army.

The proposal by Grant for an amphibious invasion of North Carolina in Grant's January 19, 1864 letter was in direct conflict with President Lincoln. Lincoln decided to let Halleck disabuse Grant of the North Carolina project:

(CONFIDENTIAL)   WASHINGTON, D.C.
February 17, 1864.

Major-General GRANT,
Nashville, Tenn.,

GENERAL: Your letter of the 12th* instant is just received. I fully concur with you in regard to the present condition of affairs in East Tennessee. It certainly is very much to be regretted that the fatal mistake of General Burnside has permitted Longstreet's army to winter in Tennessee. It is due to yourself that a full report of this matter should be placed on file, so that responsibility may rest where it properly belongs.

The condition of affairs in East Tennessee and the uncertainty of General Banks' operations in Texas and Louisiana have caused me to delay answering your former communication in regard to the operations of the campaign. <u>In one of these you suggest whether it might not be well not to attempt anything more against Richmond and to send a column of 60,000 men into North Carolina. In the first place, I have never considered Richmond as the necessary objective Point of the Army of the Potomac: that point is Lee's army.</u> I have never supposed Richmond could

---

* The correct date is Jan. 19, 1864, for the letter of Grant's which Halleck is answering.

Appendix A: Grant's Plan/Lincoln's Plan

be taken till Lee's army was defeated or driven away. It was one of Napoleon's maxims that an army covering a capital must be destroyed before attempting to capture or occupy that capital. <u>And now, how can we best defeat Lee's army-by attacking it between here and Richmond, on our shortest line of supplies, and in such a position that we can combine our whole force,</u> or by a longer line and with a force diminished by the troops required to cover Washington and Maryland?

Such movement through North Carolina alluded to by you, and also one from Port Royal on Savannah and into Georgia, have been several times suggested here, and pretty fully discussed by military men. It is conceded by those suggesting these expeditions that neither of them can be safely undertaken with a less force than that estimated by you, via, 60,000 effective men. Some require a still larger force.

If we admit the advantage of either of these plans, the question immediately arises, <u>where can we get the requisite number of troops?</u>

There is evidently a general public misconception of the strength of our army in Virginia and about Washington. Perhaps it is good policy to encourage this public error. The entire effective force in the fortifications about Washington and employed in guarding the public buildings and stores, the aqueduct, and railroads does not exceed 18,000 men. We have a few thousand more in the convalescent and distribution camps, and in the cavalry and artillery depots, but these are mostly fragments of organizations, temporarily here for equipments and distribution, and could contribute very little to the defense of the place. This force is, therefore, less than one-half of what General McClellan and several hoards of officers recommended as the permanent garrison. Considering the political importance of Washington, and the immense amount of military stores here, it would be exceedingly hazardous to reduce it still further.

<u>The effective force of the Army of the Potomac is only about 70,000.</u> General Meade retreated before Lee with a very much larger force, and he does not now deem himself strong enough to attack Lee's present army.

Suppose we were to send 30,000 men from that army to North Carolina, would not Lee be able to make another invasion of

Appendix A: Grant's Plan/Lincoln's Plan

(Halleck's Letter of February 17, 1864)

    Maryland and Pennsylvania? But it may be said that by operating in North Carolina we would compel Lee to move his army there. I do not think so. Uncover Washington and the Potomac River, and all the forces which Lee can collect will be moved north, and the popular sentiment will compel the Government to bring back the army in North Carolina to defend Washington, Baltimore, Harrisburg, and Philadelphia. I think Lee would tomorrow exchange Richmond, Raleigh, and Wilmington for the possession of either of the aforementioned cities.

    But suppose it were practicable to send 30,000 men from Meade's army to North Carolina, where shall we get the other 30,000? We have there now barely enough to hold the points which it is necessary to occupy in order to prevent contraband trade. Very few of those would be available for the field. Maryland is almost entirely stripped of troops, and the forces in Western Virginia are barely sufficient to protect that part of the country from rebel raids. The only other resource is South Carolina.

    Generals Foster and Gillmore were both of opinion at the commencement of operations against Charleston that neither that place nor Savannah could be taken by a land force of less than 60,000 men. Large land and naval forces have been employed there for nearly a year without any important results. I had no faith in the plan at first, and for months past have ineffectually urged that 10,000 or 15,000 men from Gillmore's command be sent against Texas or Mobile. And now these troops are sent upon another expedition which, in my opinion, can produce no military result.

    I always have been and still am, opposed to all these isolated expeditions on the sea and Gulf coast. It is true they greatly assist the Navy in maintaining the blockade and prevent contraband trade, but I think the troops so employed would do more good if concentrated on some important line of military operations. We have given too much attention to cutting the toe nails of our enemy instead of grasping his throat.

    <u>You will perceive from the facts stated above that there are serious, if not insurmountable, obstacles in the way of the proposed North Carolina expedition.</u> Nevertheless, as it has much to recommend it, I shall submit it with your remarks to the consideration of the President and Secretary of War as soon as

Appendix A: Grant's Plan/Lincoln's Plan

(Halleck's Letter of February 17, 1864)

troops enough return from furlough to attempt any important movement in this part of the theater of war.

Lee's army is by far the best in the rebel service, and I regard him as their ablest general. But little progress can be made here till that army is broken or defeated. There have been several good opportunities to do this, via, at Antietam, at Chancerllorsville, and at Williamsport, in the retreat from Gettysburg. I am also of opinion that General Meade could have succeeded recently at Mine Run had he persevered in his attack.

<u>The overthrow of Lee's army being the object of operations here, the question arises, how can we best attain it? If we fight that army with our communications open to Washington, so as to cover this place and Maryland, we can concentrate upon it nearly all your forces on this frontier, but if we operate by North Carolina or the Peninsula, we must act with a divided army and on exterior lines, while Lee, with a short interior line, can concentrate his entire force on either fragment.</u>

And yet, if we had troops enough to secure our position here, and at the same time to operate with advantage on Raleigh or Richmond, I would not hesitate to do so, at least for a winter or spring campaign. <u>But our numbers are not sufficient, in my opinion, to attempt this, at least for the present.</u> Troops sent south of James River cannot be brought back in time to oppose Lee, should he attempt a movement north, which I am satisfied would be his best policy.

Our main efforts in the next campaign should unquestionably be made against the armies of Lee and Johnston, but by what particular lines we shall operate cannot be positively determined until the affairs of East Tennessee are settled, and we can know more nearly what force can be given to the Army of the Potomac. In the meantime, it will be well to compare views and opinions. <u>The final decision of this question will probably depend, under the President, upon yourself.</u>*

It may be said that if General McClellan failed to take Richmond by the Peninsula route, so also have Generals Burnside, Hooker, and Meade failed to accomplish that object by the shorter and more direct route. This is all very true, but no argument can be deduced from this bare fact in favor of either

*final authority

Appendix A: Grant's Plan/Lincoln's Plan

(Halleck's Letter of February 17, 1864)

plan of operations. General McClellan had so large an army in the spring of 1862 that possibly he was justified in dividing his forces and adopting exterior lines of operations. If he had succeeded, his plan would have been universally praised. He failed, and so also have Burnside, Hooker, and Meade on an interior route; but their armies were far inferior in number to that which McClellan had two years ago. These facts in themselves prove nothing in favor of either route, and to decide the question we must recur to fundamental principles in regard to interior and exterior lines, objective points covering armies, divided forces, &c. <u>These fundamental principles require, in my opinion, that all our available forces in the east should be concentrated against Lee's army. We cannot take Richmond (at least with any military advantage), and we cannot operate advantageously on any point from the Atlantic coast till we destroy or disperse that army, and the nearer to Washington we can fight it the better for us.</u> We can here, or between here and Richmond, concentrate against him more men than anywhere else. If we cannot defeat him here with our combined force, we cannot hope to do so elsewhere with a divided army.

I write to you plainly and frankly, for between us there should be no reserve or concealment of opinions. As before remarked, I presume, under the authority of the President, the final decision of these questions will be referred to you. Nevertheless, I think you are entitled to have, and that it is my duty to frankly give, my individual opinion on the subject. It will no doubt be received for what it may be intrinsically worth; I can ask or expect nothing more.

In regard to the operations of our Western armies I fully concur in your views, but I think the condition of affairs in East Tennessee and west of Mississippi River will require some modification in your plans, or at least will very much delay the operations of your proposed spring campaign.

These, however, are delays and changes which neither of us could anticipate.

Very respectfully, your obedient servant,

H. W. HALLECK,
General-in-Chief.[8]

---

8 Official Records, Volume 32, Series 1, Part 11, Ser. No. 59, p. 411.

Appendix A: Grant's Plan/Lincoln's Plan

The Virginia campaign of 1864 can only be understood if General Halleck's letter is read carefully. The letter is important because General Halleck was unimportant. General Halleck had no power to direct events, to tell Grant what he could or could not do, to issue independent orders to any of the armies. This was a letter from President Lincoln to his new commanding general, informing him as to how the war in Virginia was to be conducted.

And finally, lest there be any doubt as to the control President Lincoln exerted over military affairs, we have an example in Sherman's letter of April 2, 1864 requesting Grant to obtain Lincoln's approval of a change in the organization of the Western army:

HDQRS MILITARY DIVISION OF THE MISSISSIPPI.
Nashville, Tenn., April 2. 1864. (Received 6 p.m.)

Lieut. Gen. U. S. GRANT
Washington, D. C.

<u>After a full consultation with all my army commanders, I have settled down to the following conclusion, to which I would like to have the President's consent before I make the orders:</u>

First, Army of the Ohio, three divisions of infantry, to be styled the Twenty-third Corps, Major-General Schofield in command, and one division of cavalry, Major-General Stoneman, to push Longstreet's forces well out of the valley, then fall back, breaking railroad to Knoxville; to hold Knoxville and Loudon, and be ready by May 1, with 10,000 men, to act as the left of the grand army.

Second, General Thomas to organize his army into three corps, the Eleventh and Twelfth to be united under Hooker, to be composed of four divisions. The corps to take a new title, viz, one of the series now vacant. General Slocum to be transferred east, or assigned to some small command on the Mississippi. The Fourth Corps, Major-General Granger, to remain unchanged, save to place Major-General Howard in command. The Fourteenth Corps to remain the same. Major-General Palmer is not equal to such a command, and all parties are willing that General Buell or any tried soldier should be assigned. Thomas to guard the lines of communication, and have, by May 1, a command of 45,000 men for active service, to constitute the center.

215

Appendix A: Grant's Plan/Lincoln's Plan

Third, Major-General McPherson to draw from the Mississippi the divisions of Crocker and Leggett, now en route, mostly of veterans on furlough, and of A. J. Smith, now up Red River, but due on the 10th instant out of that expedition, and to organize a force of 30,000 men to operate from Larkinsville or Guntersville as the right of the grand army, his corps to be commanded by Generals Logan, Blair, and Dodge. Hurlbut will not resign, and I know no better disposition of him than to leave him at Memphis.

I propose to put Major-General Newton, when he arrives, at Vicksburg.

With these changes this army will be a unit in all respects, and I can suggest no better.

<u>Please ask the President's consent, and ask what title we shall give the new corps of Hooker in lieu of the Eleventh and Twelfth, consolidated.</u> The lowest number of the army corps now vacant will be most appropriate.

I will have the cavalry of the Department of the Ohio reorganized under Stoneman at or near Camp Nelson and the cavalry of Thomas, at least one good division, under Garrard, at Columbia.

W.T. SHERMAN,
Major-General.[9]

President Lincoln was always in charge.

In the crossing of the James on June 15th, Grant executed a modified form of his original plan. He attacked Lee directly because that was what President Lincoln insisted upon, but if Grant could not destroy Lee in the field, Grant would go south of Lee and destroy his railroads.

This is clearly explained in Grant's letter of June 5, 1864 found on page 7. (and in O.R. Vol. XXXVI, Pt. 111, Ser. No. 69, p. 598).

General Grant merged his ideas with President Lincoln's ideas into a single strategic plan that met the desires of both.

---

9   Official Records Vol. 32, Series 1, Part 111, Ser. No. 59, p. 221.

Appendix B
GRANT AND SHERMAN/ GRANT AND MEADE

The close relationship between General Grant and General Sherman made possible the smooth coordination of the continent wide attack on the Confederacy in the spring of 1864.

In leaving the West in March, General Grant expressed his gratitude to Sherman:

NASHVILLE, TENN.,
March 4, 1864.

[PRIVATE.]

DEAR SHERMAN: The bill reviving the grade of lieutenant-general in the army has become a law, and my name has been sent to the Senate for the place. I now receive orders to report to Washington immediately in person, which indicates either a confirmation or a likelihood of confirmation.

I start in the morning to comply with the order, but I shall say very distinctly on my arrival there that I accept no appointment which will require me to make that city my headquarters. This, however, is not what I started out to write about.

Whilst I have been eminently successful in this war in at least gaining the confidence of the public, no one feels more than me how much of this success is due to the energy, skill, and the harmonious putting forth of that energy and skill, of those who it has been my good fortune to have occupying a subordinate position under me.

<u>There are many officers to whom these remarks are applicable to a greater or less degree, proportionate to their ability as</u>

Appendix B: Grant and Sherman/Grant and Meade

<u>soldiers, but what I want is to express my thanks to you and McPherson as the men to whom, above all others, I feel indebted for whatever I have had of success.</u> How far your advice and suggestions have been of assistance, you know. How far your execution of whatever has been given you to do entitles you to the reward I am receiving, you cannot know as well as me. I feel all the gratitude this letter would express, giving it the most flattering construction.

The word "you" I use in the plural, intending it for McPherson also, I should write to him, and will some day, but starting in the morning I do not know that I will find time just now.

Your friend
U. S. GRANT,
Major- General.[1]

Grant was a man in a hurry. Like Lincoln, he believed immediate, decisive action was necessary to sustain the war spirit of the people of the United States. Whereas the Union had achieved victory in the West, the Eastern theater had been a series of humiliating defeats for the Union. The only victories were Antietam and Gettysburg. The Civil War was dragging into its fourth year. Victory must be achieved within a year's time.

General Grant arrived in Washington D.C. on March 8th. On March 9th he received his commission as Lieutenant General, commander of all United States forces. On March 10th Grant visited General Meade with the Army at Culpepper. Virginia. Grant decided to retain Meade as Commander of the Army of the Potomac. On March 11th Grant went to Nashville, Tennessee to meet with Sherman. Together, the two old friends planned and organized the Western campaign against Atlanta. All armies would attack May 4, 1864. On March 18th General Sherman assumed command of the Western army.

On March 22nd Grant was in Philadelphia arranging a home for his family. On March 23rd Grant was in Washington D. C. On March 24th Grant established his headquarters at Culpepper Courthouse, Virginia with the Army of the Potomac and began planning, with General Meade, the 1864 Spring offensive in Virginia. All plans and preparations were completed within the month of April and the campaign began early in May, as soon as the roads were dry enough for the army to move.

---

1 Official Records Vol. 32, Series 1, Pt. 111 Ser. No. 59, p. 18.

Appendix B: Grant and Sherman/Grant and Meade

In May of 1864, the Confederacy still had two great armies in the field. The heartland of the South was untouched by the enemy. The determination of the Southern people had not wavered. Within 46 days the South's principal army was driven south 85 miles into a siege position from which it could not escape. Within six months, the Confederacy was in shambles.

The Spring offensive is best described in General Grant's letter of April 9, 1864 to General Meade:

CULPEPPER COURT-HOUSE, VA.,
April 9, 1864.

Maj. Gen. G. G. MEADE,
Commanding Army of the Potomac:

For information, and as instructions to govern your preparations for the coming campaign, the following is communicated confidentially for your own perusal alone:

So far as practicable, all the armies are to move together and toward one common center. Banks has been instructed to turn over the guarding of the Red River to General Steele and to the navy, to abandon Texas with the exception at the Rio Grande, and to concentrate all the force he can–not less than 25,000 men-to move on Mobile. This he is to do without reference to any other movements. From the scattered condition of his command, however, he cannot possibly get it together to leave New Orleans before the 1st of May, if so soon.

Sherman will move at the same time you do, or two or three days in advance. Joe Johnston's army being his objective point and the heart of Georgia his ultimate aim. If successful, he will secure the line from Chattanooga to Mobile with the aid of Banks.

Sigel cannot spare troops from his army to reenforce either of the great armies, but he can aid them by moving directly to his front. This he has been directed to do, and is now making preparations for it. Two columns of his command will move south at the same time with the general move, one from Beverly, from 10,000 to 12,000 strong under Major-General Ord; the other from Charleston, W. Va, principally cavalry, under Brigadier-General Crook. The former of these will endeavor to reach the Tennessee and Virginia Railroad about south of Covington, and if found practicable will work eastward to Lynchburg and return to it's

Appendix B: Grant and Sherman/Grant and Meade

base by way of the Shenandoah Valley or join you. The other will strike at Saltville, Va., and come eastward to join Ord. The cavalry from Ord's command will try to force a passage southward if they are successful in reaching the Virginia and Tennessee Railroads <u>to cut the main Lines of the road connecting Richmond with all the South and Southwest.</u>

Gillmore will join Butler with about 10,000 men from South Carolina. <u>Butler can reduce his garrison so as to take 23,000 men</u> into the field directly to his front. The force will be commanded by Gen. W. F. Smith. With Smith and Gillmore, Butler <u>will seize City Point and operate against Richmond from the south side of the river.</u> His movement will be simultaneous with yours.

<u>Lee's army will be your objective point. Wherever Lee goes, there you will go also.</u> The only point upon which I am now in doubt is whether it will be better to cross the Rapidan above or below him. Each plan presents great advantages over the other, with corresponding objections. By crossing above, Lee is cut off from all chance of ignoring Richmond and going north on a raid; but if we take this route all we do must be done while the rations we start with hold out, we separate from Butler so that he cannot be directed how to cooperate. By the other route, Brandy Station can be used as a base of supplies until another is secured on the York or James River. These advantages and objections I will talk over with you more fully than I can write them.

Burnside with a force of probably 25,000 men, will re-enforce you immediately upon his arrival, which will be shortly after the 20th instant. I will give him the defense of the road from Bull Run as far south as we wish to hold it. This will enable you to collect all your strength about Brandy Station and to the front.

There will be naval co-operations on the James River, and transports and ferries will be provided, so that should Lee fall back into his entrenchments at Richmond Butler's force and yours will be a unit, or at least can be made to act as such.

What I would direct, then, is that you commence at once reducing baggage to the very lowest possible standard. Two wagons to a regiment of 500 men is the greatest number that should be allowed, for all baggage, exclusive of subsistence stores and ordinance stores. One wagon to brigade and one to division headquarters is sufficient, and about two to corps headquarters.

Appendix B: Grant and Sherman/Grant and Meade

Should by Lee's right flank be our route, you will want to make arrangements for having supplies of all sorts promptly forwarded to White House, on the Pamunkey. Your estimate for this contingency should be made at once. If not wanted there, there is every probability they will be wanted on the James River or elsewhere.

If Lee's left is turned, large provisions will have to be made for ordinance stores. I would say not much short of 500 rounds of infantry ammunition would do. By the other, half the amount would be sufficient.

U. S. GRANT,
Lieutenant-General[2]

Grant's order to Meade of April 9, 1864 is the most consistently overlooked by historians of any order in the Civil War:

<u>"Lee's army will be your objective. Wherever Lee goes, there you will go also."</u>

The Army of the Potomac was to <u>seek</u> Lee and <u>engage Lee constantly</u> so that Lee could not develop any offensive plans of his own for the rest of the war.

General Grant envisioned six simultaneous attacks by 300,000 men on the Confederate armies on or about May 5, 1864. The attacks are illustrated on maps on p. 222 and 223.

1. General Meade, with an army of 120,000, would attack General Lee directly in Northern Virginia.

2. General Sherman, with an army of 100,000, would attack General Johnson in Georgia.

3. General Butler, with an army of 30,000, would make an amphibious attack south of Richmond on the James River.

4. General Siegel, with a force of 15,000, would attack up the Shenandoah Valley toward Lexington.

5. General Banks, with an army of 25,000, would attack Mobile.

6. General Ord, with 10,000, would raid Saltville and Lynchburg

---

[2] Official Records, Vol. 32, Part 111, Ser. No. 60, p 827.

Appendix B: Grant and Sherman/Grant and Meade

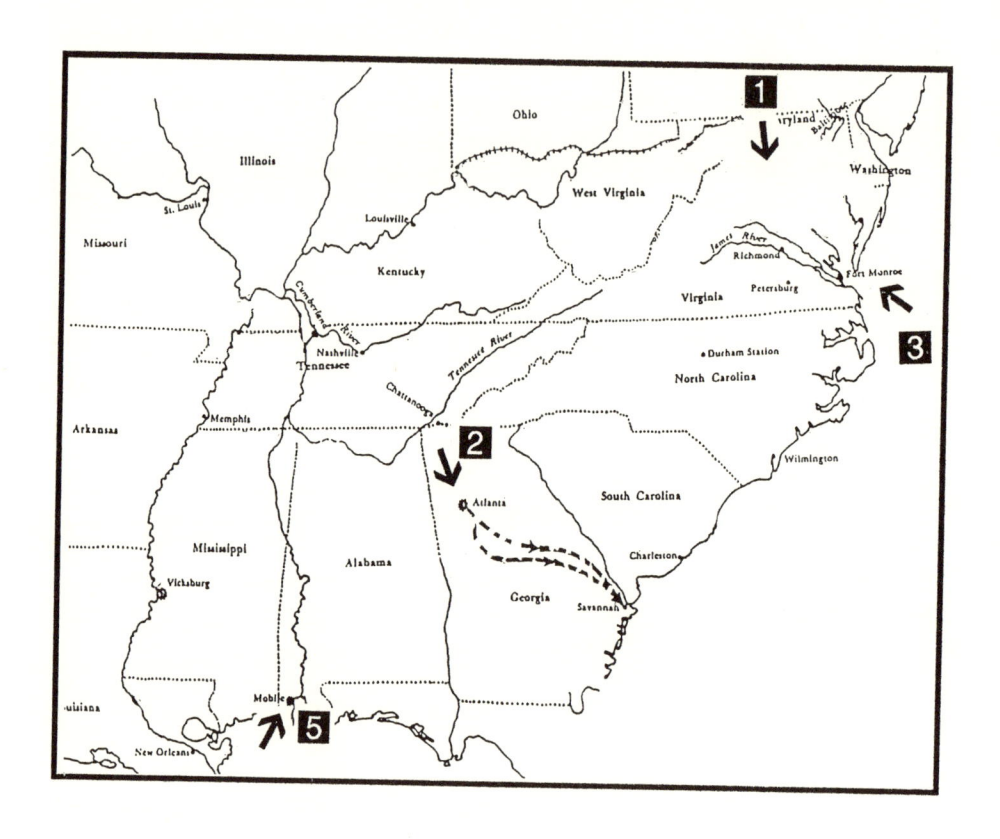

1864 Spring Offensive

1. General Meade attacks General Lee's Army
2. General Sherman attacks Atlanta
3. General Butler attacks up the James River
5. General Banks attacks Mobile

Appendix B: Grant and Sherman/Grant and Meade

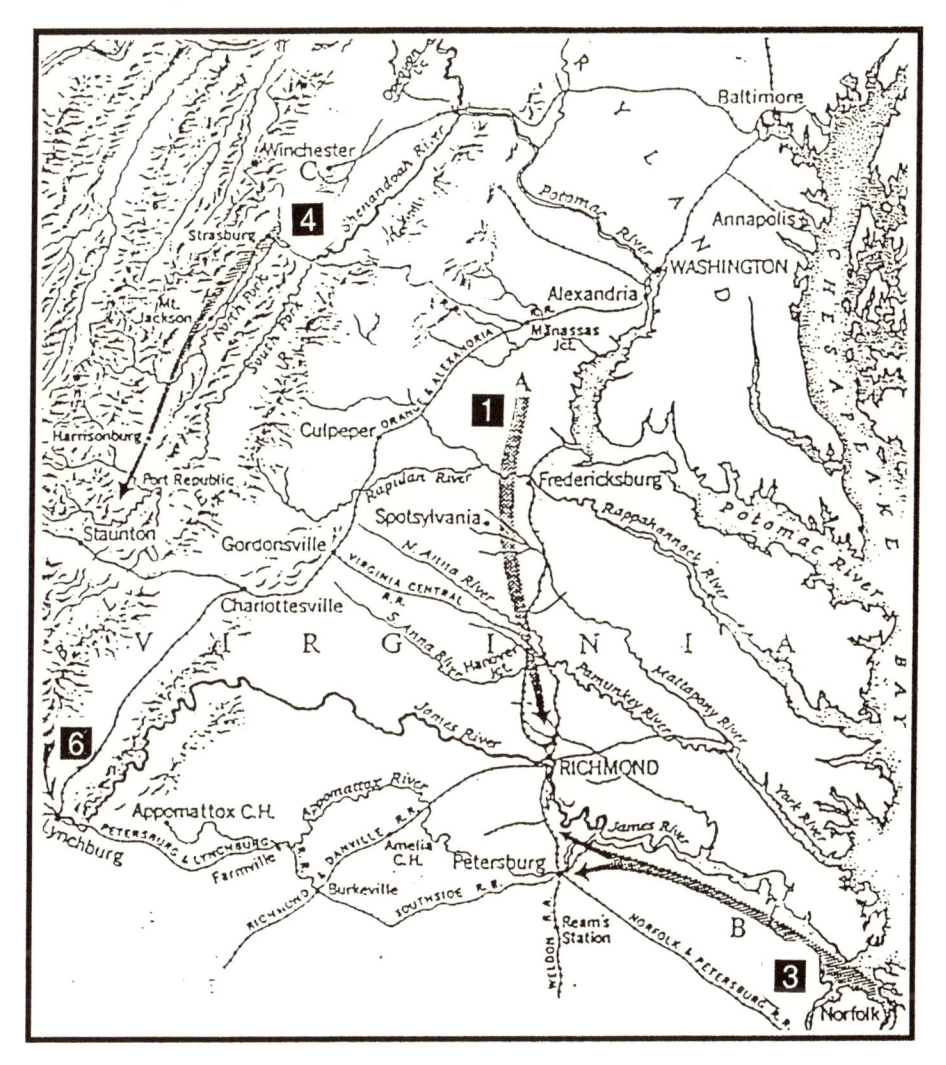

1864 Spring Offensive

1. General Meade attacks General Lee's army

3. General Butler attacks up the James River threatening Richmond

4. General Sigel attacks up the Shenandoah valley

6. General Ord raids Saltville-Lynchburg

Appendix B: Grant and Sherman/Grant and Meade

For the first time in the Civil War the full might of the United States in the form of six armies would be hurled simultaneously at the Confederacy. The Confederacy would have no opportunity to shift forces from one front to another. It had long been Grant's contention that the Confederacy had more real estate than forces to defend it. In 1864 he would test this hypothesis.

Of the six attacks on the Confederacy described in General Grant's letters of April 9, 1864, only the two great campaigns of General Sherman and General Meade were vigorously pursued to their final objectives. The four other campaigns were less than successful for a variety of reasons, but served the principal campaigns as diversions of Confederate forces.

Attack number six, General Ord's raid on Lynchburg was never launched because General Grant could not get Ord the necessary forces. It was no reflection on General Ord. Ord would later achieve fame and rise in rank in Grant's army.

Attack number five, General Bank's attack on Mobile also did not get off the ground because of Bank's inability to organize his forces. General Banks was a political general whose support President Lincoln needed and could therefore not be removed. General Grant requested that he be replaced but understood when President Lincoln refused.

Attack number four, General Siegel's movement up the Shenandoah Valley in the direction of Lexington, was turned back by an inferior Confederate force at the battle of New Market. Again, General Siegel was a political general whose support was important to the Union cause. General Grant understood.

Attack number three, General Butler's amphibious attack up the James River south of Richmond was indecisive. General Butler was an influential war Democrat from Massachusetts whose support Lincoln needed and whose political opposition Lincoln feared. In May of 1864, Butler's army made a permanent lodgment at City Point and Bermuda Hundred and unquestionably diverted Confederate troops that might have been sent to Lee. President Lincoln made it clear to Grant that Butler could not be replaced so Grant made the best possible use of him.

Attack number two, General Sherman's attack on General Johnston and subsequent conquest of Georgia was a spectacular success. Grant manifested complete confidence in Sherman and constantly told him he was one of the great generals of history. That was all Sherman needed. He proceeded to prove it.

Appendix B: Grant and Sherman/Grant and Meade

The petty jealousy backbiting and intrigue that divided the Confederate high command was noticeably absent in the relationship between Sherman and Grant. The letters between Grant and Sherman reflect the high regard they had for each other. General Grant gives his friend a complete picture of the spring campaign of which the Virginia campaign was but a part:

[PRIVATE AND CONFIDENTIAL]
HEADQUARTERS ARMIES OF THE UNITED STATES,
Washington, D.C. *April 4, 1864*
Maj. Gen. W T. SHERMAN,
Commanding Military Division of the Mississippi:
GENERAL: It is my design if the enemy keep quiet and allow me to take the initiative in the spring campaign to work all parts of the army together and somewhat toward a common center. For your information I now write you my program as at present determined upon.

I have sent orders to Banks by private messenger to finish up his present expedition against Shreveport with all dispatch; to turn over the defense of the Red River to General Steele and the navy, and return your troops to you and his own to New Orleans; to abandon all of Texas except the Rio Grande, and to hold that with not to exceed 4,000 men; to reduce the number of troops on the Mississippi to the lowest number necessary to hold it, and to collect from his command not less than 25,000 men. To this I will add 5,000 from Missouri. With this force he is to commence operations against Mobile as soon as he can. It will be impossible for him to commence too early.

Gillmore joins Butler with 10,000 men, and the two operate against Richmond from the south side of James River. This will give Butler 33,000 men to operate with W. F. Smith commanding the right wing of his forces, and Gillmore the left wing. <u>I will stay with the Army of the Potomac increased by Burnside's corps of not less than 25,000 effective men, and operate directly against Lee's army wherever it may be found.</u>

Sigel collects all his available force in two columns-one under Ord and Averell, to start from Beverly, Va., and the other, under Crook, to start from Charleston, on the Kanawha, to move against the Virginia and Tennessee Railroad. Crook will have all cavalry, and will endeavor to get in about Saltville and move east from

Appendix B: Grant and Sherman/Grant and Meade

there to join Ord. His force will be all cavalry, while Ord will have from 10,000 to 12,000 men of all arms.

<u>You, I propose to move against Johnston's army, to break it up and to get into the interior of the enemy's country as far as you can, inflicting all the damage you can against their war resources.</u>

<u>I do not propose to lay down for you a plan of campaign, but simply to lay down the work it is desirable to have done, and leave you free to execute in your own way. Submit to me, however, as early as you can, your plan of operations.</u>

As stated, Banks is ordered to commence operations as soon as he can. Gillmore is ordered to report at Fortress Monroe by the 18th instant, or as soon thereafter as practicable. Sigel is concentrating now. None will move from their places of rendezvous until I direct, except Banks. I want to be ready to move by the 25th* instant if possible but all I can now direct is that you get ready as soon as possible. I know you will have difficulties to encounter getting through the mountains to where supplies are abundant, but I believe you will accomplish it.

From the expedition from the Department of West Virginia I do not calculate on very great results, but it is the only way I can take troops from there. With the long line of railroad Sigel has to protect he can spare no troops, except to move directly to his front. In this way he must get through to inflict great damage on the enemy, or the enemy must detach from one of his armies a large force to prevent it. In other words, if Sigel can't skin himself he can hold a leg whilst some one else skins.

I am, general, very respectfully, your obedient servant,

U. S. GRANT,
Lieutenant-General.[3]

*April 25th - The Spring Offensive had to be delayed 10 days, to May 5, 1864.

With Sherman, Grant needed only to say:

> "I do not propose to lay down for you a plan of campaign, but simply to lay down the work it is desirable to have done and leave you free to execute in your own way."

to bring out the highest quality performance that the capable Sherman could produce.

---

3 Official Records, Volume 32, Part 111, Ser. No. 59, p. 245.

Appendix B: Grant and Sherman/Grant and Meade

As far the work to be accomplished Grant makes sure that Sherman will wage total war: "....get into the interior of the enemy's country as far as you can, inflicting all the damage you can against their war resources." And, evidencing additional confidence in Sherman, Grant says: "I know you will have difficulties to encounter getting through the mountains to where supplies are abundant, but I believe you will accomplish it."

In the third paragraph of the April 4th letter to Sherman (p. 225). Grant reveals his commitment to President Lincoln to personally take care of General Robert E. Lee:

"I will stay with the Army of the Potomac, increased by Burnside's corps of not less than 25,000 effective men, and operate directly against Lee's army wherever it may be found." The most difficult part of the spring offensive would be the campaign against Lee and it was to that task that Grant assigned himself. Grant assumed complete responsibility for Lee.

And Sherman's response to Grant's letter is equally cordial and demonstrates how their minds worked together:

HDQRS. MIL. DIV. OF THE MISSISSIPPI
Nashville, Tenn., April 10, 1864.

PRIVATE AND CONFIDENTIAL

Lieut. Gen. U. S. GRANT.
Commander-in Chief; Washington, D. C.

DEAR GENERAL: <u>Your two letters of April 4 are now before me and afford me infinite satisfaction. That we are now all to act in a common plan, converging on a common center, looks like enlightened war.</u>

<u>Like yourself you take the biggest load, and from me you shall have thorough and hearty cooperation.</u> I will not let side issues draw me off from your main plan, in which I am to knock Joe Johnston, and do as much damage to the resources of the enemy as possible. I have heretofore written to General Rawlins and Colonel Babcock of your staff, somewhat of the method in which I propose to act. I have seen all my army corps and division commanders and have signified only to the former viz. Schofield, Thomas, and McPherson, our general plans which I inferred from the purport at our conversation here and at Cincinnati.

Appendix B: Grant and Sherman/Grant and Meade

First, I am pushing stores to the front with all possible dispatch and am completing the organization according to the orders from Washington, which are ample and perfectly satisfactory. I did not wish to displace Palmer, but asked George Thomas to tell me in all frankness exactly what he wanted. All he asked is granted, and all he said was that Palmer felt unequal to so large a command, and would be willing to take a division, provided Buell or some tried and experienced soldier were given the corps. But on the whole Thomas is now well content with his command; so are Schofield and McPherson.

It will take us all of April to get in our furloughed veterans, to bring up A. J. Smith's command, and to collect provisions and cattle to the line of the Tennessee. Each of the three armies will guard by detachments of its own their rear communications. At the signal to be given by you, Schofield will leave a select garrison at Knoxville and Loudon, and with 12,000 men drop down to Hiwassee and march on Johnston's right by the old Federal road. Stoneman, now in Kentucky organizing the cavalry forces of the Army of the Ohio, will operate with Schofield on his left front; it may be, pushing a select body of about 2,000 cavalry by Ducktown on Ellijay and toward Athens.

Thomas will aim to have 45,000 men of all arms and move straight on Johnston wherever he may be, fighting him cautiously, persistently, and to the best of advantage. He will have two divisions of cavalry to take advantage of any offering.

McPherson will have nine divisions of the Army of the Tennessee if A. J. Smith gets in, in which case he will have full 30,000 of the best men in America. He will cross the Tennessee at Decatur and Whitesburg, march toward Rome and feel for Thomas. If Johnston fall behind the Coosa, then McPherson will push for Rome, and if Johnston then fall behind the Chattahouchee, as I believe he will, then McPherson will cross and join with Thomas. McPherson has no cavalry, but I have taken one of Thomas' divisions, viz, Garrard's 6,000 strong which I now have at Columbia, mounting, equipping, and preparing. I design this division to operate on McPherson's right rear or front, according as the enemy appears; but the moment I detect Johnston falling behind the Chattahouchee. I propose to cast off the effective part of this cavalry division, after crossing Coosa,

Appendix B: Grant and Sherman/Grant and Meade

straight for Opelika, West Point, Columbus, or Wetempka to break up the road between Montgomery and Georgia. If Garrard can do this work good, he can return to the main army; but should a superior force interpose, then he will seek safety at Pensacola, and join Banks, or after rest act against any force that he can find on the east of Mobile, till such time as he can reach me.

Should Johnston fall behind Chattahoochee I would feign to the right, but pass to the left, and act on Atlanta, or on its eastern communications, according to developed facts.

This is about as far ahead as I feel disposed to look, but I would ever bear in mind that Johnston is at all times to be kept so busy that he cannot, in any event, send any part of his command against you, or Banks.

If Banks can at the same time carry Mobile and open up the Alabama River he will in a measure solve the most difficult part of my problems-provisions. But in that I must venture. <u>Georgia has a million of inhabitants. If they can live, we should not starve.</u> If the enemy interrupt my communications, I will be absolved from all obligations to subsist on our own resources, but will feel perfectly justified in taking whatever and whenever I can find. I will inspire my command, if successful;, with my feeling that beef and salt are all that is absolutely necessary to life, and parched corn fed General Jackson's army once on that very ground.

As ever, your friend and servant,

W. T. SHERMAN,
Major-General.[4]

Sherman shows great understanding of the change in the direction of the Union war effort as a result of Grant taking command. There shall be no more random haphazard attacks. With Grant's taking over all command, the Civil War had become a modern war and would move forward much as the United States moved forward in World War II, step after step, toward defined military objectives:

> "Your two letters of April 4 are now before me and afford me infinite satisfaction. That we are now all to act in a common plan converging on a common center looks like enlighted war."

Sherman also recognizes the fact that Grant has assumed personal responsibility for the destruction of Lee and the Army of Northern Virginia:

---
4 Official Records, Vol. 32, Part III, Ser. No. 59, p. 312.

Appendix B: Grant and Sherman/Grant and Meade

"Like yourself you take the biggest load.. ."

Grant would launch a furious attack in Virginia and force the Confederate government to concentrate all available resources against him. There would be no Confederate resources which could be spared to be sent General Johnston in the West.

Nothing so beautifully illustrates General Grant's qualities of leadership as his ability to manage the Eastern theater and Western theater at the same time as revealed in his Letter of May 13, 1864; He was above petty jealousies. He is asking for promotions of both Eastern and Western officers.

SPOTSYLVANIA COURT-HOUSE. *May 13, 1864.*
Hon. E. M. STANTON,
Secretary of War, Washington D. C.:

I beg leave to recommend the following promotions to be made for gallant and distinguished service in the last eight days' battles to wit: Brig. Gen. H. G. Wright and Brig. Gen. John Gibbon to be major-generals; Col. S. S. Carroll, Eighth Ohio Volunteers, Col. E. Upton, One hundred and twenty-first New York Volunteers Col. William McCandless, Second Pennsylvania Reserves, to be brigadier-generals. I would also recommend Maj. Gen, W. S. Hancock for brigadier-general in the regular army. His services and qualifications are eminently deserving of this recognition.

In making these recommendations I do not wish the claims of General G. M. Dodge* for promotion forgotten, but recommend his name to be sent in at the same time. I would also ask to have General Wright assigned to the command of the Sixth Army Corps. I would further ask the confirmation of General Humphreys to the rank of Major-general. <u>General Meade has more than met my most sanguine expectations. He and Sherman* are the fittest officers for large commands I have come in contact with.</u> If their services can be rewarded by promotion to the rank of major-generals in the regular army the honor would be worthily bestowed and I would feel personally gratified. <u>I would not like to see one of these promotions at this time without seeing both.</u>

U. S. GRANT,
Lieutenant-General.[5]

*Western Officer

5 Official Records Volume XXXVI. Part 11, Ser. No. 68, p. 695.

Appendix B: Grant and Sherman/Grant and Meade

In April 1864, General Grant turned his attention to General Meade and the Army of the Potomac. Grant had retained Meade in command of the army because he was impressed with Meade as a competent, sincere officer who knew the Army of the Potomac, its officers, and men, and could handle the army well in combat. General Meade could execute the tactics to support the strategy that Grant had devised. What Grant needed to do was to infuse Meade and the Army of the Potomac with his own offensive fighting spirit. He must give them a determined belief that they could and would whip General Robert E. Lee.

In his letter to General Meade of April 9, 1864, General Grant emphasized that the Spring campaign would be a vigorous attack on Lee pursued to the end of the war:

"Lee's army will be your objective point. Wherever Lee goes, there you will go also."[6]

Grant's preparations for the campaign were made in great detail The fact that the campaign would probably end in a siege in Southern Virginia was evident in the planning of the Union command from the very start.

CULPEPER COURT-HOUSE, VA., *April 17, 1864*
Major-General MEADE,
Commanding Army of the Potomac.

Should a siege of Richmond become necessary, siege guns, ammunition, and equipments can be got from the arsenal at Washington and Fort Monroe very rapidly Every preparation is made for all classes of transportation by water, so that these things can be directed to any point by water we may require them. Once at the nearest landing, with the means of transportation with an army, they can be readily moved to any point where they may be wanted. The means of manning heavy artillery is always at hand with an army, as well as the means of constructing batteries. <u>I will take advantage of General Hunt's suggestion as to the proper officer to get the siege train ready and to a great extent, his suggestions as to the number, caliber, &tc of guns necessary for it.</u>

U. S. GRANT,
Lieutenant-General.[7]

---

6 Official Records Volume 32, Part 111, Ser. No. 60, p. 827. The full letter can be found on p. 219.
7 Official Records Volume 33, Ser. No. 60, p. 889.

Appendix B: Grant and Sherman/Grant and Meade

In working together in the preparations for the campaign General Grant and General Meade developed a close relationship of mutual respect and trust that would carry them through the 46 days of fierce fighting. General Meade had a notorious temper and General Grant's calm, quiet resourcefulness provided an excellent balance

HEADQUARTERS ARMY OF THE POTOMAC,
April 17, 1864

Lieutenant-General GRANT,
Commanding, &tc.

GENERAL: I desire to report that in conformity with my construction of your confidential letter of the 9th instant, the following instructions have been given by me:

The Commissary Department through its chief at these headquarters, has been notified that, at the close of the present month or early in the next, there will be required 1,000,000 of rations on shipboard in suitable vessels for being taken up the Pamunkey or James River, as may be required, and in advance of more specific instructions, Fortress Monroe has been designated as a proper point of assemblage. The Quartermaster's Department has been notified that, at the same time and place, forage and other supplies furnished by that department will be required. The Ordinance Department has been notified to have in similar readiness 100 rounds of artillery ammunition per gun and 100 rounds of small-arm per man. The Engineer Department has been instructed to have the siege trains [now at Washington] in readiness for shipment, and such engineering tools and other supplies [in addition to those carried with the army] as would be required in the event of laying siege to Richmond. A special communication has been made to you in reference to the artillery for a siege train, in case one should be required before Richmond. The Medical Department has been notified that in addition to the supplies now in depot at Alexandria, and which will be kept there as long as the Orange and Alexandria Railroad can be used, medical supplies for some 12,000 wounded should be held in readiness on shipboard, to be thrown up the Pamunkey or James, as circumstances may require. It is proper to observe, in connection with this duplication of reserve medical supplies, that in case a battle is fought within communicating distance of the

Appendix B: Grant and Sherman/Grant and Meade

Orange and Alexandria Railroad the supplies of Alexandria can be thrown forward; but if a rapid movement is made across the country, and a battle fought in the vicinity of Richmond, these supplies would have to be drawn from some other point; and the time which it would take after the battle occurs to transfer from Alexandria to this point, and the consequent suffering that might ensue, justify, in my judgment, this duplication of battle reserve supplies, and their being held in readiness at some point nearer than Alexandria.

The foregoing arrangements and instructions are based on the contingency of the enemy's falling back without giving battle. Each department has been notified to look to the quartermaster's department for intimation of the period when the different supplies ordered should be sent to any particular point.

For an immediate movement the following instructions have been given:

The ordinance department notified to have in readiness to issue, at short notice 150 rounds small arm ammunition, 50 rounds to be carried on the person and 100 in supply train. The subsistence department to have on hand for issue sixteen days' marching rations'; four of salt meat and twelve of beef on the hoof: six days to be carried on the person [three full rations in haversacks and three small rations in knapsacks]; the balance in supply trains. The quartermaster's department to have ten days' full allowance of grain for all animals. The medical department to be prepared to send the sick at short notice to the rear, and to have all necessary field-hospital supplies on hand. These preliminary instructions being given, it will require from three to four days' notice to issue and load supply trains and prepare the army to move at an hour's notice.

<u>This communication is respectfully submitted, that you may be fully advised of the steps I have taken, and that my attention may be called to the fact in case I have done more or less than is expected and required of me.</u>

Respectfully, yours,

GEO. G. MEADE,
Major-General, Commanding. [8]

---

8 Official Records Volume 33, Ser. No. 60, p. 889.

Appendix B: Grant and Sherman/Grant and Meade

Under Grant, Meade developed into an aggressive, fighting, offensive general. They remained together through the Virginia campaign and the siege of Petersburg to the very end of the war. Grant sustained Meade when the press demanded Meade's removal.

Appendix C
THE BIG SECRET: CONFEDERATE CASUALTIES

One of the great fabrications of the Civil War is that the Union army sustained 18,000 casualties in the Battle of the Wilderness and the Confederate suffered only 7,000 casualties. Shelby Foote faithfully records this myth:

> Grant lost 17,666 killed and wounded, captured and missing - about four hundred more than Hooker - while Lee, whose victory a year ago cost him nearly 13,000 casualties, was losing a scant 7800, considerably fewer than half the number he inflicted.[1]

There is no historical basis for this statement. A great area of mystery concerns Confederate casualties in the war. Of the 600,000 soldiers killed in the four terrible years of war, 250,000 were Confederates. It has been estimated that one out of eleven men in the South did not come back. The impact of the war on Southern society was devastating.

An excellent discussion of the understated Confederate casualties during the war and the devastating impact of the real Confederate casualties after the war can be found in "Attack and Die" by Grady McWhiney and Perry D. Jamieson. This study emphasizes the difficulty of establishing precise figures on the men lost in each battle.

In reading Confederate battle reports one is struck by the lack of hard facts. The Union army required prompt, accurate casualty reports from commanding officers after a battle and the Official Records reflect this. In the Confederate army, there appears to have been no such strict requirement.

---
1 Foote, Shelby, "The Civil War, 111", p. 188.

Appendix C: The Big Secret: Confederate Casualties

General Lee himself appears to have been ambivalent about reporting casualties. After the Battle of Chancellorsville, in which he suffered 13,000 casualties,[2] Lee issued the following directive:

GENERAL ORDERS, HDQRS. ARMY OF NORTHERN VIRGINIA,
No. 63   *May 14, 1863*

The practice which prevails in the army of including in the list of casualties those cases of slight injuries which do not incapacitate the recipients for duty, is calculated to mislead our friends and encourage our enemies by giving false impressions as to the extent of our losses.

The loss sustained by a brigade or regiment is by no means an indication of the magnitude of the service performed or perils encountered as experience shows that those who attack most rapidly, vigorously, and effectually generally suffer least. It is, therefore, ordered that in future the reports of the wounded shall only include those whose injuries, in the opinion of the medical officers, render them unfit for duty.

It has also been observed that the published reports of casualties are in some instances accompanied by a statement of the number of men taken into action. The commanding general deems it unnecessary to do more than direct the attention of officers to the impropriety of thus furnishing the enemy with the means of computing our strength, in order to insure the immediate suppression of this pernicious and useless custom.

By command of General Lee:

W. H. TAYLOR,
Assistant Adjutant-General.[3]

What Lee was saying was that meticulous reporting of casualties only aided the enemy. No officer in the Army of Northern Virginia would be criticized for understating his casualties. Lee's influence was enormous. After the three day battle of Gettysburg the Confederates reported losses of 20,451. Modern historians put their casualties at 28,000.[4] <u>In the Virginia Campaign many Confederate officers filed no casualty reports whatever.</u>

---

2   Esposito, Col. Vincent J. "The West Point Atlas of American Wars", Map 91.
3   Official Records, Vol. 25, Part 11, Ser. No. 40, p. 1798.
4   Esposito, Col. Vincent J. "The West Point Atlas of American Wars" p. Map 99.

Appendix C: The Big Secret: Confederate Casualties

Many Confederate officers were killed during the Virginia campaign. This caused shifts in command as Lee struggled to fill the vacancies The reports of these displaced officers reflect the pressure and confusion of these horrendous 46 days. The reports are fragmentary and inconclusive. Moreover, there was the confusion of continuous battle, and the merging of depleted units to fill out the ranks. Finally, during the winter of 1864-65, the Confederate government created reports for propaganda purposes.

General Gordon, an able, conscientious officer reported: (Regarding the Union attack on the Salient, in the Battle of Spotsylvania, May 12, 1864)

> ....I regret that a report of the casualties in these engagements has not been furnished me by the brigade commanders. Two of these brigades are not now under my command.
> I am, major, very respectably, your obedient servant,
> Maj. Campbell Brown
> J. E. Gordon
> Major-General.[5]

General Gordon was in the thick of the fight for the Salient. Of any Confederate officer, his report would have been the most valuable. But, under the stress and strain of continuous assault by the Union army, General Gordon found it impossible to properly assess the casualties of units under his command. General Gordon's report was dated July 5, 1864, two months after the battle of Spotsylvania and two weeks after the siege of Petersburg had begun. His report is fragmentary. Without the reports of officers like General Gordon who commanded the fighting units, staff people in Richmond had nothing on which to build their official reports.

General Stephen D. Ramseur, considered one on the most capable officers in the Confederate army, made the following report three months after the Battle of the Wilderness:

---

5   Official Records, Vol. XXXVI, Part 1, Ser. No. 67, p. 1079.

Appendix C: The Big Secret: Confederate Casualties

Camp Near Winchester
August 1, 1864

Lieut. Gen R. S. Ewell

....This report is very brief, and hastily written. It does not do justice to the brave officers and men under my command, but in the midst of a most active campaign it was the best I could do. Being separated from my brigade I have not been able to procure a list of killed and wounded. This list will be forwarded at my first opportunity.....

S. D. Ramseur
Major-General[6]

General Ramseur's report was written from the Shenandoah valley where he participated in General Early's raid. General Ramseur was mortally wounded Oct. 19th. Presumably his report was never completed.

This confusion should not be taken as a reflection on these fine officers. The Army of Northern Virginia was under continuous attack and did well to survive. These reports are by no means isolated but rather are typical of Confederate reports of this period.

General Armistead L. Long, CSA made the following report on the Wilderness Campaign in November 1864. General Long was also writing from the Shenandoah valley.

(Wilderness Campaign)
Staunton. November 25, 1864

Adjt. General, Lieut. Gen. Ewell's Command Richmond, Va.

.....Being absent from my command, I am unable to append a list of casualties. The chief loss was upon the capture of Cutshaw's and Page's battalions on May 12.

This report would have been submitted at a much earlier period had it not been for the difficulties incident to an active campaign in getting subreports and my own illness. I am, very respectfully, your obedient servant,

A. L. Long
Brigadier-General, Chief of Artillery
Second Army Corps. of operations
May 4-31[7]

---

6 Official Records, Vol. XXXVI, Part 1, Ser. No. 67, p. 1080.
7 Official Records, Vol. XXXVI, Part 1, Ser. No. 67, p. 1084.

Appendix C: The Big Secret: Confederate Casualties

An exception to the lack of casualty reports by Confederate officers is the report of Brigadier General McGowan. It is one of the best reports by an officer on the Salient fighting at Spotsylvania:

<u>No. 295</u>.

Report of Brig Gen. Samuel McCowan C. S. Army commanding brigade. Wilcox's division, of operations May 8-13.

We remained at the trenches in the Wilderness until Sunday afternoon, May 8, when we marched by the right flank toward Spotsylvania. Bivouacked that night near Shady Grove, and reached the Court-House on Monday morning, the 9th. We were put into position by Major-General Wilcox on the right of our line in the suburbs of the village, and immediately threw up a breast-work. Here we remained, with more or less skirmishing until the 12th.

Thursday morning, the 12th, was dark and rainy, and at a very early hour a tremendous fire of artillery and musketry was heard on the line to our left. We were moved along the breast-work toward the left until we reached a sharp angle in the works near a brick kiln, opposite to which the enemy had established a battery. I threw the sharpshooters into a wood to our front and right to pick off the gunners and horses. Here we remained until about 9 a.m., when I was directed to march with my brigade and report to General Ewell, who directed Major-General Rodes to put me in on the right of his line to support General Harris, and assist in filling up the gap which had been made by the capture of Major-General Johnson and a part of his command. At this place our line of works made a sharp angle, pointing toward the enemy, which angle the enemy held in great force, besides having the woods and ravine in front occupied by multitudes who seemed to be as thick as they could stand. The right of my brigade extended some distance up the left side of the angle and rested on nothing but the enemy, who held the point, and some portion (I never knew how much) of the right side of the angle. Besides having no support on my right, this part of my line was enfiladed from the point of the angle and the gap held by the enemy. In getting into this trench we had to pass through a terrific fire. I was wounded, and knew nothing of what occurred afterward from

Appendix C: The Big Secret: Confederate Casualties

personal observation. I am informed that the brigade found in the trenches General Harris and what remained of his gallant brigade, and they (Mississippians and Carolinians), mingled together, made one of the most gallant and stubborn defenses recorded in history. These two brigades remained there, holding our line without re-enforcements, without food, water, or rest, under a storm of balls which did not intermit one instant of time for eighteen hours. The trenches on the right in the Bloody Angle ran with blood and had to be cleared of the dead bodies more than once.

To give some idea of the intensity of the fire, an oak tree 22 inches in diameter, which stood just in rear of the right of the brigade, was cut down by the constant scaling of musket-balls and fell about 12 o'clock Thursday night, injuring by its fall several soldiers in First South Carolina Regiment.

The brigades mentioned held their position from 10 o'clock Thursday morning until 4 o'clock Friday morning when they were withdrawn, by order, to the new line established in rear.

<u>The loss of my brigade was very heavy especially in killed, being in the aggregate 451-86 killed on the field 248 wounded, many of whom have since died: 117 missing doubtless captured.</u>

Our men lay on one side of the breast-work and the enemy on the other, and in many instances men were pulled over. It is believed that we captured as many prisoners as we lost.

<u>Among the casualties are Lieut. Col. W. P Shooter and Lieut. E. C. Shooter, of the First [Infantry, Provisional Army:] Lieuts. J. B. Blackman, Jr., and J. R. Faulkenburg of the Twelfth Col. B. T. Brockman and Capt. J. K Brockman, of the Thirteenth Lieuts. A. M. Scarborough and H. N. Hunter, of the Fourteenth, and Capt. G. W. Fullerton, of the [First] Rifles, killed.</u> Col. C. W. McCreary. Lieuts. A. F. Miller, James Armstrong, Capt. W. Kelly, and Lieut. M. R. Tharin of the First Infantry. Provisional Army,] Lieut. W. B. White and Captain Stover, of the Twelfth; Capt. J. Y. McFall and Lieut. W. J. Rook, of the Thirteenth. Capt. G W. Culbertson, Lieuts. J. M. Miller and D. E. Brown, Capts. E. Cowan and J. M. Mc Carley, of the Fourteenth; Capts. L. Rogers and R. S. Cheshire, Lieuts. L. T. Reeder and A. C. Sinclair, and Lieut. Col. G. Mc D. Miller, of the Rifles, <u>wounded.</u>

Appendix C: The Big Secret: Confederate Casualties

In all these operations I take pleasure in acknowledging the great assistance of my staff. Maj. A. B. Wardlaw, brigade commissary; Maj. Harry Hammond, brigade quartermaster, and Lieut. C. G. Thompson, ordnance officer, were active and efficient in their appropriate departments

Capt. L C. Haskell, assistant adjutant-general, and Lieut. G. Allen Wardlaw, aide-de-camp, were everywhere on the field of battle where honor and duty called (both of these officers had their horses killed under them in the Wilderness), and were always conspicuous for coolness and gallantry, &c.

S. McGOWAN.[8]

General McGowan's report might well have been representative of the missing casualty reports. Without the missing reports we will never know the hard facts.

Reports by Confederate Corps Commanders

Not only are reports of brigade and division commanders missing on casualties but there are no reports from higher levels of Confederate command. Lee made no report to Richmond on his casualties in the Virginia campaign. Nor did most Confederate Corps commanders. General Longstreet, severely wounded, made a very late report on the campaign dated March 23, 1865, that does not mention casualties. General A. P. Hill was ill during a great deal of the fighting and did not report casualties.

The most detailed report of casualties by a Confederate Corps commander was made indirectly by General Ewell: his report tells how the second Corps was drastically depleted by the fighting.

(Battle of Spotsylvania) January 5, 1865

Col. W. H. Taylor
Assistant Adjutant General
(Army of Northern Virginia)

.....On May 19 General Lee directed me to demonstrate against the enemy in my front, as he believed they were moving to his right and wished to ascertain. As they were strongly entrenched in front I obtained leave to move around their right. After a detour of several miles through roads impassable for my artillery I came

---

[8] Official Records, Vol XXXVI Part 1 Ser. Mo. 67, p. 1093.

Appendix C: The Big Secret: Confederate Casualties

on the enemy prepared to receive me. <u>My force was about 6,000, his much larger.</u> His position being developed and my object attained, I was about to retire, when he attacked me. Part of my line was shaken, but Pegram's brigade, of Early's division (Colonel Hoffman commanding), and Ramseur's of Rodes', held their ground so firmly that I maintained my position till nightfall, then withdrew unmolested. My loss was about 900 killed, wounded, and missing

Next day General Early returned to his division and General Gordon was put in command of one composed of his own brigade and the remnants of Johnson's division. Hoke's brigade (Colonel Lewis commanding) returned to Early's division, and the Twenty-first....

Very respectfully, your obedient servant,

R. S. EWELL,
Lieutenant-General.[9]

Col. W. H. TAYLOR
Assistant Adjutant-General.

According to General Ewell's report, the 2nd Corps, which had represented one third of Lee's army on May 5th, had shrunk from 17,000 men to 6,000 and then suffered 900 additional casualties in the battle at Harrison's farm. Ewell's Corps was devastated by the intense fighting in the first 15 days.

In sharp contrast with General Ewell's report is an "official report" from the Confederate War Department, dated 1865, six months after the battles. These figures published in Richmond have an air of authority but when examined, do not have any basis in fact. This report was made by the Medical Director of the Confederate States Army dated January 5, 1865:

Report of Medical Director Lafayette Guild, C. S. Army, of casualties in month of May.

MEDICAL DIRECTOR'S OFFICE, ARMY OF N. VIRGINIA,
January 5, 1865.

SIR: Your communication of the 2d instant has been received. In reply I transmit the following summary of casualties occurring in the Second Corps during the month of May, 1864:

---

[9] Official Records, Vol. XXXVI, Part 1, Ser. No. 67, p. 1069.

Appendix C: The Big Secret: Confederate Casualties

Command	Killed	Wounded	Total
Johnson's Division	177	744	921
Rodes' Division	347	1534	1881
Early's Division	228	1322	1550
Artillery of Second Corps	15	86	101
Total	767	3686	4453

Any other information which may be required can be obtained by reference to my reports,* which have been forwarded to the Surgeon-General's Office.

I am, sir, very respectfully, your obedient servant,

L. GUILD,
Medical Director Army of Northern Virginia.

Maj. CAMPBELL BROWN,
Asst. Adjt. Gen. Department of Richmond.[10]

*Not found

Director Guild's report omits any reference to "captured" or "missing" but describes itself as a "summary of casualties." Director Guild's report is worthless. No mention is made of Johnson's Division of 3,000 men which were captured in the Salient at Spostylvania.

Importance of Confederate Casualties

In trying to understand the Virginia campaign it is of key importance to come to grips with Confederate casualties. The campaign was one thing prior to May 21, 1864. The campaign changed entirely after May 21, 1864. Lee fought Grant vigorously in Northern Virginia in the battles of Wilderness and Spotsylvania. In both battles the Confederate Army took a terrible toll of attacking Union troops. But the Union army took a terrible toll of Confederate troops. After May 21st, the end of the Battle of Spotsylvania, the Army of Northern Virginia was a changed army. The Army of Northern Virginia had no offensive striking power left. Lee was never again able to launch an offensive with his army. Lee fought from trenches for the balance of the war. General Lee could not be lured out of trenches. He could only defend a prepared position.

This fact had enormous implications for the Confederate cause. Lee had dominated the Eastern theater during the first three years of the

10 Official Records, Vol. XXXVI, Part 1, Ser. No. 67, p. 1075.

Appendix C: The Big Secret: Confederate Casualties

war. With lightning maneuvers, he had moved around the Union army. Lee had been able to overcome the Union advantage in numbers by shifting his forces rapidly and attacking. Lee had been able to keep the larger Union army off balance. Lee had been able to dominate his opponents and control the battle by striking at them and keeping them confused. Now Lee was relegated to the defense. Now it was Grant who could control the fighting, and force Lee to constantly react to movements by the Union army.

The basic change that took place in the Confederate army after Spotsylvania can only be explained by enormous casualties sustained in the first three weeks of fighting: (May 4-May 21) the loss of 25,000 veteran troops which could never be replaced. These were the troops that had given Lee the cutting edge for maneuver and attack. Lee had suffered a second Gettysburg in May, 1864. The failure to recognize the enormity of Confederate casualties in the first three weeks of the campaign is the key mistake made by contemporary historians. They make the error of concentrating on Union casualties and ignoring Confederate casualties.

The West Point Military Atlas states that at the beginning of the campaigns General Lee had approximately 64,000 soldiers with which to oppose General Grant's army of 120,000 men.

General Longstreet	1st Corps	10,000 (approx.)
General Ewell	2nd Corps	17,000
General Hill	3rd Corps	22,000
General Stuart	Cavalry	8,400
Artillery, engineers, etc.		6,200
		63,900
	Guns	274[11]

There are many estimates of Confederate casualties by respected authorities. The National Park Service Handbook, "Where a Hundred Thousand Fell," gives the following figures:

---

11 Esposito Col. Vincent J, "The West Point Atlas of the Civil War", Map 120.

Appendix C: The Big Secret: Confederate Casualties

A. In the Battle of the Wilderness:
The Federals lost 15,387 of 118,000 in killed, wounded and missing. The Confederates 11,400 out of 62,000. (This would mean that General Lee lost 18% of his army in the Wilderness.)

B. In the Battle of Spotsylvania:
Union losses in killed, wounded and missing were 17,555. Confederate losses are unknown.[12]

"The West Point Atlas of the Civil War" gives these figures:

A. In the Battle of the Wilderness:
Union losses had been between 15,000 and 18,000. Confederate records are fragmentary, estimates varying from 7,750 to 11,400.[13]

B. In the Battle of Spotsylvania:
Union losses during the fighting around Spotsylvania Court House are variously reported but appear to have been between 17,000 and 18,000. Confederate casualties are unknown, but since their forces fought behind fortifications during most of these engagements, their losses must have been considerably less, possibly between 9,000 and 10,000.[14]

Although Confederate casualties at Spotsylvania are more elusive, the fighting at the Salient gives simple clues. In "The Killing Ground," part of the Time Life series on the Civil War, the following casualty figures are given for the fighting at the Salient:

The inconclusive battle for the Mule Shoe had ended. In the two days of fighting at Spotsylvania, May 12 and 13, close to 6,000 of Lee's veterans had been killed or wounded. Nearly 4,000 men had been captured. Grant's total was equally devastating, 10,920 killed, wounded or captured.[15]

---

12 Cullen, Joseph P. "Where a Hundred Thousand Fell," National Park Service, Series 39. 1966, p. 45, p. 53.
13 Esposito, Col. Vincent J., "The West Point Atlas of the Civil War," map 125.
14 Ibid., Map 133.
15 Gregory, Jaynes, "The Killing Ground", Time-Life Books, p. 105.

Appendix C: The Big Secret: Confederate Casualties

In other words, the fighting in the Salient on two days, May 12, 13th, cost the Confederate army 10,000 casualties. The battle of Spotsylvania lasted for 13 days, May 8 through May 21, so that the figures cited are by no means complete. Upton's attack netted 1,000 Confederate prisoners on May 10th. It must again be borne in mind that these figures of Southern casualties are estimates pieced together from fragmentary reports.

It is the author's contention that most of the estimates of Confederate casualties for the Wilderness campaign are low and that General Lee suffered at least 25,000 Confederate casualties in Wilderness/Spotsylvania. General Lee suffered these enormous casualties fighting to maintain his position in Northern Virginia. He failed. It is also the author's conclusion that those 25,000 Confederate casualties, 40% of Lee's army, were veteran shock troops, the very best troops he had. They represented the offensive striking force of the Army of Northern Virginia. As replacements, Lee got garrison troops from the deep South which could never replace battle hardened veterans and battle hardened officers. Garrison Confederate officers with limited experience could never replace the superb officer corps Lee had developed over three years.

In the Civil War, it was very important that the officers lead their men forward in combat. An officer led by example. If the officer was not brave he could hardly expect his men to be brave. This practice meant heavy officer casualties in the big battles. Loss of Confederate officers at Gettysburg was appalling. Wilderness and Spotsylvania were a second Gettysburg.

For information on the Army of Northern Virginia, Robert K. Krick, Chief Historian of the Fredericksburg Battlefields, is the authority without peer. In his book, "Lee's Colonels--A Biographical Register of the Field Officers of the Army of Northern Virginia," Krick traces the careers of 2,000 field officers who attained the rank of colonel, lieutenant-colonel and major. The book covers officers who survived the war and tells of their post war activities. The book also reveals those officers killed and the circumstances. Forty seven officers of the rank of colonel, lieutenant colonel or major became casualties in the Wilderness/Spotsylvania fighting. The figures are from the first edition of Mr. Krick's book:

Killed in action	25
Mortally wounded	10
Prisoners of war	11
Wounded	1 [17]

---

[17] Krick, Robert, "Lee's Colonels-A Biographical Register of Field Officers of the Army of Northern Virginia." Note: these figures vary from figures presented by Douglas Southall Freeman, see p. 248.

Appendix C: The Big Secret: Confederate Casualties

This says nothing about the captains, lieutenants and sergeants who were killed leading troops forward. When colonels were killed, their subordinates were presumed to be nearby. A careful combing of Confederate reports in the Official Records tells the story. It reveals report after report of the cost of heavy fighting:

> Captain Smith and 94 of his men were captured. 3 killed and 19 wounded. Major Watson was wounded while working one of Smith's guns and died of his wounds some four or five days later.[18]

The intensity and violence of the fighting in Wilderness/Spotsylvania were such that higher levels of officers became casualties:

Brigadier General John M. Jones	KIA
Brigadier General Leroy Stafford	severely wounded
Brigadier General John Pegram	KIA
Brigadier General Micha Jenkins	KIA
Lt. General Longstreet	severely wounded
Major General J.E.B. Stuart	MWIA
Brigadier General John Gordon (cavalry)	MWIA
Major General Edward Johnson	POW
Brigadier General George H. Stewart	POW
Brigadier General Perrin	KIA
Brigadier General Daniel	KIA
Brigadier General Walker	severely wounded

With these losses the whole burden of the campaign descended on Lee. More and more he was exposing himself in battle, running the danger of losing the war immediately by one well placed bullet. There was no one left for Lee to lean on, no General capable of doing more than obeying orders. The generals Lee had depended upon to grasp opportunities when they saw them, to improvise, to read Lee's mind and act for him without specific orders were gone. This loss of Confederate officers is described by Douglas Southall Freeman in his monumental,"Lee's Lieutenants":

> "How much the Army command had suffered in the Wilderness and at Spotsylvania, no statistician set forth at the time. The list was longer than in any previous campaign: the summary was nothing short of terrifying..

---

18 Official Records, Vol. XXXVI, Part 1, Ser. No. 67, p. 11089.

Appendix C: The Big Secret: Confederate Casualties

(Douglas Southall Freeman)
"THE END OF THE OLD ORGANIZATION

General Officers of the Army of Northern Virginia whose Troops were present throughout the Campaign, May 4-June 3, 1864.

	Present	Killed	Wounded	Captured
Army Headquarters	1	–	–	–
First Corps	11	1	3	–
Second Corps	16	4	4	2
Third Corps	16	1	5	–
Cavalry Corps	11	2	–	–
Artillery	3	–	–	–
Total	58	8	12	2

"The killed were: First Corps. Micah Jenkins: Second Corps, Junius Daniel, George Doles, John M. Jones and Leroy A. Stafford; Third Corps, Abner Perrin; Cavalry Corps, "Jeb" Stuart and James B. Gordon. The following sustained wounds severe enough to incapacitate them for command, temporarily or permanently: First Corps, James Longstreet, E. M. Law and Henry L. Benning; Second Corps, Harry Hays. Robert D. Johnston, John Pegram and James A. Walker; Third Corps, John R. Cooke, James H. Lane, Samuel McGowan, Edward L. Perry and Henry H. Walker The captured Generals were Edward Johnson and Geo. H. Stuart.

"By rank the casualties ran in this manner: Killed, one Major-General and seven Brigadiers, wounded, one Lieutenant General and eleven Brigadier Generals; captured, one, Major General and one Brigadier, in addition, the commanding General had been almost incapacitated by diarrhea for a week, one corps commander, Hill, had been too sick for almost a fortnight to direct his troops; and another corps chief, Ewell, had been failing so steadily in vigor that he had to be relieved of duty. In the First and in the Second Corps, two experienced divisional leaders, R. H. Anderson and Early, had been separated from their commands and Corps, for a part of the campaign, in order to direct other Corps.

These changes were more far reaching than anyone seems to have realized at the time. Faith in the Army itself was so unshakable that the President, the War Department and General

Appendix C: The Big Secret: Confederate Casualties

Lee apparently believed the normal process of training would be reversed: instead of the Generals instructing the troops, the veterans would school their new commanders. Within the limits of the tactics of everyday combat, this might prove true, but it could not be true of discipline and morale in time of continuing discouragement and waning hope. Nor could the change have been made at a time much more critical. A new development, a stern challenge, was to be expected daily. When Grant launched another direct drive on Richmond or undertook a turning operation South of the James, liaison with Beauregard and his newly arrived troops would be imperative. At a time when experience would be required to effect swift cooperation, two of the Corps of Lee's Army would be in the charge of men who had exercised that command less than a month. Of the nine Divisions, two in the First Corps were under promising men, Kershaw and Field though they scarcely could be regarded as fully seasoned at their higher rank. Two of the divisional leaders of the Second Corps were entirely new to that duty, Gordon and Ramseur. One of the three divisional chiefs of the Third Corps, Mahone, had never acted in that capacity for any length of time before the 8th of May. The only Major Generals left with one Army who had led Divisions as recently as Gettysburg, eleven months previously, were Pickett, who now was returning from detached service, Rodes, who had done admirably in Spotsylvania county, and Harry Heth, who carried some new odium for the events of May 6. None or these older Major-Generals had directed as many as four Brigades in any hard action before Chancellorsville.

The battles of a single month had put 37 percent of the general officers of the Army of Northern Virginia hors de combat. Except as Lee himself embodied it, the old organization was gone!"[19]

Even Shelby Foote conceded that the Army of Northern Virginia took a terrific battering in the 46 day Virginia campaign and was not the same army it had been in April:

"…..Close though resemblance was between the situations then (1862) and now, there were differences, none of them advantageous from the Confederate point of view. One was that

---

19 Freeman, Douglas Southall, "Lee's Lieutenants," Vol. 111, p. 512.

Appendix C: The Big Secret: Confederate Casualties

"Jackson, Lee's right arm was no longer available to carry out the suppression and another was the present depleted condition of the Army of Northern Virginia which had lost in the past forty days a solid forty percent of the strength it had enjoyed at the beginning of the campaign. Its casualties totaled about 27,000, and though it had inflicted a precisely tabulated 54,929-a number greater than all its original infantry and artillery combined-the forty percent figure, unlike Grant's forty-five percent, applied at the higher levels of rank as well as at the lower. Of the 58 general officers in command of troops on the eve of conflict, back in early May, no less than 23 had fallen in battle, eight of them killed, thirteen gravely wounded, and two captured. Nor was the distribution of these casualties, high and low, by any means even throughout the three corps. Hardest hit of all was the Second, just the one Lee had in mind to detach, since it contained, as a nucleus, the survivors of Jackson's old Army of the Valley and was therefore more familiar than the others with the region Hunter was laying waste. Not only had the corps commander been replaced, but so had the leaders of two of the three divisions, while of the twelve original brigade commanders only one remained at his post, two having been promoted and the other nine shot or captured. At Spotsylvania the corps had lost the equivalent of a full division, and this contributed largely to the reduction, by half, of its outset strength of just over 17,000. There now were barely 8,000* infantry in its ranks, distributed through three divisions with only three brigades in each, all but one under leaders new to their responsibilities."[20]

–Freeman

*General Ewell reported 6,000.

Confederate General Edward Porter Alexander wrote one of the best memoirs of the Civil War. It is interesting to note that General Alexander was quite clear on Confederate casualties in the Wilderness but would not speculate on figures at Spotsylvania or total Confederate casualties for the two battles. General Alexander's account was as follows:

Wilderness & Spotsylvania

".....That was the end of the battle of Spotsylvania & before entering upon Grant's next movement I will give the casualties

---

20 Foote, Shelby "The Civil War, A Narrative", p. 310.

Appendix C: The Big Secret: Confederate Casualties

"of the two armies in the following table. <u>The Confederate casualties were never formally reported & tabulated. The campaign work was so incessant & pressing from now until the surrender, that but few reports were made, meanwhile the officers who should have made many were killed. So the Confederate figures all through this campaign must be understood to be largely made up from partial returns & estimates made on various circumstantial indications.</u> There are, also, often conflicting statements as to the Federal losses. I shall not bother to give authority or to seek to reach exact accuracy, in either case, but will adopt my estimate which seems substantially correct & is vouched for by what seems careful & impartial authority.

(Gen'l. Alexander, CSA)
"Casualties Battle of the Wilderness & Spotsylvania
May 5 to May 20th 1864

Battle	Force	Killed	Wounded	Missing	Total
Wilderness	CS	2,000	6,000	3,400	11,400
	US	2,246	12,037	3,383	17,666
	Total				
Spotts.	CS				
	US	2,725	13,413	2,258	18,396
	Total				
Both	CS				
	US	4,971	25,450	5,641	36,062

"Aggreg.
C. S. genls. killed: Jones, Stafford, Jenkins, Stuart, Perrin, Daniel
[C. S. genls.] wounded: Longstreet, Pegram, Benning, Perry, Hill (?) Hays, Ramseur, Johnson, R. D., Walker, W. W. Walker, H. H., McGowan, Walker, J. A.
U. S. [genls.] killed: Hays, Wadsworth, Sedgwick, Rice, Stephenson
[U. S. genls] wounded: Carroll, Getty, Baxter, Robinson, Morris, Wright, Webb.
Genls. captured: Shaler, Seymour, Johnson, Stuart.

(General Alexander, C.A.S.)
    I quote Gen. Humphreys (USA):
"This account of the operations shows in what manner the contest between the two armies was carried on. The marching was done

Appendix C: The Big Secret: Confederate Casualties

chiefly at night, & the contact was so close as to require constant vigilance day & night & allow but little time for sleep. The firing was incessant-the fatigue, the loss of sleep, the watchfulness, taxed severely the powers of endurance of both officers & men. Usually, in military operations, the opposing armies come together, fight a battle, & separate again, the strain lasting only a few days. In a siege, it is only a small part of the opposing troops that are close together. But with these two armies it was different. <u>From the 5th of May to the 9th of June, they were in constant close contact, with rare intervals of brief comparative repose.</u>"[21] Gen. Humphrey, U.S.A.

General Alexander is in agreement with the author regarding the incompleteness of Confederate casualty reports: "So the Confederate figures all through this campaign must be understood to be largely made up from partial returns & estimates made on various circumstantial indications."[22]

Confederate Prisoners

The most significant evidence of large Confederate casualties is the number of prisoners taken by the Union army. Prisoners are a classification of casualties who have names and dates and faces and can be documented. Prisoners are "casualties in hand." Accurate figures on prisoners are one of the surest indicators of total casualties. They are also indicators of sagging morale.

At the conclusion of the battles of Wilderness and Spotsylvania, all Confederate prisoners were shipped north to Federal prison camps. The assembly point for Confederate prisoners was at Belle Plain, Virginia, in a circular valley known as the Punch Bowl. In his excellent book of photographs of the Virginia campaign, William A. Frassanito gives the following description:

> "Approximately 7,500 Confederate prisoners passed through the Punch Bowl at Belle Plain from May 13, 1864, when the first and largest group arrived, through May 18, when the last

---

21 Gallagher, Gary W. editor, "Fighting for the Confederacy," The Personal Recollections of General Edward Porter Alexander, p. 385.
22 Ibid

Appendix C: The Big Secret: Confederate Casualties

group boarded steamers for Point Lookout. Although detailed accounts and reminiscences of Southerners detained at Belle Plain during this five-day period are close to nonexistent, it is fairly certain that the prisoners were well cared for-or at least were cared for as well as possible, considering the military situation. A blowup of a portion of view 5 is reproduced here to show what appears to be a number of supply wagons parked at the rim of the Punch Bowl while prisoners queued up along the edge of the hollow in a series of closely packed lines, await the distribution of supplies."[23]

–Frassanito

There are excellent pictures in William Frassanito's book of Confederate prisoners lining up for food in the Punch Bowl.

The 7,500 Confederate prisoners shipped north from the Punch Bowl at the conclusion of the Battle of Spotsylvania is also cited in "The Killing Ground" by Jaynes Gregory.[24]

These 7,500 Confederate prisoners shipped in five days represent 11% of Lee's army. In many battles the prisoners account for one third of the casualties. Prisoners are taken as battle lines are overrun. Battle lines are overrun as men are killed and wounded. Prisoners are a sign of collapse. The author estimates that there were 25,000 Confederate casualties in the combined battles of Wilderness/Spotsylvania.

Purely A Defensive Force

After May 21, 1864, the Army of Northern Virginia was only capable of fighting defensively. The Confederate army could only retreat and entrench, retrench and entrench:

<u>May 21, 1864</u> At dawn at Spotsylvania, Confederate skirmishers discovered that the Union army (100,000) had stolen away in the night and was Southeast of the Confederate position.

<u>May 21-22, 1864</u> To avoid being cut off from Richmond, General Lee ordered an immediate 25 mile retreat South to the North Anna River.

---

23 Frassanito, William A., "Grant and Lee-the Virginia Campaigns 1864-1865," p. 57.
24 Gregory, Jaynes, "The Killing Ground" Time-Life Books, p. 112.

Appendix C: The Big Secret: Confederate Casualties

<u>May 23, 1864</u>   After retreating 25 miles South General Lee entrenched his army in a giant V shaped position at North Anna and awaited attack.

<u>May 24-25, 26th</u>   General Grant evaluated the Confederate position and determined that it was too strong to attack. The Union army spent the three days destroying Southern railroads. The Confederate army spent three days in their trenches.

<u>May 26, Nightfall</u>   General Grant again stole away from Lee in the night and marched his army Southeast along the North bank of the Mattapotomi River.

<u>May 27, 1864</u>   At dawn on May 27th Confederate skirmishers found that Grant's army was gone. In order to avoid being cut off from Richmond, General Lee immediately ordered an 18 mile retreat Southeast to Totopotomi Creek.

<u>May 28, 1864</u>   General Lee entrenched his army along Totopotomi Creek, 10 miles North of Richmond and awaited attack. Lee's cavalry clashed with Union cavalry.

<u>May 29-30, 1864</u>   The Army of the Potomac moved South and closed with the Confederate position along Totopotomi Creek.

<u>May 31, 1864</u>   General Grant decided that the Confederate position at Totopotomi Creek was too strong to attack. General Grant decided to make one last effort to draw Lee out of his entrenchments to fight a battle in the open before forcing Lee into a prolonged siege. General Grant sent General Sheridan and the cavalry 10 miles Southeast to seize the town of Cold Harbor, located 9 miles East of Richmond.

<u>June 1, 1864</u>   Units of the Confederate army and the Union army began to concentrate at Cold Harbor. Both armies were in motion. Gen. Lee ordered another 10 mile retreat South to Cold Harbor.

Appendix C: The Big Secret: Confederate Casualties

June 1, 1864 — General Grant ordered an attack at dawn on June 2nd at Cold Harbor by the entire Union army. On June 2nd Lee's army was not concentrated or entrenched and the attack might well have succeeded.

June 2, 1864 — General Hancock's U. S. 2nd Corps got lost on a 10 mile night march from Totopotami Creek and arrived at Cold Harbor at dawn June 2nd too exhausted to attack. The Union attack was delayed until June 3rd

June 2, 1864 — In the 24 hour delay, the Confederate army entrenched heavily, establishing elaborate crossfire positions backed by artillery.

June 3, 1864 — When the Union army attacked at dawn on June 3rd it was repulsed decisively in one hour with heavy casualties.

June 4-11, 1864 — General Grant made elaborate preparations for a 50 mile movement South by his 100,000 man army to Petersburg. Grant would immobilize General Lee's army in siege. He would position the Union army South of Lee where it could attack and destroy the Southern railroads.

June 12-18, 1864 — In one of the greatest military moves in American history, General Grant carried out his design from the beginning of the campaign: to cross the James and capture Lee's rear.

June 12-17, 1864 — The Army of Northern Virginia did absolutely nothing to impede Grant's army's move to Petersburg.

June 17-18, 1864 — The Army of Northern Virginia filed into the trenches of Petersburg, ending field operations and entering a siege that would last until the end of the war.

General Lee's appraisal of his position at Petersburg was very gloomy: (To Davis)
 "I hope your Excy will put no reliance in what I can do individually, for I feel that will be very little. The enemy has a strong position & is able to deal us more injury than from any other point he has ever taken."

R. E. Lee[25]

---
25 Freeman, Douglas Southall, editor, "Lee's Dispatches," G. P. Putnam's Sons, 1957, p. 253.

Appendix C: The Big Secret: Confederate Casualties

The military performance of the Army of Northern Virginia in Southern Virginia is characterized by the avoidance of battle. Only rarely did the Confederates leave their trenches. Every move of the army, with minor exceptions, was either retreat South to avoid being cut off from Richmond and/or to entrench heavily to avoid the danger of meeting the Union army in the open field.

This performance of Lee's army from May 21st through June 18th is totally out of character for General Robert E. Lee. His reputation was built on aggressive attack. After Spotsylvania, the Confederate army could only retreat.

Ultimately, it is important to touch on the matter of the disproportionate Union casualties to Confederate casualties in the Virginia campaign. Union casualties were consistently higher. Was the difference due to greater Confederate martial skills and valor? Shelby Foote would have it so:

> "Leaving Spotsylvania on May 21, however, after sixteen unrelenting unavailing days of combat (waged at an average cost of 2,300 casualties a day, as compared to Lee's 1100) the blue marchers had been discouraged by this second tacit admission that, despite their advantage in numbers and equipment and supplies, whenever the tactical situation was reduced to a direct confrontation, face to face, it was they and not their ragged, underfed adversaries who broke off the contest and shifted ground for another try, with the same disheartening result.
>
> "Now what is the reason that we cannot walk straight through them with our far superior numbers?" a Michigan soldier asked and after ruling out individual skill as a factor in the equation - "We fight as good as they" - came up with two possible answers: "They must understand the country better, or there is a screw loose somewhere in the machinery of our army."[26]

Mr. Foote commits an incredible historical omission. He fails to mention that the Confederate soldiers are fighting from trenches and the Union soldiers are attacking across an open field. This provided a 5 to 1 advantage to Confederate soldiers. Backed by cannon on the line it provided a 10 to 1 advantage. Mr. Foote does not mention this fact. Since it is seldom described by sectional historians, Confederate trenches must be considered as a factor.

---
26 Foote, Shelby, "The Civil War - A Narrative," Vol. 111, p. 268.

Appendix C: The Big Secret: Confederate Casualties

The Confederate trenches are still quite evident today at Spotsylvania, Cold Harbor and Petersburg. After May 6th, Lee's army consistently fought from trenches and could not be lured out of them. On the third day of the Battle of the Wilderness (May 7), Lee withdrew his army and entrenched west of the Brock Road. After that, Confederate soldiers fought from trenches. Confederate soldiers would not come out in the open. In the Battle of Spotsylvania, the Confederate army stayed in their trenches for twelve solid days. The Confederates did not attack or maneuver. They remained below ground. General Lee refused open battle. After the devastating loss of 25,000 casualties in Wilderness/Spotsylvania, Lee realized that, if he fought Grant in the open, Grant would destroy him.

In southern Virginia, North Anna, Totpotomy Creek, Cold Harbor and Petersburg, Lee constructed elaborate fortifications for his men. Lee planned no brilliant maneuvers or counter charges. Lee ordered his men to stay underground. Lee's army was so depleted that he could not hazard his precious manpower in open battle. Lee's strategy in southern Virginia was to create large killing zones in front of elaborate fortifications in the hope that Grant would frontally attack

Lee was a brilliant engineer. In the Virginia campaign, Lee constructed fortifications which were masterpieces of the art. A Confederate trench in 1864 was an awesome thing. The attackers first encountered "abatis," trees cut down in the direction of the attack with branches slashed and sharpened. (See illustration pages 260-261) The attackers would have to hesitate as they crossed the abatis, presenting better targets. The next obstacle would be forward pickets who picked off attackers and warned the main line. All the while the wave of attackers would be taking rifle and cannon fire, suffering casualties and still unable to fire at an unseen enemy secure in its trenches. Each defending Confederate soldier could get off five to ten shots at the advancing Yanks before they reached the trenches and could fire back. It was literally a shooting gallery for the Confederates with Yankees as targets that could not shoot back and could not harm them.

Appendix C: The Big Secret: Confederate Casualties

The attackers next encountered the "palisade," sharpened sticks planted in the ground, forming a sharp fence in front of the Confederate trenches. The palisade acted as barbed wire. It slowed the wave of attackers down, making them even better targets for the increasing Confederate fire. The final fifty yards in the open presented the attackers as close targets. The ditch in front of the trench presented the last obstacle before the Yankee soldiers could jump into the Confederate trench with bayonets. The obstacle of an elaborate Confederate trench line threw fear into the hearts of the bravest men. It took seasoned soldiers of proven courage to press a charge home.

At Cold Harbor the casualties from the June 3, 1864 attack were 7,000 for the Union and 1,500 for the Confederacy, a perfect 5 to 1. At Gettysburg, Picket's charge reversed the process and produced 5 to 1 Confederate casualties. The illustration, on pages 260-261, shows the probable ratio of kills per man in a trench against the attacking forces.

Grant had a two to one advantage in numbers, but General Lee had a five to one advantage in defensive position. If Grant would continuously attack the killing zones, Lee could have destroyed the whole Union army.

Appendix C: The Big Secret: Confederate Casualties

Grant was well aware of the advantage of the entrenched defense; in his report dated May 26, 1864, Grant describes General Lee's elaborate fortifications at the North Anna River:

> "To make a direct attack from either wing would cause a slaughter of our men that even success would not justify...I have determined therefore to turn the enemy's right by crossing at or near Hanover Town. This crosses all these streams at once and leaves us still where we can draw supplies...."
>
> U. S. Grant[27]

Confederate General A. L. Long gives one of the most honest explanations of the battle of Spotsylvania:

> "The Confederate losses, though severe, were much less, this being due to the fact that the Confederates were protected by secure breastworks, from behind which they could with comparative safety repel the assailants.[28]"

This admission that the Confederate Army fought exclusively from trenches after May 6th is rare among Southern historians of the Virginia campaign.

---

27 Simon, John T., "The Papers of Ulysses S. Grant," Vol. 10, p. 490.
28 Long, A. L., "Memoirs of Robert E. Lee" (1886) Reprinted by The Blue and Grey Press, p. 341, Secaucus, N. J., 1983.

1864 TRENCH WARFARE

An Attack—Union Point of View

Shots taken by Confederate soldiers before Union soldiers could even see them.

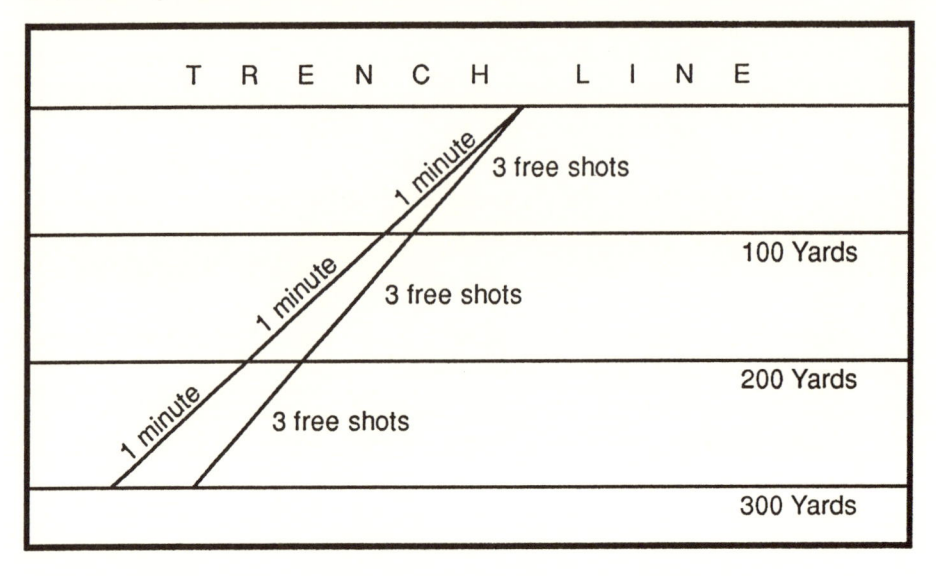

TRENCH LINE	
1 minute — 3 free shots	
1 minute — 3 free shots	100 Yards
1 minute — 3 free shots	200 Yards
	300 Yards

An Attack—Confederate Point of View

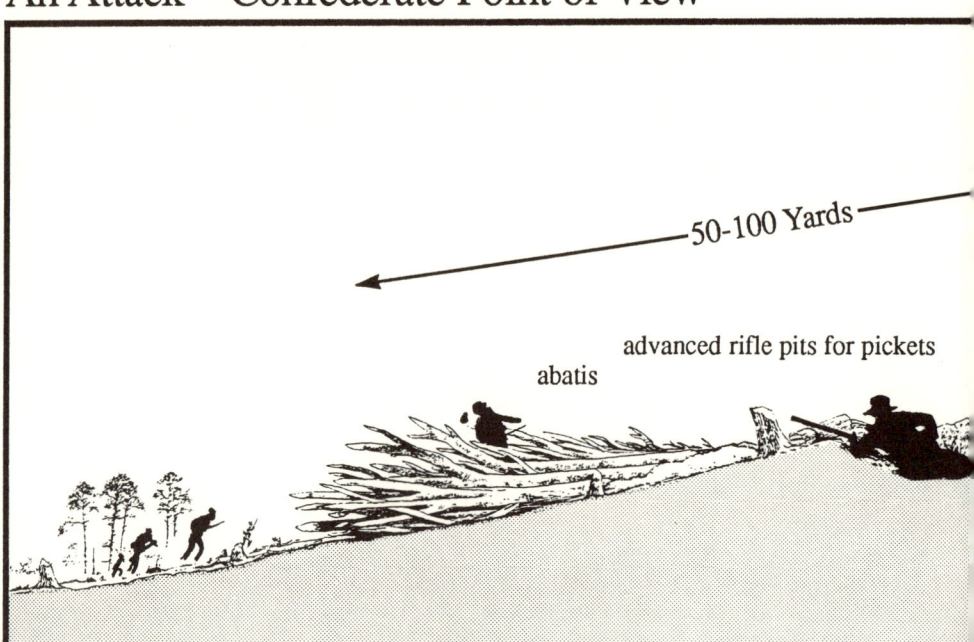

50-100 Yards

advanced rifle pits for pickets

abatis

An Attack—Union Point of View

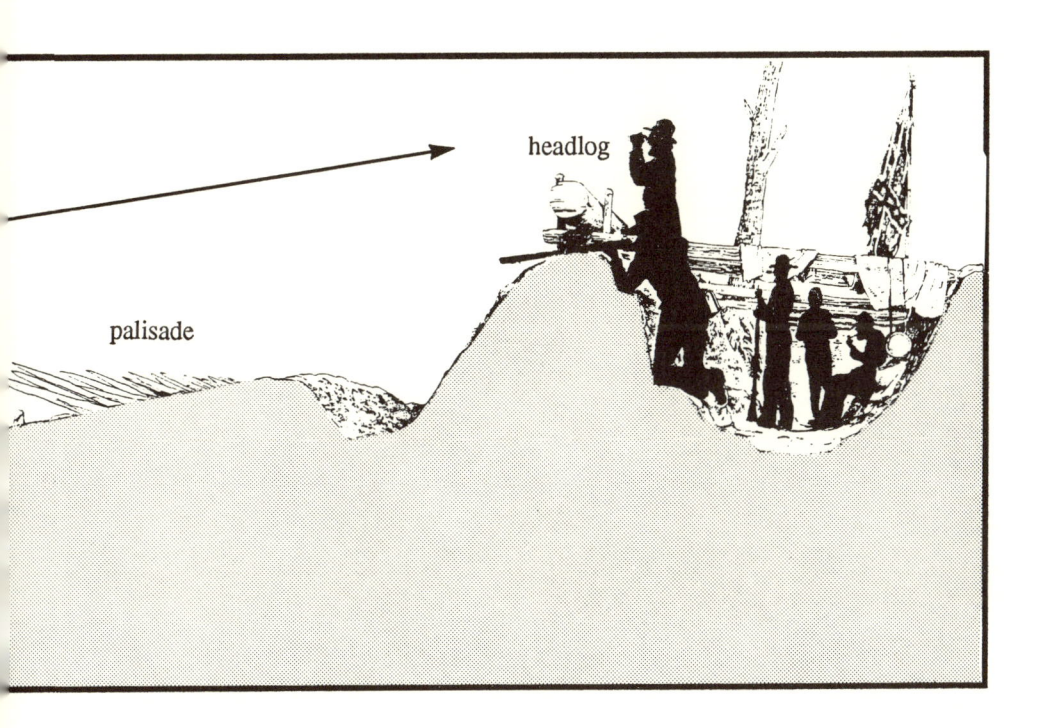

Confederate Line

headlog

palisade

Appendix D
COLD HARBOR LETTERS

There were actually two battles of Cold Harbor. The first battle of Cold Harbor was the union attack at dawn on June 3, 1864. The second was the struggle between the Army of the Potomac and General Robert E. Lee to allow the Union Army to retrieve its wounded from the battlefield on June 3, 4, 5, 6, 7, 1864. General Lee won the first battle. What is not so generally known is that General Lee won the second battle as well by devious means.

What Lee wanted is not clear. General Grant had driven the Confederate army out of Northern Virginia 60 miles south to the gates of Richmond. General Grant had destroyed half of the Confederate army, which included many of Lee's close friends. General Grant was laying waste large parts of Lee's beloved Virginia. Lee was emotionally disturbed.

This unique correspondence between Lee and Grant has not been reviewed in its entirety by historians. Some historians take the erroneous view the General Grant was indifferent to his own wounded and made little effort to recover them and that it was General Lee who called Grant's attention to their suffering. This is, of course, a misreading of the letters. Once brought into what should have been a routine matter, General Grant very energetically pursued the objective of getting the wounded back and was only frustrated by General Lee.

Shelby Foote, in his "Civil War - A Narrative," presents the following historical misrepresentation that has been allowed for one hundred years. Nothing in the following passage has any historical substance. Northern soldiers cared as much about their dead and wounded as did Southern

Appendix D: Cold Harbor Letters

soldiers. The struggle to recover the wounded was between the Army of the Potomac and General Robert E. Lee. After all, it was Lee who gave the order to shoot.

(Foote)

Horror was added to bitterness by the suffering of the wounded, still trapped between the lines, and the pervasive stench of the dead, still unburied after two sultry nights and the better part of third day under the fierce June sun. "A deserter says Grant intends to *stink* Lee out of his position, if nothing else will suffice," a Richmond diarist noted, but a Federal staff colonel had a different explanation: "An impression prevails in the popular mind, and with some reason perhaps, that a commander who sends a flag of truce asking permission to bury his dead and bring in his wounded has lost the field of battle. Hence, the resistance upon our part to ask a flag of truce."

No more willing to give that impression here in Virginia than he had been a year ago in Mississippi, following the repulse of his two assaults on the Vicksburg fortification, the Union general held off doing anything to relieve either the stench or the drawn-out agony of his fallen soldiers until the afternoon of June 5, and even then he could not bring himself to make a forthright request for the necessary Confederate acquiescence. "It is reported to me," he then wrote to Lee, "that there are wounded men, probably of both armies, now lying exposed and suffering between the lines." His suggestion was that each side be permitted to send out unarmed litter bearers to take up its casualties when no action was in progress, and he closed by saying that "any other method equally fair to both parties you may propose for meeting the end desired will be acceptable to me." But Lee, who had no wounded out there, was not letting his adversary off that easy. "I fear that such an arrangement will lead to misunderstanding and difficulty," he replied. "I propose therefore, instead, that when either party desires to remove their dead or wounded a flag of truce* be sent, as is customary. It will always afford me pleasure to comply with such a request as far as circumstances will permit."

*All correspondence with Lee was sent by a flag of truce, Lee's meaning is not all clear.

Appendix D: Cold Harbor Letters

(Foote)

 Thus admonished, Grant took another night to think the matter over – a night in which the cries of the injured, who now had been three days without water or relief from pain, sank to a mewling – and tried a somewhat different tack, as if he were yielding, not without magnanimity, to an urgent plea from a disadvantaged opponent. "Your communication of yesterday is received," he wrote. "I will send immediately, as you propose, to collect the dead and wounded between the lines of the two armies, and will also instruct that you be allowed to do the same." Not so, Lee answered for a second time, and after expressing "regret to find that I did not make myself understood in my communication," proceeded to make it clear that if what Grant wanted was a cease-fire he would have to come right out and ask for it, not informally, as between two men with a common problem, but "by a flag of truce in the usual way." Grant put on as good a face as he could manage in winding up this curious exchange. "The knowledge that wounded men are not suffering from want of attention," he responded, "compels me to ask a suspension of hostilities for sufficient time to collect them in; say two hours."

 By the time Lee's formal consent came back across the lines, however, the sun was down on the fourth day of exposure for the wounded and even the mewling had reached an end. Going out next morning, June 7, search parties found only two men alive out of all the Federal thousands who had fallen in the June 3 assault; the rest had either died or made it back under fire, alone or retrieved by comrades in the darkness. At the end of the truce – which had to be extended to give the burial details time to roll up the long blue carpet of festering corpses – Grant fired a parting verbal shot in concluding his white-flag skirmish with Lee: "Regretting that all my efforts for alleviating the sufferings of wounded men left upon the battlefield have been rendered nugatory, I remain, &c., U. S. Grant, Lieutenant General."

 Lee made no reply to this, no doubt feeling that none was called for, and not even the northern commander's own troops were taken in by a blame-shifting pretense which did little more than show their chief at his worst. They could discount the Copperhead charge that he was a butcher, "a bull-headed Suvarov," since his

Appendix D: Cold Harbor Letters

methods so far had at least kept the rebels on the defensive while his own army moved forward more than sixty airline miles. But this was something else, this sacrifice of brave men for no apparent purpose except to salve his rankled pride. Worst of all, they saw in the agony of their comrades, left to die amid the corpses on a field already lost, a preview of much agony to come, when they themselves would be left to whimper through days of pain while their leader composed notes in defense of conduct which, so far as they could see, had been indefensible from the start."

–Foote*

Strangely, this nonsense has been allowed to stand for 100 years with no one taking the trouble to examine the facts, arrange the correspondence in sequence and expose the game that General Lee was playing. It has always been assumed that General Lee wanted the Army of the Potomac to recover its wounded. The actual facts show – Lee didn't! Lee did everything he could to delay the recovery of the Union wounded!

Mr. Foote's account of the efforts to recover the union wounded at Cold Harbor is an example of the limited scholarship and misrepresentation on this subject that has gone unchallenged and should not be allowed to continue.

The "usual way" of removing wounded men from a battlefield in the Civil War was by informal, unofficial arrangements between frontline troops. Examples of these arrangements are found on pages 279, 280 and 281. What is different about Cold Harbor is that a high ranking Confederate general issued specific orders to his troops forbidding such arrangements.

There is very little question that without direct interference by General Lee, Union wounded could easily have been removed from the Cold Harbor battlefield and many lives saved through normal processes.

At Cold Harbor, once he was brought into the problem of recovering battlefield wounded, General Grant addressed himself to the process as directly, honestly, and aggressively as possible. He tried to solve it. In fact he sent five messages to Lee solely on this subject. General Grant's side of the correspondence stands on its own merits. Efforts to discredit it are futile. Viewed as a complete record it demonstrates masterful use of language and self control.

*Foote, Shelby, "The Civil War-A Narrative", Vol. 3 Random House, N.Y. 1974 p. 295

Appendix D: Cold Harbor Letters

Table of Correspondence
Between General Grant and General Lee
At the Cold Harbor Battlefield
On June 5,6,7,1864
In Regard to the Removal of the
Union wounded from the Battlefield

Cold Harbor Correspondence – Union Wounded
Letters of Gen. Grant and Gen. Lee – June 5, 6, 7, 1864

	Date 1864	Time Issued		Substance	Delivered	Page in Book	Page in Official Records Vol. XXXVI Ser. No. 69
Letter 1	June 5	3:00 pm	Grant to Lee	Allow unarmed litter bearers to pick up wounded without being fired upon. (Sent by flag of truce)	At 10 pm news of the Union messenger still being sought.	p. 270	p. 600
Letter 2	June 5	12 Midnight(?)	Lee to Grant	When either party desires to remove wounded a flag of truce be sent, as is customary	Received by Grant 3:00 am(?) (allow 3 hrs.)	p. 272	p. 600
Letter 3	June 6	4:00 am(?)	Grant to Lee	As you propose between 12 and 3 pm today all parties bear white flags. Not go beyond wounded. (Sent by flag of truce)	Received by Lee 7:00 am(?) (allow 3 hrs.)	p. 273	p. 638
Action	June 6	12 noon		No response from Lee. Lee gives no indication of accepting truce.			
Letter 4	June 6	after 3:50 pm	Lee to Grant	Regret I did not make myself understood. When either party desire permission it shall be asked for by flag of truce in the usual way.	Received by Grant 4:00 pm(?)	p. 275	p. 638
Letter 5	June 6	4 pm(?)	Grant to Lee	Ask for suspension of hostilities for 2 hours to collect the wounded. Any time you select. (Sent by flag of truce)	Received by Lee 7:00 pm(?)	p. 276	p. 638 p. 638

Cold Harbor Correspondence – 2
Letters of Gen. Grant and Gen. Lee – June 5, 6, 7, 1864

	Date 1864	Time		Substance	Time to Deliver	Page Footnote	Page in Official Records Vol. XXXVI Ser. No. 69
Letter 6	June 6	7:00 pm	Lee to Grant	Any parties you may send between Hours of 8 and 10 pm June 6 shall not be molested. (Truce expired before message received)	Received by Grant 11 pm June 6	p. 277	p. 639
Letter 7	June 7	10:30 am	Grant to Lee	Your note of 7 pm yesterday received at nearest headquarters after the hours expired. Regreting my efforts rendered nugatory.	Time received 1:30 pm	p. 278	p. 666
Report of unofficial truce - Afternoon - June 6, 1864 - On General Wright's Sixth Corps Sector							p. 280
Report of unofficial truce - Afternoon - June 6, 18654 - On General Smith's Eighteenth Corps Sector							p. 281
Letter 8	June 7	2:00 pm	Lee to Grant	Hours between 6 and 8 this afternoon. You will send parties…with white flags permitted to collect the dead and wounded.*	Received by Grant 5:00 pm? Not in time for Grant to prepare or issue orders.	p. 282	p. 667
Letter 9	June 7	5:30 pm	Grant to Lee	Impossible to communicate the fact of the truce by the hour named by you.	Received by Lee 8:30 pm?	p. 283	p. 667

Where a time is underlined there is a record.
Where there is a (?), the time is estimated but no record exists.
*General Lee is offering General Grant the same terms he rejected in Grant's Letter #3.

269

Appendix D: Cold Harbor Letters

On June 4, 1864 the very somber task was pushed forward. <u>Immediately</u> after the Union attack at dawn on June 3, 1864 the army of the Potomac began its efforts to recover its wounded. Confederate soldiers were particulary vicious. They fired on unarmed litter bearers. Their conduct was unusual. No informal truces could be arranged with any brigade, division or Corps commanders. Removal of the wounded in the Civil War was customarily worked out unoffically by front line units of each army among themselves with agreements not to fire.

Civil War soliders were not stupid. They knew that tomorrow they might be lying wounded on the battlefield, depending on the mercy of the enemy. But at Cold Harbor it was different. Confederate troops fired mercilessly, all along the front. Someone high in the Confederate command had given specific orders that the Union army was not to be allowed to recover its wounded.

<u>Preliminary Communications</u>

Headquarters Second Division,
June 4, 1864 3 p.m

Major-General Hancock:

General: The sharpshooters I sent out this morning have discovered the body of Colonel McKeen lying in front of the enemy's works in a postion from which they will not be able to remove it until after dark. They succeeded, however, in removing the papers (by which the body is recognized), watch, & c., which are to be brought to me this evening.

JOHN GIBBON,
Brig. Gen. of Volunteers, Commanding Division.[1]

June 5, 1864

General Williams,
Assistant Adjutant-General, Army of the Potomac:

General Gibbon reports that Colonel Smyth's brigade left some of its wounded very near the enemy's works, and that others were wounded in the attempt to get them off. It is probable that a considerable number of dead remain behind the line.

D. B. Birney,
Major-General.[2]

---

1   Official Records, Vol. XXXVI Part III, Ser. No. 69, p. 574.
2   Official Records, Vol. XXXVI Part III, Ser. No. 69, p. 608.

Appendix D: Cold Harbor Letters

General Hancock, commanding the 2nd Corps, turned to General Meade for help. It was in frustration at this point that the comanding general became involved in a matter heretofore resolved at a Corps or division level by frontline troops.

Second Corps,
June 5, 1864 - 1 p.m.

General Williams:*

Can any arrangement be made by which the wounded in front of Barlow can be removed? I understand men wounded on the 3d are still lying there.

WINF'D S. HANCOCK,
Major-General, Commanding.[3]

*General Meade's adjuctant.

[First endorsement]

Respectfully referred to Lietenant-General Grant.

Is it possible to ask, <u>under flag of truce,</u>*for permission to remove the wounded now lying between our lines, and which the enemy's sharpshooters prevent me bringing off?

The wounded are lying in front of the Second, Sixth, and Eighteenth Corps.

Respectully,

GEO. G. MEADE,
Major-General.

[Second endorsement]

<u>A flag</u>* might be sent proposing to suspend firing where the wounded are, until each party get their own. I have no objection to such a course.

U. S. GRANT,
Lieutenant-General[4]

General Meade replied to General Grant:

---

3 Official Records, Vol. XXXVI Pt. III, Ser. No. 69, p. 603.
4 Official Records, Vol. XXXVI Pt. III, Ser. No. 69, p. 604
5 *Note: Referenced to a white flag of truce.

Appendix D: Cold Harbor Letters

Headquarters Army of the Potomac,
June 5, 1864 - 1:30 p.m.

Lieutenant-General Grant:

General: Any communication by flag of truce will have to come from you, as the enemy do not recognize me as in command whilst you are present.

GEO. G. MEADE,
Major-General.[6]

This was the first time that General Grant was informed that Union wounded were still on the field. General Grant acted immediately when he became aware of the problem. The total lack of compassion by the Confederate army was unusual in the Civil War and could not have been anticipated. Without the slightest hesitation General Grant sent the following message to General Lee.

<u>Correspondence Between Lee and Grant</u>

<u>Letter 1</u>

Cold Harbor, Va., *June 5, 1864*

General R. E. Lee,
Commanding Confederate Army:

It is reported to me that there are wounded men, probably of both armies, now lying exposed and suffering between the lines occupied respectively by the two armies. Humanity would dictate that some provision should be made to provide against such hardships. I would propose, therefore, that hereafter when no battle is raging either party be authorized to send to any point between the pickets or skirmish lines, unarmed men bearing litters to pick up their dead or wounded without being fired upon by the other party. <u>Any other method equally fair to both parties you may propose for meeting the end desired, will be accepted by me.</u>

U.S. GRANT,
Lieutenant-General[7]

---

6 Official Records, Vol. XXXVI Pt. III, Ser. No. 69, p. 599.
7 Official Records, Vol. XXXVI Pt. III, Ser. No. 69, p. 600.

Appendix D: Cold Harbor Letters

General Grant was forthright and honest. He, as General in Chief, was appealing to General Lee to allow Union litter bearers to retrieve the wounded men from the battlefield.

Difficulties

The difficulty of getting messages across the no man's land of the Cold Harbor battlefield cannot be overstated. It took a minimum of three hours to communicate from Grant's headquarters to Lee's headquarters. Col. Lyman of Meade's staff carried General Grant's appeal to General Lee.

(1) Col. Lyman described his mission to Lee.

At three o'clock on June 5, 1864 General Meade summoned Col. Lyman to his tent and gave him the following orders:

(underlining by the author)

"Lyman, I want you to take this letter from General Grant and take <u>it by a flag of truce</u>, to the enemy's lines. General Hancock will tell you where you can carry it out."[8]

Col. Lyman then tells of the long delays of getting to the Confederate lines and getting a response from the Confederate command.

(2) At 7:10 PM Col. Lyman had still not gotten to General Lee.

Headquarters Second Army Corps,
June 5, 1864 - 7.10 p.m.

General Williams:

Colonel Lyman sends word that he had communicated with the enemy, and is waiting to know how soon he will be received.

WINF'S S. HANCOCK,
Major-General.[9]

(3) At 10 pm that night General Meade was still trying to locate Col. Lyman.

---

8 Agassiz, George R., editor "Meade's Headquarters," 1863-1865. (Letters of Theodore Lyman) Atlantic Monthly Press 1922, p. 149.
9 Official Records, Vol. XXXVI Pt. III, Ser. No. 69, p. 607.

Appendix D: Cold Harbor Letters

Headquarters Army of the Potomac
June 5, 1864-10 p.m.

General Hancock:

What has become of Lyman? He need not wait for an answer. We can receive and forward it when delivered.

GEO. G. MEADE,
Major-General, Commanding

Headquarters Second Army Corps,
June 5, 1864.

General Meade:

Nothing has been heard of Colonel Lyman since he went beyond my picket-line with one of my staff. I do not know that I will be able to communicate with him.

WINF'D S. HANCOCK,
Major-General.[10]

When General Lee's response to General Grant's appeal was received it appeared reasonable and cooperative. Lee had modified Grant's proposal just as General Grant had invited him to.

<u>Letter 2</u>

Headquarters Army of Northern Virginia,
June 5, 1864.

Lieut. Gen. U. S. GRANT,
Commanding U. S. Armies

General: I have the honor to acknowledge the receipt of your letter of this date proposing that hereafter, except in time of action, either party be at liberty to remove the dead and wounded from between the lines. I fear that such an arrangement will lead to misunderstanding and difficulty. <u>I propose, therefore, instead, that when either party desires to remove their dead or wounded, a flag of truce be sent, as is customary.</u> It will always afford me pleasure to comply with such a request as far as circumtances will permit.

Very respectfully, your obedient servant,

R. E. LEE,
General[11]

---

10 Official Records, Vol. XXXVI Pt. III, Ser. No. 69, p. 608.
11 Official Records, Vol. XXXVI Pt. III, Ser. No. 69, p. 600.

Appendix D: Cold Harbor Letters

General Lee's letter was received some time after 10 pm on **June 5th** in light of General Meade's efforts to locate Col. Lyman. (see top p. 274)

General Grant's response went back to General Lee very quickly, early on the morning of June 6th by messenger under <u>flag of truce.</u>

<u>Letter 3</u>

Cold Harbor, VA., *June 6, 1864.*

General R. E. Lee,
Commanding Army of Northern Virginia:

Your communication of yesterday's date is received. I will send immediately, as you propose, to collect the dead and wounded between the lines of the two armies, and will also instruct that you be allowed to do the same. I propose that the time for doing this be between the hours of 12 m. and 3 p.m. today. I will direct all parties going out to bear a white flag, and not to attempt to go beyond where we have dead or wounded, and not beyond or on ground occupied by your troops.

U.S. GRANT,
Lieutenant-General[12]

In regard to the question of whether a <u>white flag</u>, <u>a flag of truce</u>, being used, it must be noted that General Grant's original request to General Lee for permission to remove Union wounded went forward under a <u>white flag</u> carried by Col. Lyman's aid, <u>a flag of truce</u>. General Grant's second message to General Lee in which he accepted General Lee's terms went back to General Lee under a <u>white flag</u>, <u>a flag of truce</u>. General Grant set out a specific time in which the wounded would be recovered (a truce) and also specified that the recovery parties would bear <u>white flags</u>, <u>flags of truce</u>.

The <u>entire</u> Army of the Potomac was informed regarding the truce:

[Circular.]   Headquarters Fourth Brigade,
June 5, 1864.

Regimental commanders are informed that <u>a flag</u> has been sent out from army headquarters proposing a cessation of hostilities for a short time, to enable our troops to bring off the wounded in

---
12 Official Records, Vol. XXXVI Pt. III, Ser. No. 69, p. 638.

Appendix D: Cold Harbor Letters

our front. The command will be held in readiness to cease firing at a moment's notice. During the truce, not a man or officer will be permitted outside the works, nor will they show themselves to the enemy in any manner. Regimental commanders will be held rigidly responsible that these orders are fully carried out. Notice will be given in due time if the truce is agreed upon. This information is published for the present for the information of regimental commanders only.

By order of Colonel Beaver, commanding brigade:

CHAS. P. HATCH,
Lieutenant and Acting Assistance Adjutant-General.[13]

On June 6th the recovery of the men wounded on June 3rd and still on the battlefield was uppermost in the minds of the Army of the Potomac. Preparations were made for parties of litter bearers to move out on the battlefield. Ambulances and medical facilities were made ready. Nothing happened. There was no reply from General Lee confirming the truce. The hours dragged by.

Headquarters Ninth Army Corps,
June 6, 1864.

Major-General Humphreys:

Has the proposition for flag of truce been accepted? If so, for what time?

A. E. BURNSIDE,
Major-General.

Headquarters Army of the Potomac,
June 6, 1864-3:10 p.m. (Received 3:50 p.m.)

Major-General Burnside,
Commanding Ninth Corps:

The commanding general directs me to say that you will be notified as soon as the flag of truce is accepted.

A.A. HUMPHREYS,
Major-General and Chief of Staff[14]

---

13 Official Records, Vol. XXXVI Pt. III, Ser. No. 69, p. 608.
14 Official Records, Vol. XXXVI Pt. III, Ser. No. 69, p. 655.

Appendix D: Cold Harbor Letters

Later in the afternoon came a letter from General Lee. It was one of the strangest letters of the Civil War. It reveals a side of General Lee's character that had remained hidden and is at sharp variance with the popular concept of Robert E. Lee. It revealed a Lee that was very cold and very hard.

<u>Letter 4</u>

Headquarters Army of Northern Virginia,
June 6, 1864.

Lieut. Gen. U. S. Grant,
Commanding U. S. Army:

General: I have the honor to acknowledge the receipt of your letter of this date and regret to find that I did not make myself understood in my communication of yesterday. I intended to say that I could not consent to the burial of the dead and the removal of the wounded between the armies in the way you propose, but that when either party desire such permission it shall be asked for by <u>flag of truce</u> in the usual way.

Until I receive a proposition from you on the subject to which I can accede with propriety, <u>I have directed any parties</u> you may send under white flags as mentioned in your letter <u>to be turned back</u>.

Very repectfully, you obedient servant,
R. E. LEE,
General.[15]

In his letter General Lee says:

"<u>I could not consent</u> to the burial of the dead and the removal of the wounded between the armies in the way you propose..."

"<u>I have directed</u> any parties you may send under <u>white flags</u> as mentioned in your letter to be turned back."

General Lee is frankly admitting that he ordered ("directed") that Union litter bearers not be permitted to recover wounded soldiers. The firing on unarmed litter bearers has not been accidental. It has been "directed" by General Lee. This is an incredible admission that has no parallel in the Civil War.

Having delayed matters three days, and gotten two pleas from General Grant, General Lee called off the recovery because he did not believe that the request had come "<u>by flag of truce.</u>" This is incredible!

---
15 Official Records, Vol. XXXVI, Pt. III, Ser. No. 69, p. 638.

Appendix D: Cold Harbor Letters

It is General Lee's own words that create confusion.

> "I intended to say that I could not consent to the burial of the dead and the removal of the wounded between the armies in the way you propose, <u>but that when either party desire such permission it shall be asked for by flag of truce in the usual way.</u>

Colonel Lyman delivered Grant's first letter by <u>flag of truce</u>. All communications with Lee have gone to him under <u>a white flag</u>. In Grant's second letter the terms of the truce could not be spelled out more clearly. All of the internal communications within the Army of the Potomac referred to "a truce," "a cessation of hostilities" to recover the wounded.

Grant's careful work had gone for nothing. It was his own men who were dying. What did Lee want? What was his purpose? Had he insulted Lee by setting a time for the truce?

General Lee states, "(I) regret to find that I did not make myself understood in my communication of yesterday." (June 5th) Neither does he make himself clear in his letter of June 6th.

General Grant had no choice but to make one last attempt to reach the dying men. He composed the most humble letter he could devise leaving it to General Lee to set the time for the truce in case that had been the sticking point.

Letter 5

Cold Harbor, VA., *June 6, 1864.*

General R. E. Lee,
Commanding Army of Northern Virginia:

The knowledge that wounded men are now suffering from want of attention, between the two armies, compels me to ask a suspension of hostilities for sufficient time to collect them, say two hours. Permit me to say that the hours you may fix upon for this will be agreeable to me, and the same privilege will be extended to such parties as you may wish to send out on the same duty, without further application.

U. S. GRANT,
Lieutenant-General.[16]

---

16 Official Records, Vol. XXXVI Pt. III, Ser. No. 69, p. 638.

Appendix D: Cold Harbor Letters

General Grant's letter asking General Lee to set any hours and any conditions could not have gotten off before mid afternoon on June 6th and would probably have taken three hours to cross no man's land to General Lee. General Lee's reply is marked 7 pm June 6, 1864.

If there is any doubt as to Lee's lack of sincerity in getting the wounded men off the battlefield, General Lee's letter of June 6, 1864 - 7 pm should dispel it. General Lee's letter written at 7:00 pm could be expected to take three hours to make its way across the battlefield to General Grant's headquarters.

Letter 6

Headquarters Army of Northern Virginia,
June 6, 1864-7 p.m.

Lieut. Gen. U. S. Grant, Commanding U. S. Armies:

General: I regret that your letter of this date asking a suspension of hostilities to enable you to remove your wounded from between the two armies was received at so late an hour as to make it impossible to give the necessary direction so as to enable you to effect your purpose by daylight.

In order that the suffering of the wounded may not be further protracted, I have ordered that any parties you may send out for the purpose between the hours of 8 and 10 p.m. today shall not be molested, and will avail myself of the privilege extended to those from this army to collect any of its wounded that may remain upon the field. I will direct our skirmishers to be drawn close to our lines between the hours indicated, with the understanding that at the expiration of the time they be allowed to resume their positions without molestation, and that during the interval all military movements be suspended.

Very respectfully your obedient servant,

R. E. LEE,
General[17]

What General Lee had actually done, hidden in rhetoric and flowery words, was a clever subterfuge. After three days of barring the Union army from its wounded at gunpoint, something he should never have

---

17 Official Records, Vol. XXXVI Pt. III, Ser. No. 69, p. 639.

Appendix D: Cold Harbor Letters

done in the first place. General Lee had given General Grant a worthless piece of paper. Under the guise of being helpful General Lee had given nothing. The truce he offered expired at the time if was delivered to Grant. General Lee had been communicating with Grant for two days. General Lee had a very good idea how long it took to get messages from one headquarters to another. General Lee timed his offer perfectly <u>so that it would be worth nothing</u>.

Confirmation of General Lee's duplicity can be found in the records of the Army of the Potomac:

> Note in Letter Book, Headquarters Armies of the United States.
> This letter of General Lee* was not delivered at the outposts of General Hancock until after 10 o'clock, the hour fixed by General Lee for the expiration of the armistice. Notwithstanding, the rebel pickets were drawn in as proposed, and a burial party sent out shortly after 8 o'clock, but as our pickets had received no instructions on the subject, the party was captured. On the report of these facts, General Grant has just sent the subjoined letter to the rebel commander.
> * Letter #6, p. 279, dtd June 6, 1864-7 p.m.

<u>Letter 7</u>

Cold Harbor, Va., *June 7, 1864-10:30 a.m.*
General R. E. Lee, Comdg. Army of Northern Virginia:

I regret that your note of 7 p.m. yesterday should have been received at the nearest corps headquarters to where it was delivered after the hour that had been given for the removal of the dead and wounded had expired. 10:45 p.m. was the hour at which it was received at corps headquarters, and between 11 and 12 it reached my headquarters. As a consequence, it was not understood by the troops of this army that there was a cessation of hostilities for the purpose of collecting the dead and wounded, and none were collected. Two officers and six men of the Eighth and Twenty-fifth North Carolina Regiments, who were out in search of the bodies of officers of their respective regiments were captured and brought into our lines owing to this want of understanding. I regret this, but will state that as soon as I learned the fact I directed that they should not be held prisoners, but

Appendix D: Cold Harbor Letters

must be returned to their commands. These officers and men having been carelessly brought through our lines to the rear, I have not determined whether they will be sent back the way they came or whether they will be sent by some other route.

Regretting that all my efforts for alleviating the sufferings of wounded men left upon the battlefield have been rendered nugatory,

I remain, &c.,

U.S. Grant,
Lieutenant-General.[18]

Despite General Lee's efforts to frustrate the proceedings some of the Union wounded were recovered.

Fortunately for the Union wounded some of General Lee's soldiers disobeyed him. Some of the Confederate units had compassion and there was an unofficial truce on the section of the battlefield held by General Wright's 6th Corps. This informal truce occurred at approximately 1:00 p.m. June 6, 1864.

Report of Unofficial Truce

Headquarters Army of the Potomac,
June 7, 1864-11 a.m.

Major-General Wright,
Sixth Corps:

I am informed unofficially, based on the report of Colonel Tompkins, that there was yesterday some time on your lines a suspension of hostilities, on some kind of informal agreement between your forces and the enemy, during which your dead and wounded were removed. You will please report whether you have any knowledge of the existence of such a state of affairs, of any communications being held with the enemy, and, if so, by whose authority the same was done.

Respectfully, yours,

Geo. G. Meade,
Major general.

(Same to Major-General Smith, Eighteenth Corps.)

---

18 Official Records, Vol. XXXVI, Pt. III, Ser. No. 69, p. 666.

Appendix D: Cold Harbor Letters

Headquarters Sixth Army Corps,
June 7, 1864-11:05 a.m.

Major-General Meade,

I had already inquired into the report referred to in your dispatch of 11 a.m. and am assured that no agreement whatever was entered into with the enemy for a cessation of hostilities, but that some time before the cannonading of <u>yesterday afternoon men from both sides brought in their dead lying between the lines, both parties refraining form firing as if by tacit consent, and that this condition of things existed for an hour or more</u>, when the fire of the enemy above alluded to commenced, and was followed by firing along the line. I shall call on Colonel Tompkins for a further report in the matter.

H. G. Wright,
Major-General, Commanding.[19]

Report of Unofficial Truce

A second informal truce occurred along the section of the battlefield held by General Smith's 18th Corps. This informal truce was on the afternoon of June 6th.

Headquarters Eighteenth Corps,
June 7, 1864.

Major-General Meade,
Commanding Army of the Potomac:

General: I have the honor to acknowledge receipt of your dispatch of 11 a.m., and in answer to furnish the following information: General Brooks, commanding First Division, states that an officer went out from his front during yesterday p.m. and at his own risk brought in a wounded man. General Matindale, commanding Second Division, states that <u>the enemy ceased firing and stood upon their works and our men did likewise, supposing a cessation of hostilities was going on according to the request of the commanding general of the army</u>. A rebel officer advanced and informed one of the officers of Second Brigade that unless work was suspended on a battery we were building hostilities would be resumed. Our men and the enemy then resumed their old positions. General Ames, commanding Third Division, states that there was no communication along his front.

---

19 Official Records, Vol. XXXVI, Pt. III, Ser. No. 69, p. 679.

Appendix D: Cold Harbor Letters

During the afternoon on yesterday, between 2 and 3 o'clock, I visited my lines, and was informed by the troops of the first line that an informal agreement had been made with the enemy in their front to stop picket-firing. As this was very much in accordance with my own ideas, I expressed a wish that this state of affairs would extend all along my lines, as my men in the rear lines were suffering severely from such firing. While I was down there an officer of my corps went out under fire to exchange papers. <u>During the night, while our dead were being buried, our men were so near as to hear a rebel officer give orders not to fire on burying parties</u>. This is all with regard to cessation of hostilities or communication with the enemy on my front that I am informed of officially or otherwise.

I am, general, very respectfully, your obedient servant,

W. F. Smith.
Major-General, Commanding.[20]

Whether or not any of these Confederate officers were disciplined for disobeying Lee's orders and allowing Union soldiers to recover their wounded is not known.

General Lee had been successful in blocking the rescue of the wounded men for four days, June 3, June 4, June 5, June 6. There was very little hope that they were still alive. General Grant had concluded his letter of June 7th.

"Regretting that all my efforts for alleviating the sufferings of the wounded men left on the battlefield have been rendered nugatory."[21]

U. S. Grant

Surprisingly, General Lee responded.

---

20 Official Records, Vol. XXXVI, Pt. III, Ser. No. 69, p. 687.
21 Official Records, Vol. XXXVI, Pt. III, Ser. No. 69, p. 666.

Appendix D: Cold Harbor Letters

Letter 8

Headquarters Army of Northern Virginia,
June 7, 1864-2 p.m.

Lieut. Gen. U.S. Grant,
Commanding U.S. Armies:

General: Your note of 10:30 a.m. today has just been received. I regret that my letter to you of 7 p.m. yesterday should have been too late in reaching you to effect the removal of the wounded.

I am willing, if you desire it, to devote the hours between 6 and 8 this afternoon to accomplish that object upon the same terms and conditions as set forth in my letter of 7 p.m. yesterday. If this will answer your purpose, and you will send parties from your lines at the hour designated with white flags, I will direct that they be recognized and be permitted to collect the dead and wounded.

I will also notify the officers on my line that they will be permitted to collect any of our men that may be on the field. I request you notify me as soon as practicable if this arrangement is agreeable to you. Lieutenant McAllister, Corporal Martin, and two privates of the Eighth North Carolina Regiment, and Lieutenant Hartman, Corpl. T. Kinlow, and Privates Bass and Grey were sent last night, between the hours of 8 and 10 p.m. for the purpose of recovering the body of Colonel Murchison, and as they have not returned, I presume they are the men mentioned in your letter. I request that they be returned to our lines.

Very respectfully, your obedient servant,

R. E. Lee,
General.[22]

Again, General Lee's letter (Letter 8) deserves close scrutiny. General Lee was still playing games with words. General Grant's letter to General Lee was marked June 7, 1864 10:30 a.m. (see, Letter 7, page 278) General Lee's letter of response was marked June 7, 1864 2:00 p.m. Surely General Lee could see that if it took three and a half hours for him to respond to General Grant's letter brought by messenger over a

---

22 Official Records, Vol. XXXVI, Pt. III, Ser. No. 69, p. 667.

Appendix D: Cold Harbor Letters

battlefield, it would take his own letter at least three hours to reach Grant. And yet, General Lee plays the same game twice. The truce he is offering Grant expires soon after it is delivered. General Grant would have no time to prepare or give the necessary orders. <u>General Lee is trying</u> to establish for the record that he is cooperating while he is actually doing everything he can to keep the wounded men unattended on the battlefield. It is fascinating to watch Lee's mind at work.

General Grant barely hides his disgust with Lee. In his letter to General Lee he points out the impossibility of complying with Lee's timing. Grant's note is very short. Lee has done nothing to help. Grant knows it.

Letter 9

Cold Harbor, Va. *June 7, 1864-5:30 a.m.*

General R. E. Lee,
Commanding Army of Northern Virginia:

Your note of this date just received. <u>It will be impossible for me to communicate the facts of the truce by the hour named, by</u> you (6 p.m.), but I will avail myself of your offer at the earliest possible moment, which I hope will not be much after the hour. The officers and men taken last evening are the same mentioned in your note and will be returned.

U. S. Grant,
Lieutenant-General.[23]

The last truce that General Lee proposed on June 7, 1864 2 p.m. (Letter 8, page 282) was in the exact terms that General Grant had originally proposed to Lee on June 6th (Letter 3, page 273) and which Lee had so rudely refused. (Letter 4, page 275). General Lee's inconsistency is apparent. He is playing with words. He is toying with Grant. He sends him meaningless truce proposals designed to expire before they can be carried out.

General Lee was aware that wounded men were dying and he by his own orders delayed their rescue. June 3, June 4, June 5, June 6, June 7 .

General Lee's last letter (Letter 8, page 282) was not motivated by any interest in the Union wounded. On the contrary, General Lee's interest was in getting eight of his own men back.

Nonetheless the Union army made use of whatever means were available to recover its wounded.

---

23 Official Records, Vol. XXXVI, Pt. III, Ser. No. 69, p. 667.

Appendix D: Cold Harbor Letters

[Endorsement]

June 7, 1864

Referred to General G. G. Meade, Commanding Army to the Potomac.

I will notify General Lee that hostilities will cease from 6 to 8 for the purposes mentioned. You may send the officers and men referred to as you deem best. Please return this.

U.S. Grant,
Lieutenant-General.[24]

[Circular.]   Headquarters Army of the Potomac,
June 7, 1864.

Corps commanders are notified that a <u>flag of truce</u> exists from 6 to 8 p.m. today, and they will immediately send out, under a white flag, medical officers with stretcher bearers to bring in the dead and wounded. No other officers or men will be permitted to leave the lines, and no intercourse of any kind will be held with the enemy, and the medical officers and attendants will be enjoined not to converse upon any subject connected with the military operations or likely to give information to the enemy.

By command of Major-General Meade:

S. Williams,
Assistant Adjutant-General.[25]

Headquarters Ninth Army Corps,
June 7, 1864-8:30 p.m.

General Humphreys:

The enemy in my front did not respect the <u>flag of truce</u>. My medical director was fired upon as he advanced with a white flag and a continual fire kept up by the enemy during the whole period covered by the flag.

Respectfully,

A. E. Burnside,
Major-General.[26]

---

24 Official Records, Vol. XXXVI, Pt. III, Ser. No. 69, p. 667.
25 Official Records, Vol. XXXVI, Pt. III, Ser. No. 69, p. 669.
26 Official Records, Vol. XXXVI, Pt. III, Ser. No. 69, p. 684.

Appendix D: Cold Harbor Letters

At the close of the day on June 7, 1864 General Lee reported:

> Headquarters Army of Northern Virginia,
> *June 7, 1864-7:00 p.m.*
>
> Hon. Secretary of War,
> Richmond, Va.:
> Sir: The operations of today have been unimportant. Slight skirmishing has taken place along the lines.
> Very respectfully, your obedient servant,
>
> R. E. Lee,
> General.[27]

In General Lee's mind nothing of significance had happened. His correspondence with Grant was unimportant. The recovery of Union wounded was unimportant. Lee outmaneuvered Grant. Lee won the second battle of Cold Harbor.

---

27 Official Records, Vol. XXXVI, Pt. III, Ser. No. 69, p. 877.

BIBLIOGRAPHY

Agassiz, George R. *Meade's Headquarters 1863-1865*, Letters of Colonel Theodore Lyman from The Wilderness to Appomattox, The Atlantic Monthly Press, Boston 1922

Ambrose, Stephen E. *Halleck - Lincoln's Chief of Staff*, Louisiana State University Press, Baton Rouge 1962

Black, Robert C. III, *The Railroads of the Confederacy*, Chapel Hill, The University of North Carolina Press, 1952

Basler, Roy P., ed. *Abraham Lincoln - His Speeches and Writings*, The World Publishing Co. Cleveland & New York, 1946

Beringer, Richard E. *Why the South Lost the Civil War*, University of Georgia Press, Athens and London, 1986 N. Jr

Burne, Alfred H. Lt Col. *Lee, Grant and Sherman*, Introduction by Douglas Southall Freeman, New York, Charles Scribners Sons 1939

Churchill, Winston S. *A History of the English Speaking Peoples, The Great Democracies*, Dodd, Mead & Co. New York, 1966

Catton, Bruce *Grant Takes Command*, Little, Brown and Co. Boston, Toronto, 1968

Catton, Bruce *A Stillness at Appomattox*, Doubleday & Co. Garden City, New York, 1953

Davis, William C. & the Editors of Time Life Books, *Death in the Trenches*, Time Life Books, Alexandria, Virginia 1946

Dowdey, Clifford and Manarin, Louis H., Editors *The Wartime Papers of R.E. Lee*, Virginia Civil War Commission, Little Brown and Co. Boston, Toronto 1961

Esposito, Colonel Vincent J. Chief Editor *The West Point Atlas of the Civil War*, (Adapted from the West Point Atlas of American Wars, Vol. 1) Frederick A. Praeger, Publisher, New York 1962

Grant, U.S. *Personal Memoirs of U. S. Grant*, Edited with notes and introduction by E.B. Long The World Publishing Co., Cleveland & New York, 1952 (Original New York, July 1, 1883)

Freeman, Douglas Southall *Lee's Lieutenants*, 3 vols. Charles Scribners Sons 1944

Foote, Shelby *The Civil War - A Narrative,* 3 vols. Random House, New York, 1974

Freeman, Douglas Southall and McWhiney, Grady *Lee's Dispatches*, unpublished letters of General Robert E. Lee, CSA to Jefferson Davis and the War Department of The Confederate States of America 1862-1865 C.P. Punam's Sons, New York 1957

Frassanito, William A. *Grant & Lee*, Charles Scribners Sons New York 1983

Fuller, General J.F.D. *The Generalship of Ulysses S Grant*, Indiana University Press, Civil War Centennial Series, Kraus Reprint Co., Millwood, N.Y. 1977 (Copyright 1929)

Gallagher, Gary W. ed. *Fighting for the Confederacy*, The Personal Recollections of General Edward Porter Alexander, The University of North Carolina Press, Chapel Hill/London 1989

Hart, B.H. Liddell *Strategy*, Frederick A. Praeger Publisher, New York - Washington 1967 (Faber & Faber Ltd London, 1954)

Humphreys, Maj. Gen. Andrew A., *The Virginia Campaign of '64 and '65*, The Army of the Potomac and The Army of the James, Charles Scribners's Sons, New York 1883

Gibbon, Brig. General *Personal Recollections of the Civil War*, Morningside Book Shop Dayton, Ohio 1988 (original 1885)

Haskell, John Cheves, Edited by Goyan, Gilbert E and Livingood, James W. *The Haskell Memoirs*, G.P. Putnam's Sons, New York 1960

Hathaway, Herman *How the North Won*, University of Illinois Press, Urbana Chicago London 1983

Jaynes, Gregory and the Editors of Time Life Books *The Civil War (a Series) The Killing Ground, Wilderness to Cold Harbor*, Time Life Books, Alexandria, VA 1986

Jones, Rev. J. William, D.D. *Life and Letters of Robert Edward Lee, Soldier and Man*, Harrisonburg, Virginia, Sprinkle Publications, 1978 (1906)

Jones, Rev. J. William, D.D. *Army of Northern Virginia - Memorial Volume*, Morningside Book Shop 1976 (1879)

Krick, Robert K. *Lee's Colonels*, A Biographical Register of the Field Officers of the Army of Northern Virginia Morningside Book Shop 1979

Lee, Captain Robert E. *Recollections and Letters of General Robert E. Lee*, Doubleday, Page & Co. 1904

Longstreet, James, Lt. Gen. CSA, Edited Robertson, James J. Jr. *From Manassas to Appomattox*, Memoirs of the Civil War in America, Indiana University Press 1976

Morrison, James L, Jr. Ed *The Memoirs of Henry Heth*, Greenwood Press, Westport, Connecticut 1974 Heth, Henry 1825-1899 (begun 1897)

Miller, J. Michael *The North Anna Campaign*, Even to Hell Itself May 21-26, 1864 H.E. Howard Inc. Lynchburg, VA 1989

McWhiney, Grady and Jamieson, Perry D. *Attack and Die*, Civil War Military Tactics and the Southern Heritage. The University of Alabama Press, 1982

Porter, General Horace *Campaigning with Grant*, edited with Introduction and Notes by Wayne C. Temple Bonanza Books, New York March 1861 Indiana University Press 1958 Civil War Centennial Series Originally published - The Century Magazine 1897

Official Records
               Operations in Southeastern Virginia
                   May 1-June 12, 1864
             Series 1 Vol. XXXVI Part 1 No. 67
             Series 1 Vol. XXXVI Part 2 No. 68
             Series 1 Vol. XXXVI Part 3 No. 69
                Junes 13-July 31, 1864
             Series 1 Vol. XL Part 1 No. 80
             Series 1 Vol. XL Part 2 No. 81
             Series 1 Vol. XL Part 3 No. 82
Official Records
                Operations Western Theater
             Jan. 1, 1864 to April 30, 1864
             Series 1 Vol. 32 Part 2 No. 58
             Series 1 Vol. 32 Part 3 No. 59
             Series 1 Vol. 33 Part 3 No. 60

Schaff, Morris *The Battle of the Wilderness*, Houghton Mifflin Co., Boston and New York, The University Press, Cambridge 1910

Scott, Robert Garth *Into the Wilderness with the Army of the Potomac*, Indiana University Press, Bloomington, Indiana 1957

Sheridan, P.H. General U.S. Army *Personal Memoirs*, Charles L. Webster & Co. 1888

Sherman, William T. By Himself *Memoirs*, D. Appleton and Company 549 and 551 Broadway 1875

Simon, John Y. *The Papers of Ulysses S. Grant*, 18 volumes Southern Illinois University Press, Carbondale and Edwardsville, Illinois, Particularly Vol. 10, Jan 1-May 31, 1864 (1982)
Vol. 11, June 1-Aug 15, 1864 (1984)

Trudeau, Noah Andre *Bloody Roads South*, The Wilderness to Cold Harbor, May, June 1864, Little Brown & C. Toronto, London 1989

Trudeau, Noel Andre *The Last Citadel*, Petersburg, Virginia June 1864-April 1865 Little Brown and Co. 1991

Williams, T. Harry *Lincoln and His Generals*, New York Alfred A. Knoff 1952

Williams, T. Harry *McClellan, Sherman and Grant*, Rutgers University Press New Brunswick, New Jersey, 1962

Wilson, James Harrison LLD, Maj Gen. *The Life of Charles A. Dana*, Harper & Brothers Publishers, May 1907